THE PAPERBOY'S WAR

TED EGAN

KERR

First published 1993
Kerr Publishing Pty Ltd
3/37 Duke Street
Balmain 2041 Australia
Telephone (02) 555 1811
Fascimile (02) 818 5206

Cover artwork Hall & Jones, Brisbane
Typeset in 12/15 Century Schoolbook by DOCUPRO, Sydney
Printed by McPhersons Print Group, Maryborough, Vic

Distributed by TOWER Books nationally
Distributed in New Zealand by Fiesta, Christchurch

National Library of Australia cataloguing-in-publication data:

Egan, Ted. 1932
  Paperboy's war.

  ISBN 1 875703 08 X.

  1. Egan, Ted—Childhood and youth. 2. Country
  music—Australia—Biography. 3. Entertainers—
  Australia—Biography. I. Title.

781.642092

To my parents,
whose sacrifice gave me
a better kind of life
than they enjoyed

Contents

1
Window of Opportunity

I reckon throwing that rock through the window of Phelan's butcher shop was one of the best things I ever did. But I didn't think so at the time.

We didn't call them 'rocks'. We called them 'yonnies' or 'brinnies' in suburban Melbourne — Coburg, to be precise — and we Grade 4 boys prided ourselves on our accuracy at hitting lamp-posts, trees or other inanimate objects. Occasionally, we'd have 'wars' when we threw rocks at one another. Not too seriously, mind, but practising just in case we met up with a bunch of State school kids at the railway crossing. Then she'd be on, 'yonnies' flying, and them chanting at us:

> Catholic dogs, jump like frogs
> In and out the water logs

to which we'd reply

> States, states, ring the bell
> All the Proddos go to hell

Our lot went to St Paul's in Sydney Road, Coburg. It's now a Muslim school — Doctor Mannix would turn in his grave—but in our day it was run by the Sisters of Mercy, and the kids from our part of Coburg, which was

9

called 'Co-ee', used to walk home westwards along
O'Hea's Road, and then branch off, one by one, into our
respective side streets. I lived in Higinbotham Street,
and the eminent judge after whom the street was named
would have been displeased, I suppose, if he'd known
we referred to it as 'Itchybottom Street'.

Not many things got their proper names in the 1940s.
Especially boys. Nowadays boys get called Michael and
Robert and James and Thomas, but in our day it was
Tommy Way, or Jimmy Quill, or Bobby Sullivan, or Mocka
(Maurice) Sheehy, or Jacky Rogan or Flipper (Philip)
Cerini. Mickey Williamson, who lived in Molesworth
Street, eventually became Michael, and later Mike, when
he was with Channel 7. But he was Mickey to us. I was
always Teddy Egan and hated it, dreading the inevitable
Teddy Bear jibes.

And nicknames: if they didn't have one my Dad, Joe
Egan, would invent one for them. He was one of the great
nicknamers, Dad. His workmates gloried in names like
Hitler, Foo, Funf and Lightning. He even gave himself a
nickname. He called himself Bugger McGoogle, which
lovingly, especially to his many grandchildren, became
Google. We all hooted with laughter when Mrs O'Keefe
(Pop dubbed her Farting Fanny) said authoritatively one
day 'Joe Egan's nickname is McDougall.'

Our family loved to pick people up on little mistakes
or slips or foibles like that. Sometimes we could be cruel
about it, too, but never to their face. No fear. Any public
misdemeanor from us kids would result in our Mum
administering at least 'a screw of the flesh'. A screw of
the flesh was an almighty pinch which she could apply
with the most benign smile on her face as she kept
praying at Mass, or carried on a conversation, 'Yes, it is
a lovely day, Mrs O'Brien'. While we would writhe in silent
agony, well aware that any sound or indication that the
flesh was being screwed might take us to stage two's

introductory command: 'Go into the wash house.' That meant a belting with the strap.

Not that it happened to the girls much. Peggy (Margaret) occasionally; Paddy (Patricia) and Sal (Shirley) never, as I recall. But for me it seemed a daily event, the odd pinch, a predictable trip to the wash house (nowadays they're called 'laundries') and a bit of a belting. I was quick on my feet and Grace (Mum, although strangely we were allowed to call her 'Grace') was not really a sadist, she just liked to let us know who was boss. A few whacks around the legs with the razor strop, inordinately loud yells from me to establish that I was in fact being slaughtered, and then her final admonition ' . . . and don't you dare tell your father. Now, go and do your homework/cut the wood . . . whatever.' And she'd invariably say to the girls: 'My Godfather, he's a defiant boy that Teddy Egan.'

Teddy Egan! That's what Mr Phelan bellowed as he stormed out from among the snags and the sides of lamb hanging in his butcher shop. Silly me was still standing there, frozen at the sight of the shattered window.

I had done it a hundred times before. 'Watch this, Wacker,' I'd say to Tommy Way, and I could hit the lamp post outside Phelan's butcher shop every time. Deadly Tedly. But this day the rock hit the post and ricocheted straight through the window.

'Yes, Teddy Egan,' roared old Phelan as he grabbed me by the ear. 'Your mother will be hearing from me about this, my boy.' A good tug at my ear and he hurled me on my way. I slunk home, and Mum thought I was sick when I said 'No thanks' to her customary 'Do you want a piece?' (One slice of bread and jam, but it was always called a 'piece'.) I even sat at the kitchen table and started to do my homework without being told. I couldn't sleep that night, trying to guess the extent of the bill he would present.

When I came home from school the next day there was

Grace, the letter in her hand. She said nothing, but grimly handed me the envelope. Inside was an account:

TO WINDOW BROKEN BY TEDDY EGAN — £5-5-0.

Five guineas: an immense amount of money for a nine-year-old boy. It was some consolation that Grace didn't want the details of the breakage, but simply asked, 'And where do you think I'll find money like that?' Always a quick thinker I replied, 'I'll sell papers.' So the next day I was sent back to old Phelan to ask if I could pay off the debt at two shillings a week. I had signed up as a *Herald* boy at Morley's Newsagency, opposite the Coburg Post Office. I had been assigned to the prestigious Brown's Pub corner, and I would start the next day. Fourpence a dozen was the wage.

Grace was not all that keen on the idea of me selling papers. For one thing it would mean I would be 'on the streets' and the streets, we were constantly told, were the source of temptation. Our lot were always very strong on temptation. For another thing it would mean I would have to do my homework 'after tea' and thus would get to bed later. But the main objection to having a paper boy in the family was that this might stamp us as a 'common' family. To be poor was one thing, but to be common . . .

There was no alternative. Pop was working, but received only the basic wage: I think it was about £3 per week. There were five kids — the three girls, me, and my new brother Geoffrey who was not yet called 'Tim'. There were house payments, food and clothing costs, the normal extras like water, electricity and medical bills, and the expense of having four of us at St Paul's in the days before State Aid. We not only had to take 'school' money but extra payments for 'drill' and 'singing' where the nuns had to bring in specialist teachers. And it was a source of pride to an Irish-Catholic family like ours to have our name up in black-and-white in the parish gazette as weekly contributors to paying off the parish debt as well as providing a stipend for old Peter McGee.

Peter McGee. Father McGee. Pete. Soggarth Aroon, a fiery old fellow in his eighties who should have been retired years ago. But where could an old priest go? Back to Ireland? That would have been nice for the poor old bloke, but the problem was he felt he was still in control. He delivered fiery if somewhat incoherent sermons at early Mass on Sunday mornings. I remember that we all had a good laugh (a silent laugh, for it was a sin to talk or laugh in church) when old Peter in his confusion harangued the congregation about the parish debt: 'Out of tree hondred in the parish, only a tousand have paid their parish dues.'

Grace would have preferred a morning paper round for me, whereby I would deliver the *Sun* (hardly anyone in Coburg took the *Age* or the *Argus*, the other morning papers). This could have been achieved on my bike in the early morning, so I would not be 'on the streets' in the same sense as the evening job would put me on them. But I was an altar boy, regularly rostered to serve daily Mass at St Paul's, usually assigned for 7 a.m. While there was Mass with Father McGee, a morning paper run was out of the question.

Even at the time I only ever felt sorry for old Pete. A nine-year-old boy could see that this once fine man was sick and old and tired, and what we called 'mental'. But none of that sympathy allayed the absolute fear that enveloped me as I either walked, ran or rode my bike to church at 6.30 a.m., especially on those foggy or frosty mornings in Melbourne when you were chilled to the bonemarrow and your breath exploded into clouds as you blew on your hands trying to instil some warmth. The altar boy on duty had to be standing outside the sacristy by 6.45 a.m. to turn on a light to enable Pete to see his way across from the Presbytery. 'Good morning, Father' was the required greeting as the old man walked arthritically up the outside stairs, wearing his cassock and biretta and sometimes concealing the fact that he still had his pyjamas on underneath. He would occasionally grunt a reply. Deftly the door would be opened when he handed over the key. To delay was inviting trouble.

He would go into the sacristy to don the vestments and prepare for Mass, and I would be busy filling the cruets with water and wine, lighting the candles, and putting on my own soutane and surplice. The soutane was the caftan-length black garment, and over the top went the surplice, a white square-necked shirt, three-quarter sleeves with lace. There was also lace at the bottom of the shirt. I felt I looked a bit like St Aloysius Gonzaga. And we wore black slippers, for the mark of a good altar boy (so the nuns told us) was that nobody must notice you. You must be so unobtrusive nobody was reminded of you, nobody heard your footsteps, and your Latin responses were always suitably muted. Never forget you are assisting at the Divine Sacrifice. Speak clearly, but never intrusively. The nuns were assigning their similar roles of 'passive contributors' to us, I realised later.

Right on the dot of 7 a.m. Pete would be ready. Well, I sometimes had to point to his biretta, or something else that he might have forgotten. Then we were ready. He gave a curt nod, and into the sanctuary we swept. Usually there were only five or six people, one of them my Aunty Kit, kneeling in the dark cold church for 'Seven', which was what early Mass was always called. A fairly large crowd, kids especially, used to attend the next Mass at about 7.45 a.m. depending on when Pete finished. The kids could fit Mass in before school. Pete went into his rapid-fire Latin, and because we altar boys knew the priest's Latin as well as our own Latin responses, I was aware Pete used to skip great passages, or make bits up, and I was often left pondering whether he had in fact legally 'said' Mass in accordance with Canon Law. But I knew God would judge all of that. Right, stay with him, Ted; we're off!

> Pete: *In nomine Patris et Filii, et Spiritui Sancti Amen. Introibo ad altare Dei.* [or words to that effect]
> Me: *Ad Deum qui laetificat juventutem meum.*

and we'd go through a form of the Mass.

And then afterwards 'the lecture'. When we re-entered the sacristy at the end of Mass I would be especially busy, in the hope Pete might be so impressed he would forget to deliver 'the lecture'. But he never did. Usually it happened when I was washing the cruets. He would suddenly swing round and then descend on me. This big, still powerful old man would go into an absolute, irrational rage as he remembered some real or imagined error:

'You didn't hold the cruets correctly as you poured the wine.'

Or:

'You didn't put the book in the right place when you crossed over from the epistle to the gospel side.'

Or:

'Who taught you to genuflect, you little bugger?'

I would try to stand there meekly, telling myself to put up with it, offer it up as an 'act of atonement' for other — perhaps more real — sins, make allowances because the poor old coot was mental, but I don't mind admitting that on a few occasions I wet my pants I was just so frightened. At all times I could hear Grace's voice:

'Respect for the cloth, Teddy. Always have respect for the cloth.'

This meant, we were told, that while the human wearing the religious habit might show signs of human frailty, the religious orders themselves had been created by Christ through His Apostles. Well, Pete's lectures were bad enough, but often he would punctuate his tirade with left hooks which the parents of the altar boys tolerantly called 'boxes on the ears' — fine for them, but they weren't on the receiving end of what were quite hefty punches. If I ducked he'd say, 'Stand still you little bugger.' This was the man who had just held the Body of Christ in those same hands!

And yet, one of the highlights of my school life occurred when I was selected to sing at Pete's diamond anniversary — sixty years a priest. I sang an old Irish song — 'Soggarth Aroon, the Parish Priest'.

> Who in the winter's night?
> Soggarth Aroon
> Who, when the snow is white?
> Soggarth Aroon
> Who, when the shadows fall?
> Who, when the people call?
> Who serves us one and all?
> Soggarth Aroon

As I sang I looked down from the stage at the old man sitting in the front row of the old bluestone parish hall. He wore his silk black suit, black shirt front and white dog-collar, and he held his black Homburg hat and his walking stick in his blue-veined chilblained hands. His eyes were closed, and I speculated that probably he was thinking of his boyhood in far-off Ireland. But then, perhaps he was thinking of supper. Or beautiful Sister Mary Josepha? Or nothing at all? It didn't matter to me. I was having my moment of nervous glory, and I knew — didn't I? — that one day I too would be a priest.

2

Herooooodasportingglobesmithsweekly

Oh, didn't I practise it!

'*Herooooodasportingglobesmithsweekly!*'

You had to have a personal style as a paper boy, I could see that, so I modelled myself absolutely on that doyen of paper boys: Nigger O'Reilly.

I am appalled nowadays that we called him that, to his face, and thought there was nothing wrong with calling a young Aboriginal boy 'Nigger' or, more affectionately we felt, 'Nig'. He used to sell morning and evening papers at the busy Moreland Road-Sydney Road intersection, and did he have *style* ! As the number 20 Coburg tram reached Moreland Road, heading for the city, Nig would swing aboard.

'Paper! Read all about it,' he'd chant. He would flick his fingers and a folded newspaper was offered to all and sundry.

'Gooday, Nig,' most people would say as he covered the entire length of the tram, no matter how crowded. Nobody was vindictive to him for all held him in absolute awe. After all, Aboriginals were already very scarce in Victoria, and the only Aboriginals we ever saw as kids were Nigger, Pastor Doug Nicholls — who was often in the news in the

17

football pages – and the man in the 'Mine Tinkit They Fit' advertisements for Pelaco shirts. Nigger had a gruff voice and he treated everybody laconically.

'Ar there, Ace,' or 'G'day Champ,' he'd respond, but he would be concentrating on the hands, watching for the proferred coins which represented a sale. He could sell twenty papers while the tram was waiting to cross Moreland Road. Often another tram would be crossing, and this meant the conductor had to lever the lines across or we'd have finished up in Carlton. Having covered the tram Nig would move for the doorway. Just when you thought the tram was going so fast he wouldn't dare dismount, he would casually complete his last sale, swing off the tram like a ballet dancer, and be gone. I suppose Nig was about twelve, and what an artist.

Mr Morley, the newsagent, told me I had to be at the shop by 3.50 p.m each day, Monday to Friday, ready to sell the CITY EXTRA edition of the *Herald*. That was the first edition. Because my 'stand' at Brown's Pub was only a few doors from the newsagency I would only take a dozen papers and replenish as required. Try carrying a dozen newspapers and you find out how heavy paper is. And I could see from studying Nigger that mobility was the key. On and off those trams, Ted. (I never thought of myself as Teddy, of course.) I had a leather strap across my chest, and this helped hold the papers. A leather money bag with a clip was over the other shoulder. Mr Morley would give me my change — usually enough to cover the contingency of being given two shillings for a twopenny *Herald* early in the day's sales — and away I'd go, working from 4 to 6.30 p.m., when the pubs had emptied.

'Heroooda paper,' I self-consciously said to myself on the first couple of days, but confidence came quickly. Most nights it was just the *Herald* for sale, but on Wednesday there was the pink *Sporting Globe* and on Thursday the

"Mine Tinkit They Fit"

`Mine Tinkit they Fit' ads for Pelaco shirts would be considered racist
today, but in Melbourne in the 1940s we thought nothing of them.

less popular *Smith's Weekly*. Occasionally, one of the
women in the Ladies' Lounge at Brown's would ask for a
New Idea, a *Woman's Mirror* or the *Women's Weekly*, and
it was easy enough to dash down to the shop and get
special orders like this. There could well be a tip in a
special sale like that, and I'd turn on the style.

'Isn't he well-mannered?' I'd smugly hear them say, as
they drank their little five-ounce beers or sipped furtively
on their 'fourpenny darks' — muscat to wine buffs.

Business was slow until 5 p.m so I had the chance to
read through the paper myself, studying the headlines,
looking at the race form and glancing through the comics.
Then, suddenly, the trams and the pub would be full as
people went home from work. I quickly got used to the
amazing level of noise as the strident voices of the men
echoed from the tiled walls and floors of the pub. It was
the time of the six o'clock swill and women were not
allowed to drink in the public bars. The men all had this

frenetic air to them: come on, let's get as many as we can
into us. I was dumbfounded at first, for there was never
any alcohol in our house, and I, recently 'confirmed' by
Doctor Mannix, had already taken a 'sacred oath' which
meant that 'under pain of mortal sin' I promised never to
touch alcohol until my twenty-fifth birthday. But I came
to accept the noise, the pervading smell of stale beer, the
cigarette smoke and the jostle. These were my customers,
and I was soon on a first-name basis with many of them.

'Gooday, Teddy,' they'd say. Or, perhaps:

'Howyergoin', Snowball.' All boys were called Snowball
if you didn't know their names. It didn't matter if your
hair was jet-black, as mine was, you'd be 'Snow' or
'Snowball'.

I was nine when I started at Morley's. It was 1941
and the war had been going two years. I was still at St
Paul's school so I didn't get all that much opportunity to
study Nigger O'Reilly except when I'd travel as a passenger on the tram. There would be the occasional trip to
Brunny — Brunswick, the next suburb on the way to the
city — and about once a month our family would travel
by tram to Carlton to see 'the aunts' who lived at 170
Neill Street. That would mean changing trams at Moreland Road, and I would have the chance to watch Nigger's
total strategy as he worked the intersection. He never
seemed to walk much, he just swung on and off trams,
and he'd be at one of the four corners whenever a crowd
had converged to wait for a tram.

I vowed to become as good as Nig at swinging from
one moving tram to another going in the opposite direction. Eventually, I could do it and I worked the Bell
Street-Sydney Road intersection with absolute flair.

'Paper! Read all about it! Latest report from the Middle
East! Sixth Divvy has Eye-ties on the run! Read all about
it! Dicky Reynolds injured!' And always a penny in the
same hand that proferred the folded *Herald*, so that when

they gave me the predictable threepenny coin I would drop the penny change into their hand at the same time I passed the paper. You never got tips on the trams, so there was no point in trying to milk them. Tips only came from the tipsy, in the pub. Speed was vital on the trams, for they moved quickly away from Bell Street, and it was a long walk back from Victoria Street, the next stop on a southbound tram, or O'Hea's Road on a northbound. On you go, Ted. Couple of quick sales and try if possible to swing off the wrong side of the tram if the conny isn't watching, preferably on to the wrong side of a tram going in the opposite direction, couple more sales and swing off, making sure everybody was watching. Three skips off the tram, straight into the public bar at the pub.

'Getyerpaperrrr! Harold Badger riding Ajax in the Futurity!'

I loved it.

Melbourne was already a bustling place in war terms. Service personnel were everywhere, going to and coming from the war. No Yanks yet, and the actual fighting was a long way away from Australia, but we followed every minute detail. We knew every color patch of every unit in the Australian army. We knew the insignia for every rank in the three services. We could identify every type of German ship and submarine, for there were charts telling us how to spot the enemy, and where to report. We obeyed the admonition:

DON'T GOSSIP. WALLS HAVE EARS

for we were on the lookout for spies at all times. A lot of shops had already boarded up their windows, and poor old Tony Lopes, an Italian fruiterer who had a fruit shop in O'Hea's Road, had a large sign consisting of a pair of crossed Union Jacks and:

A. LOPES, NAT'ZED AUSSIE

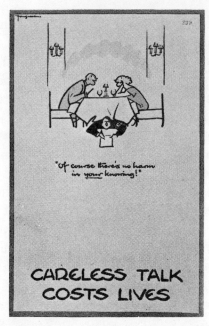

Typical wartime poster, warning us of the spies in our midst

written underneath. It was not a good time for people with Italian or German names.

I had been chosen as St Paul's School's entrant in a national handwriting competition where we had to write, in best Sisters of Mercy style, lightly up, firmly down,

Lend to defend. Buy War Savings Certificates.

I didn't win, and I recall that the winner's entry was absolute copperplate. I look at my handwriting today and shudder, but in those times handwriting was a big thing from the first day at school when you made strokes, then butcher's hooks, on your slate, squeaking away and gradually progressing to 'running writing'. The nuns produced some wonderful handwriters, my three sisters included, and I have a cousin, Laurie Dwyer, who to this day uses the old wooden pen with the steel nib, dipping it neatly into the ink and flour-

ishing his arm before launching into one of his beautifully written letters.

Because we were of Irish-Catholic stock we had lots of
relations, and our house became a focal point for cousins
who had joined up when war was declared. Pat and Peg
were already attractive teenagers, and both played the
piano by ear. Sal was eleven and was 'learning music'. My
Dad loved to play the squeezebox, so parties were common
in our house from that time until the end of the war. Not
that we needed a party to start us singing. I realise now
that Pop (I never called him Google) and Grace were not
only wonderful parents, they were amazingly good con-
trollers of children in their different ways. We would often
just sit on around the kitchen table after tea, and they'd
get us singing. While a song was going Grace would
unobtrusively steer one of us to the sink to wash and then
she'd pass teatowels to whoever was drying the dishes.
So much did we enjoy singing I can remember prolonging
it by drying a single knife, fork or plate for minutes.
Because we knew that the next part of the routine was
'Pat! Ted! Shirley! Peg! Soap, flannel, towel and dish.' I
don't know whether Grace genuinely got our names mixed
up. I suspect it was a foible she knew was always good
for a laugh.

The wherewithals for a wash would be brought from
the bathroom to the kitchen. The kettle would be boiling
gently on the wood stove. Put the cold water in first. Never
the hot water first, you'll scald yourself. Sal and I would
have a wash in the kitchen, the bigger girls would then
add extra hot water and take the same dish to the
bathroom for their wash. Geoffrey, who would soon be
called Tim, was long since washed, in his pyjamas, probably asleep. After our wash, off to bed, but occasionally
I'd be allowed to wait up and watch Pop shave.

Nowadays kids watch TV. Because he had to get up
early, and we didn't have hot water on tap, Pop took

advantage of the fire still going in the wood stove. The kettle was reheated after the kids' wash, and he would prepare for the wonderful ritual he created in the simple business of having a shave.

Into the bathroom he'd go to collect his shaving mug, soap, brush, razor, mirror and towel. He would lean his mirror against the sugar tin, and spread his towel so that half was a mat and the other half he could use as a towel, which he would tuck into his shirt front. He would unpack his Gillette safety razor, take his razor blade from its wrapping and briskly hone the blade on the inside of a medicine glass he always had for this purpose. He could make a razor blade last for *months*. Then, after assembling the razor, he poured boiling water into his shaving mug, dipped the brush, rubbed it on the stick of shaving soap and started lathering. I've never seen a barber do it with such flourish. His face would double its size. So thick was the foamy white cover Pop looked like a giant cream bun. A flourish of the arm like the conductor of an orchestra, dip the razor into the water, and start slicing away at his face. As each stripe was removed his face would be revealed pink, scalded and absolutely gleaming. At the other end of the table I would be watching, entranced, mentally practising every move. Usually Pop had a 'oncer' but if he knew the shave must last until the next night when he might be going to Lodge or playing cards, he would have a 'twicer', re-lathering his face and doing another lap. Every bit of lather would be peeled away, the razor would twirl in the shaving mug, and then he would turn his face to different angles in the mirror to admire his handiwork. I suspect he rather liked me watching him, but I'm certain the ritual would have been as elaborate with no spectators. There would only be a couple of spots of shaving soap in his ears, or in his nostrils. He'd dab these away with the towel, unscrew the razor, dry every component part, re-wrap his razor blade, pack it all into its bakelite case, throw the towel over his arm and repair to the bathroom. Going past me he would wink, nod his head and say 'Right. Off to bed.' He would then start to roll his five cigarettes for the next day. In a couple of years I'd be allowed to help.

I'd leave the kitchen and head for bed. I slept on what we called 'the back verandah' but it was more an enclosed porch than an open verandah. Before retiring there was always the last piddle, over the little hedge which grew near the dunny, directing a squirt at our cocker spaniel Roger when he was silly enough to come within range. Or perhaps a hold-it-back, let-it-go spurt to see how high up the back wall of the house I could hit. I didn't prolong things too much, for to 'play with yourself' was very definitely a mortal sin, one of the worst. The priests at Confession always seemed to want to know detail when you slipped in 'And I committed impure actions once, Father' in among the 'Missed my morning prayers' and 'I was disobedient three times, Father'. They didn't seem to care who it was you had disobeyed, or the circumstances, but they always wanted chapter and verse on the impure actions. What could you say? 'I was playing with my dick?' That would have been another sin. No, it was *'mumble mumble mumble* private parts, Father', which always attracted a hefty penance and the requirement to ask Our Lady to purify one's thoughts, words and actions. Now say a good Act of Contrition.

If I wasn't already up next morning getting ready for Mass, the next sound I'd hear would be Grace getting Pop off to work at about 6.30 a.m. I would strain my ear to try to get details of conversation as Grace cut sandwiches for lunch (or 'dinner' as the midday meal was called then) for Pop and us kids.

Pop would have been up earlier to make the porridge if it was winter — and it always seems to have been winter in Melbourne. He made magnificent porridge, my

dad, having soaked the oats overnight. Next morning he'd
stir the pot on the stove until the texture was perfect. In
between stirs he would rub his hands together in front of
the stove to stimulate some warmth. He'd ladle out his
porridge, add sugar and milk, tap his spoon three or four
times in the palm of his hand — I now do that — and
eat. The pot would be on the side of the stove when the
rest of us got up. Then he'd prepare his boiled egg and
toast, perhaps singing along with the hillbillies on the
wireless or, if it was Shirley Thoms or June Holmes
singing, offering a comment like 'Squarking bloody
females.'

Only my sister Pat can make and butter toast as well
as Pop. It sounds silly to list toastmaking as an art form,
but you should try my sister Pat's toast. Pop was a great
man for ritual as I've said. Although there would still be
a tablecloth on the kitchen table from last night he would
spread out some newspaper and use it as people use table
mats today. He'd read the newspaper as he decapitated a
soft-boiled egg as precisely as a guillotine would lop a
head. He would butter his thick toast from edge to edge,
then scoop out the soft centre with his finger and thumb,
turn the toast over and butter the other side. He then cut
off all the crusts into delicate 'fingers' which he would dip
into his meticulously salted and peppered egg. It was all
done with absolute relish.

His pot of weak black tea would be handy and, if Grace
was there, he'd make a great thing of pouring 'long' tea
as he called it, aiming the stream of boiling tea from about
two feet away, into his special cup — no saucer, to save
the washing-up. He would do this in the knowledge that
Grace would feign alarm. 'Oh, careful, Poppy,' she'd say,
and then, a profoundly shocked 'Joe!' when he'd deliber-
ately slurp his tea, something he'd never otherwise do.
He and Grace would play these little role-games all the
time. There was absolutely no doubt Grace was the boss

in our home, but she liked to play this demure suburban housewife role to Pop's mischievous little boy.

It was probably to convince herself she was happy, whereas she was the most unfulfilled of women, a victim of her age and environment, a woman who could have been anything, given today's opportunities. And unlike a lot of women of her day Grace knew where she was missing out. She'd always had to live in the shadow of her sister Mary, who had travelled the world — working like a slave to achieve it, mind — but when Mary left the family farm to travel the world Grace became the next 'Mother's help' in a large family of boys. Unlike Mary, Grace never escaped life's humdrum: in her case, marriage, kids, the Depression, poverty. I felt we were kindred spirits, and that I could read into the active mind which she felt it was necessary to sublimate in otherwise boring chores like ironing, given that there was no chance of any other lifestyle. I lit the fire late one afternoon, and made her a cup of tea. She sat for a moment in the dim light and said to me, 'You know, Teddy, I'd have made a great surgeon.' I looked at her and thought, Yes, you would.

In the mornings if I was still in bed Pop poked his head around the door to say 'Hooroo'. Never 'Goodbye' or 'See you later'. Always 'Hooroo'. Grace would give him a perfunctory kiss, and I'd wait in anticipation for the click of the front door as Pop left, for then would come the first laugh of the day.

Without fail, as soon as Pop was gone, Grace would let fly with one of her almighty farts. It was a shock at first. You think your mother is like the queen or the nuns, and doesn't fart, but Grace was a beauty. Once I got used to the fact of her flatulence I anticipated each day's fusillade with delight and would inevitably roar with laughter when it was fired. One day Grace heard me. She stormed onto the back verandah with a 'Fart? What fart?' look on her face and a simulated sternness to add weight to her warning 'If you're not ready for school in ten minutes it's not too early to take you into the wash-house, young man.'

3
Before The War

My Mum constantly said, 'Teddy, you were born on the coldest day for thirty years.' But when I eventually looked up the newspapers of that day, 6 July 1932, I discovered it was merely a normal Melbourne winter's day — early morning frosts and fogs, rain later. No colder than average. It's funny how we reminisce about things that never happened. I guess it seemed colder than normal to Grace, having a fourth baby in the middle of winter in the middle of the worst economic depression Australia had known. I was born at home, at 4 Higinbotham Street, and Nurse Regan, who lived on the corner of O'Hea's Road and Higinbotham Street, was the midwife. I weighed in at a fairly hefty 5 1/2 kilograms (12 pounds in those days).

My Dad was out of work due to the Depression, and we were fairly lucky to have our own home in those troubled days. Dad was in the Irish National Foresters (always referred to as 'The Lodge') which covered us for health and sickness benefits. We were very proud of a large photograph of all the members of the lodge, wearing green sashes, for Dad and Phil Fury, a family friend, were the two leading officials. I guess all funding and lending institutions had to be flexible in those lean times, for we survived even though Dad was unemployed for a couple of bitter years.

Our house was mortgaged to the State Savings Bank of Victoria (later called The State Bank) and Pop often said, 'If it wasn't for the bank in the Depression we'd have lost the house for sure. There were times when I could only pay sixpence a week off our debt, sometimes nothing at all, but the manager said he understood. He just wanted me to keep in touch with him at all times'.

My sisters tell me they were initially thrilled at the arrival of a baby brother, but their enthusiasm waned when they discovered they had to mind me and sing me to sleep. Pat was aged nine — born on St Patrick's Day 1923, so a good Irish-Catholic family had her baptised Patricia. Peg, whose real name is Margaret, was seven, and Sal, correctly Shirley, was almost two. My Mum was thirty-one and my Dad thirty-four when I was born.

Grace was born Grace Brennan at Banyena, in the Wimmera region of Victoria, on 8 March 1901. Her parents were Peter Brennan, an Irishman from Chequer Hill, near Dunmore, County Galway, and Martha Williams, who was a 'native' of Australia, as white people born in this country were then described. Martha Williams' parents were Robert Williams, a sailor from Mousehole, Cornwall, who had jumped ship at Portland, and Honorah Corcoran, from County Cork, Ireland, who had come to Australia as one of Caroline Chisholm's emigrant girls, called by Mrs Chisholm 'God's Police'. Robert Williams finished up a fairly wealthy farmer at Dunkeld, near the Grampian Mountains in rich western Victoria. But he started life as the first prisoner in Portland Goal and went on to work for Victoria's famous pioneers, the Henty Brothers for a time.

Joseph Egan was born at Timboon, in the western district of Victoria, on 26 January 1898. He, and of course we, thought his parents were John Egan, from Thurles,

Tipperary, Ireland and his wife Elizabeth. Years later we learned otherwise.

Grace and Joe had both been reared in large Irish-Catholic families, and were 'good' Catholics themselves. Being a 'good' Catholic did not necessarily mean that you were 'good' in the real sense of the term, but that you 'went to Mass and the Sacraments'. My parents met at a dance at Camperdown, married there in 1922 and moved to Melbourne just as the Depression started. Straight into the dole queues.

Our neat little house was built in weatherboard, painted beige, with chocolate-brown trimming. It had a galvanised iron roof, which allowed us as kids the ecstasy valued so much by Australians, the delightful sound of rain on a tin roof as you lay snug in your bed. No other elemental sound equals it, this ongoing Australian baptism. There was a front verandah, and a hallway through the house, which had a lounge room, main bedroom, the so-called 'dining room' which did in fact have a dining table, but was usually the bedroom for my sisters, as well as having two or three spare beds for visitors. There was a bathroom, but we did not have hot water laid on. When it was bath-time we would carry hot water in buckets from the copper in the washhouse. We had a modestly equipped kitchen with a wood (and later, a gas) stove, sink, table and chairs, and a wooden 'dresser' to store cutlery, crockery and food. We did not have an ice chest until about 1941. I used to sleep on the back porch, which was next to the washhouse. In the back yard there was a lavatory, which was sewered, fortunately. We had lots of relations in the country who still used the old 'dunnycan' and we city-ites used to dread 'going to the lav' when we visited them. (When did we start to say 'go to the toilet' in Australia? During the war I guess.) Later, we had a little 'bungalow' as we called it, a little cabin built in the backyard. In the backyard there was room for a clothes line, cricket pitch, a big plum tree and, from time to time, chooks and a vegetable garden.

Mum and Dad each had just a few years of primary education at small schools in the bush. Like all ex-country people they constantly reminded us how they had to milk cows before walking miles to school, but it was all very true in their case.

I have no infantile memories, and my first clear recollection is starting school at St Paul's in 1936, learning to write on a scratchy slate in 'The Bubs', as the first year of school was called. I certainly don't remember the day my sisters love to recall, when, aged about two and a half, I apparently pooped my pants on a tram one day when Grace had taken me to the Shrine of Remembrance. The story gets better and better each year the girls tell it. It seems I was screaming, 'It's running down my legs' in the middle of a crowded tram. Grace had to get off the tram in Royal Parade, Parkville, and hose me down with a sprinkler hose she disconnected, getting soaked herself in the process. It must have provided a good laugh for the passengers, but Grace was like Queen Victoria — 'not amused'.

I don't remember, either, another occasion when I apparently caused a public laugh, this time on a train. I was about three, I'm told. My Dad was taking me into the city by train, and we passed through a little tunnel at North Melbourne. Apparently all was quiet on the train, and I asked in a quite loud voice: 'Is this what it's like inside the Black Maria, Dad?' All eyes on the train apparently turned to have a good look at 'Dad'.

To this day, I can't work out why I started school at age three and a half, in 1936. But I did. It meant I was always the youngest in my class, right through school and it was a handicap right through school. I became an absolute 'smart-arse', convinced I could get away with murder because, although young, I never had problems with lessons or passing exams. I look back on my entire school life with regret, for I gave some nice teachers hell, and didn't learn the fundamentals of anything, in real terms. I quickly absorbed the techniques of passing exams, so I breezed through school, eventually doing incongruous things like being First in Victoria in economics — a real joke, as anybody who knows me well will affirm. But then, economics in Victoria has become a long-standing joke in itself.

I was born into a narrow xenophobic lifestyle, which nonetheless provided a secure existence and lots of laughs. As Irish Catholics we felt very free to ridicule anybody who was not like us. Our house was always full of friends and relations, very definitely just like us. They all seemed to take absolute guidance from Archbishop Daniel Mannix, affectionately called 'Dinky Dan' — the tall, aloof, fiery Irish Archbishop of Melbourne who constantly confronted the Australian Establishment. If we weren't having a 'party' (which was not a lavish affair, but singing and dancing in the lounge room at home), it would be political talk concentrating on the vital question 'What did the English do to the Irish?' Or there would be card-games. Two Irish priests, Fathers Lynch and Duggan, were regular visitors for a game called 'Forty-Fives' and the kitchen table resounded to the thumps as they trumped one another's cards. Our family delights in recalling a night when at about 11.30 p.m. Father Lynch remembered he had not finished saying his Office, the Latin panegyric all priests had to say daily, and aloud. He retired briefly from the game, knelt in the corner of the room where he rattled off the remainder of the Office, and then returned to the table saying:

'Right, now who led that bloody ace?'

School at St Paul's was an extension of family life. Many of the Sisters of Mercy were Irish, and formidable. The nuns either walked to school from the convent in pairs, or travelled in the little black 'Nuns' Bus' driven by a cadaverous man named Mr Perry. The nuns had long black habits with a leather belt, and long rosary beads which rattled ominously from their waists. Starched white wimples framed their faces and gave them an awe-inspring countenance. Very occasionally a wisp of hair would erotically be exposed, but the most striking thing was that they had no ears.

Usually the nuns recited the Rosary aloud as they walked to school, and 'teachers' pets' would ingratiate themselves, carrying the nuns' cases and joining in the Rosary. Unlike today, most of the teachers at Catholic schools were nuns, although we had a couple of long-term lay teachers, Miss White in Grade Five and 'Cocky' Reardon in Grade Three. Cocky was a great favorite, even though her nickname derived from her high-pitched voice, and we used to vie to carry her case for her when she came into O'Hea's Road at May Street. She knew all of Coburg's gossip, and we would have a great old chat as we walked to school with her. She was kind and an excellent teacher, much loved for her mannerisms, her beautiful handwriting and sound teaching methods

It's interesting to me that I have such precise memories of the war, yet I only remember a few specific things prior to 1939.

I remember getting a Coronation Medal in 1937. I remember seeing the Australian world-champion cyclist Hubert Opperman — the immortal 'Oppy' — riding from Melbourne to Sydney on a three-wheeler kid's bike. 'Oppy' was raising funds for charity, and we all lined up in Sydney Road outside St Paul's to give him three cheers as he rode past. I remember being introduced to a new word — 'glut' — when we were given apples and pears daily as a result of this glut announced by the Apple and Pear Board. And I remember the outbreak of infantile paralysis because my school mate Marty Mullins contracted polio — although it wasn't called 'polio' in those days — and Marty was wheeled to school on a big flat trolley and then later had his legs in irons.

I remember hearing the names of Hitler and Franco, Andrew 'Boy' Charlton, the Australian Olympic swimming champion, and Jesse Owens, the immortal American athlete.

But that's about the sum total of specific recollections.

From the outset to the present I have enjoyed incredible health. Rarely a day's sickness, good hard bones, good teeth until a kick in the mouth in a schoolboy football match removed a couple of teeth and broke my jaw — but that was later. I loved games, particularly the fundamentals of games, and I would practise catching and throwing or bowling for hours, on my own if necessary. I became adept at kicking with either foot before it was accepted practice, as we kicked 'paper footies' made from tightly-rolled newspapers for endless hours. In the summer we played cricket, either in the backyard for 'Sheffield Shield' games, or on the street for the 'Tests'. It was normal for kids to play on the street, and was quite safe then.

Higinbotham Street ran north and south between Gaffney Street and O'Hea's Road. There were around sixty weatherboard houses, thirty on either side of a quite attractive bitumen street, which had cobble-stone guttering, brick paved footpaths, and big gum trees every forty yards on both sides of the street. The residents of Higinbotham Street were all working-class people, and only two or three people in the street had cars. Those with cars had a driveway. Cars were never parked on the street. That provided the kids of the street with a huge communal playground, where you could put a rubbish tin up for a cricket wicket, and have a good unimpeded game of cricket for hours, without any sign of a truck or car. Usually the only traffic was the various horse-drawn carts.

The milkie came with his four-wheel cart in the early hours of the morning and filled the billycan left on the front verandah. He carried a big bucket of milk together with a half-pint scoop. His horse walked slowly along the street, usually with a nose-bag on, and the milkie ran swiftly and quietly from house to house, signalling to his patient, obedient horse with low whistles or clicking noises. A steamy snort into the nosebag and clip clop would go the docile horse, walking quietly until told to 'Whoa there.'

The baker was a different turnout altogether. His was a light, two wheeled high-framed horse-drawn jinker, with a bread box at the back of a high, precarious seat. He came during the morning, travelling at a brisk trot, coming to absolute stops, whereupon he would run to deliver bread from a basket to about six houses at a time. 'Baker,' he shouted cheerily, as he delivered the lovely, hot, crusty 'high-tin' loaves that still had that straight-from-the-oven smell. Someone would come from each house to collect the bread, and then the baker would move on.

One of life's great challenges for young boys was to 'whip behind' the baker's cart, which meant that, with perfect timing, you sneaked onto the little step at the back of the cart just as the baker climbed into the front seat, so the hopefully unseen passenger got an exciting ride as his playmates yelled, 'Whip behind the baker's cart'. You had to get off with equally precise timing before the baker caught you and gave you what I later in the Northern Territory heard referred to as 'the Scobie Send Off' — an arse full of leather.

Mr Howlett delivered wood in the winter and ice in the summer to those lucky enough to have ice-chests. We didn't know what a refrigerator was, and we only got an ice-chest during the war. Mr Howlett was a kind man who always gave us a piece of ice, chipped from a big block with his ice pick. What a thrill that was! We would wrap the ice in our hankies or a piece of rag to make it last longer as we slurped and sucked appreciatively. Mr Howlett's wagon was always pulled by two Shetland ponies, and we loved to pat these sturdy little animals.

Melbourne, we felt, manifested its 'superiority' over Sydney in many ways. One of these was that we referred to the garbage collector as 'the dustman' whereas we were sure the vulgar Sydneysiders called him 'the garbo'. The dustman had a dray pulled by a big Clydesdale draught horse, and he collected the rubbish twice a week. We looked forward to those days, especially on school holidays, as there was always the prospect of collecting some horse manure for the garden. Not that we were great gardeners, but we kids used to stand fascinated as the horse shuffled, shook its harness and chains, and then, without a care in the world, disdainfully lifted its tail and had a chaffy, steaming shit. Then the horse waited patiently while the dustman emptied the rubbish tins, swept the gutter, and shovelled the dirt from the gutter into his dray. The horse seemed very contented. He would let us pat him as his bitted mouth ground away at his nosebag of chaff. His tail relentlessly swished the flies away. His huge steel-shod hairy hooves seemed at first to be stamping out a message of impatience, but as we watched closely we could see that the horse never ever moved once instructed to 'whoa'. The little stamps and the rattle of harness was just to keep the flies moving, and to assert a bit of equine authority too, we felt, for they were such noble animals.

Occasionally there would be a fish man, or a fruit man, with scales on the back of the cart, but in the main, meat, fruit and vegetables were purchased at the nearby shops in O'Hea's Road. Fish and chips, vital to Catholics who were not allowed to eat meat on Fridays, were bought at the fish and chip shop near the railway line. Men often came on bicycles to sharpen knives and scissors. They put their bikes on a stand and then operated a grindstone by pedalling the stationary machine as they did the sharpening. Other men came periodically to sell clothes props — long, forked sticks to push the wire clothes line to maximum height. In those days before telephones and fax machines, the postman came twice a day, on his bike. He blew his whistle as he put mail into your letter box. Letter-writing was definitely the means of communication for people like us, and it is sobering to reflect that in those days a letter posted in Geelong in the late afternoon would be delivered at Coburg the next morning.

Our games on the streets were great fun, as plenty of kids were always attracted, and it was a good lesson in organisation and control. Older kids organised the games and picked the teams. Two captains would call the names and you went to stand behind your captain. I was good at games and always selected early, but it must have been agonising for kids like Fat Stoneham, always left forlorn, last to be chosen, and taken into a team on sufferance. Away we'd go into spirited games of cricket, Keepings off, Branders, Tip-cat, Release and dozens of different team games with balls or skipping ropes or hop-scotch courses. On the long summer evenings we would play Hidey or Kick the tin. Girls had a few 'girls only' games mainly focussing on skipping and hopscotch, and the 'boys only' games included Cherry bobs, Footy cards and Alleys (marbles) but the main concentration for boys was cricket in the summer and footy or Hoppo bumpo in the winter. Fat Stoneham was hopeless at most games but he was invincible at Hoppo bumpo where you had to hop through a team of hopping defenders and cross a line. Fat would just steer a straight line and leave a pile of bodies in his wake.

My Dad loved Fat Stoneham. Fat believed everything Pop told him, implicitly, so of course he was the recipient of many confidential secrets. 'For your ears only, Fat.' Fat gave us all a good laugh one evening when a large crowd of both kids and parents were having a lively game of cricket in the street. For some reason we were using a hard 'compo' ball, made of solid rubber. I was batting and smacked the ball straight at Fat, and it hit him on the head, knocking him over.

'Well fielded, Fat,' Pop shouted.

'Yes,' said Fat as he got to his feet, ruefully rubbing his head. 'Thanks, Mr Egan. I'm glad I got to it, or he'd have scored a four.'

Isn't it strange how large the things of your childhood are written in your mind? I am sure the gum trees growing in Higinbotham Street were huge. They certainly had to be pruned back from the power lines regularly, and it was quite an adventure to climb them, particularly in the evenings when we were playing Hidey. I go back to Higinbotham Street now and there are no trees. Not only that, the street is so narrow you wonder how all those marvellous games were played on such a grand scale. You try to imagine trees, but there just isn't any room. It's the cars. They've displaced the trees and stopped the games.

I feel so sorry for kids today, with all their video games and expensive toys and electronic gadgets. Their constant plaintive cry is: 'I'm bored'. Never once was I bored as a child. Never once.

4

Glimpses Under
The Surface

It's fascinating to talk to my three sisters and my brother
Geoffrey, who nowadays is called Tim. As adults we all
look back on a very happy childhood. We love to get
together, sing the songs of our childhood and go over a
few standard reminiscences about Grace smiling benignly
while 'screwing the flesh' or Pop's propensity for puns and
poetry (and alliteration! I wonder where I inherited it?).
But although we agree we were a very close family I find
it staggering how little actual detail I know of the lives
and thoughts and worries and ambitions of my brother
and sisters. I guess it's all part of the Celtic tradition. You
do things like singing spontaneously, yet try to conceal
your private emotions and personal feelings behind a
gregarious front.

I mentioned my Mum taking me to the Shrine of
Remembrance at age two. Pooping my pants notwith-
standing, I realise I shared experiences with Grace that
none of the other children had. I feel sure my brother Tim
would say the same. But my sisters have been genuinely
surprised to hear me tell of things that Grace did and
things she told me.

In particular I became aware of her abhorrence of war,

41

based on her intrinsic cynicism about politicians, and the experiences of her three brothers in the carnage of World War 1. When in later years I wrote my 'Song for Grace' (in the first person) other members of the family expressed surprise that I had been Grace's confidant to this level as she expressed her feelings about the 'war to end all wars'.

When Grace died we found among her cherished possessions a little box marked 'Last Messages from Brothers'.

It was typical of Grace for she had a very orderly mind, and knew what was worth keeping. Among various letters there was only one thing from her brother Jack. A standard Christmas card issued to Australian soldiers in Egypt in 1914. It bore no message other than 'From Jack to Gracie'. She treasured it all her life and wept for him every Anzac Day. When I was about twelve I cried with her as she told me the story I have written into her song, of how her stern Irish father could not have her see him mourn the loss of his son.

Jack Brennan was probably a typical enlistment in the Australian Light Horse when war broke out in 1914. Born of Irish-Australian stock he was reared in rural Victoria. He was very fit (you had to be, even to be accepted into the Army in the first days of the war) and rode a horse gracefully and naturally. He would have been attracted by the sense of adventure suggested by the war, for our family are typical Celts, restless, looking for what we call romance. The lure of the uniform, and the once-in-a-lifetime chance to do something other than work on a farm would undoubtedly have appealed. He certainly would not have been endowed with any love of England, but he would have felt himself, as an Australian, to be part of the British Empire.

He joined the 9th Light Horse, had the standard studio photograph taken in Melbourne prior to embarkation, and sailed to Egypt, never to return. Like so many of the

Australian Light Horse he was sent to Gallipoli without his horse. After five months of hell, for he finished up a stretcher bearer so heavy were the casualties, he died of wounds on 16 October 1915. When one reads his last letter, written on 7 October to his sister Mary, it is poignancy itself to know that he was blinded and had a leg blown off in the nine days between writing the letter and his death.

The Dardanelles,
7th October 1915

My dear Sister,

I rec'd your very welcome letter of 13th August yesterday. Glad to hear that all were well. I am surprised that Bob passed the Docs. The exams cannot be so stringent now, for I nearly got fired out on account of the left eye being a bit weak. I hope this will be over before Bob gets here, for the sake of humanity in general. The loss of life is horrible and the dead ones are lucky in my opinion compared with those who lose their eyesight or limbs etc. Bob will probably get into the reinforcements to the 10th Reg. I hope he does for I would have a good chance of meeting him as they are of our Brigade and always near us, that is if I am still alive when he reaches here. I told you in my letter last week that I had met Martin. I see him frequently as they are not very far from us. He has been here 5 wks or so. Takes it all very philosophically of course. They have not been in any willing goes as yet.

I got a letter from the Mater, too. They have been having a rather trying winter apparently. I have received about six or seven letters from you so far but the letters from home are not very regular somehow, although I know they write enough. I see by the papers that good numbers are still enlisting. They will all be wanted for it seems that we are in for another twelve months of war at least. Looks as though a good harvest were assured throughout Aust. Had they had another bad season goodness knows what would have happened. The majority would have faced starvation.

Well, I'll conclude this, hoping it finds you in the best of health. My address is the same No. 378 Tpr etc, C Sqd 9th L H Reg, 3rd L H Brigade, A I E F is quite sufficient, Sqd, Reg and Brigade etc fully lettered of course.

What's left of the old Reg. of us are looking forward to a spell soon. We have had nearly five months strenuous. It tires one out and jangles the nerves. Well, goodbye dear sister.

Best love from
Jack.

When her brother Jack was killed at Gallipoli, Grace was the eldest child of her family still living with their parents. My song for her records her painful childhood experience:

The telegram came, my mother collapsed, and I had
The terrible task of breaking the news to my Dad.
With our old draught horse, Punch,
My father was ploughing the land.
I ran to the paddock,
The telegram clutched in my hand.
The Irishman read it, said 'Thank you,
Now leave me alone
Go on back to the house, help your mother,
She's there on her own.'
He called: 'Stand up Punch,
We have to get on with this job.'
But I saw his slumped shoulders
And I heard his heart-rending sob.

My song for Grace finishes with her denunciation of war:

Well, Robert was gassed
And he always had pains in his head

Martin was shell-shocked
And he'd have been better off dead
And I? I'm just an old lady
Who watched them all go
But I am the one you should ask
About war, for I know,
That all of these years have gone by
And I know the grief yet.
Yes, I will remember them
I can't forget.

Grace and I visited the Shrine of Remembrance regularly. Not that she agreed with the place conceptually. When it was built during the Depression years, by politicians looking for self-aggrandisement, Grace felt the money raised by public subscription should have been distributed among the many returned diggers then out of work. Spoils to the victors, indeed! I felt that Grace visited the Shrine mainly to leave the book which listed the men killed in the service of Australia open at the page where the name 'Brennan, John, 9th Light Horse' appeared. Then she would sit and have a little weep in the gardens. One Anzac Day she told me the story which almost word for word became my song in her honor.

Mothers and sons. Fathers and daughters. I saw a softer side of Grace that my sisters probably didn't, although I think they shared things with Pop that I didn't.

It wasn't that I was denied time or care or interest on the part of my Dad, for we played cricket and cards together and he was always very interested in my progress and achievements at school. I loved to sit and watch him shaving, mending our shoes, or doing his very lovely calligraphy in our books.

We shared a common interest in sport, and so I barracked for Richmond with him in the football, and in return he respected my judgement when it came to racehorses, for I was from an early age an avid student of breeding and racing form, and was very good at picking winners. When he took his 'four placed horses' card each week the selections were often mine.

He encouraged me each week to enter the tipping competition run by the *Sporting Globe*. The mid-week *Globe* came out on Wednesday, so between Thursday and Saturday morning the entries in the competition had to be posted or dropped into the *Herald* office in Flinders Street, Melbourne. The prize money jackpotted each week. They paid out a smaller amount for the highest number of winners selected, with the principal amount rising all the time against the prospect of anyone picking all the winners.

I was seven. Pop worked for F H Stephens, the shipping agents. He would get one of the Stephens drivers to drop my entry in at the *Herald* office each week. One particular Saturday afternoon, as Pop mended some shoes, we sat by the wireless, listening to the races. Race by race our excitement mounted, and we watched the wireless, unbelieving. The last race was run, and I'll never forget it. I had picked every winner of the seven races. The family spoke in hushed tones of the incredible sum of money I had just won.

'Three hundred and sixty quid,' said Pop as he checked the previous week's *Globe* for details. That was almost two years wages for a working man. We were rich!

But on the Monday evening Pop came home from work, pale and despondent. He looked at me as though he felt he had betrayed me.

'I'm so sorry,' he said. 'The bloody driver didn't put your entry form in.' To my amazement I took it all very philosophically, and fortunately I have always been like that with money. It's a handy commodity, but that's as far as it goes. I won't let it stuff up my life. But health! Now, there's something to be concerned about.

The greatest thing my Dad ever did for me was to inculcate a great love of cricket. During the summer months I would sometimes go to work with him on the Saturday morning, which was great because I got to travel around Melbourne with some of the drivers (I never did find out which one forgot the form), do simple little clerical jobs, or help load or unload the trucks. Often I would go with the drivers to exciting places like the wharves. And then, when Pop knocked off at midday, we'd go to the cricket, usually to the Melbourne Cricket Ground. There we'd meet Hec Brown and other friends who shared with my Dad a great affection for the game. They wouldn't like today's flamboyance, all the carry-on and the sledging, for they were men from a period when cricket equalled the ethics of life: you tried your best, you competed fiercely, but you didn't cheat or take any unfair advantage. And at the end of the game you shook hands with your opponent. Jardine, they felt, was the exception who proved the rule. Douglas Jardine, the architect of bodyline bowling, which was intended to fix the mighty Don Bradman, to knock him out if they couldn't get him out.

'Arrogant Pommy bastard,' was the opinion of Jardine my Dad ventured to Hec Brown one day.

'Stop praising him, Joe,' rejoined the phlegmatic Hec.

It was just marvellous for an impressionable boy to sit with these eloquent men. The generally slow pace of the great game of cricket provided ample opportunity for them to articulate their preferences for particular players, and to express their concern that players should never consider themselves more important than the game itself. They didn't have to go into the negatives, the it's-not-as-good-as-it-used-to-be stuff, for we were living the golden years of cricket when Don Bradman and Bill 'Tiger' O'Reilly reached heights never since attained by other players. In 1937 I was taken to see Don Bradman make 200 at the MCG. It was the Third Test against the old

enemy, England. As I was only five years of age I have
to acknowledge I don't remember the detail of the great
man's innings, but I do remember Pop saying:

'You're watching the greatest batsman the world will
ever know.' Little wonder I subsequently wrote my song
'The Tiger and The Don':

> When I was a kid each summer meant
> Long days at the MCG,
> With my dear old Dad and his Gladstone bag
> And his thermos of sweet black tea,
> Sandwiches, fruit cake, sitting up in the stand
> With my Dad and his mates at the cricket,
> I tell you, it was grand.
> There'd be a big post-mortem
> As every wicket fell,
> They'd pick their 'greatest-ever' teams
> And they wove me in their spell.
> They'd argue, but there was one point
> They all agreed upon,
> There'd never be a pair to match
> The Tiger and The Don
>
> My Dad said: 'Feast your eyes upon
> The Tiger and The Don
> You'll never see a pair like them again.
> Don's the greatest bat of all
> And when The Tiger's got the ball,
> He puts the fear of God in all those Englishmen.'

When I wrote and recorded the song in 1990, I sent a
copy of the recorded version to Sir Donald Bradman and
to Bill 'Tiger' O'Reilly. Typical of such great men, they
both wrote by return mail to say they had enjoyed the
song, and felt thrilled that their cricketing exploits had
obviously given such pleasure to so many people. I
cherish their letters, which are mounted with photos of
the two cricketing heroes. With them in the same frame
is a photo of my Dad in his cricket flannels. As a result

of his influence and enthusiasm I have enjoyed thousands of hours of watching, listening to and talking about the greatest game of all.

I am intensely proud of my Celtic inheritance, but we Celts certainly are embarrassed by displays of personal emotion, yet will sing songs that bring tears to our eyes as we approach jingoism in professing our Celtishness. If I record that neither of my parents once said 'I love you' to me, that further provokes the embarrassment, for I never tell my own kids that I love them. I think you *demonstrate* to kids that you love them by unstintingly and patiently giving them your time and your interest, trying to teach them and, equally importantly, letting them teach you. I only hope my kids know I love them, just as I knew, without needing to be told, that my parents loved me.

'Actions speak louder than words,' Grace would say.

'Example is better than precept,' Joe often told me. I guess he was telling me he loved me. I wonder if he realised that I loved him?

Paradoxically, we were reared to the tune of Grace's many precepts:

'Ask no questions and you'll be told no lies.'

'Show me your companions and I'll tell you what you are.'

'The more you stir, the more they stink.'

These are just a few that I recall her explaining in the periods after school when I seem to remember just Grace and me, in the kitchen, she ironing, me peeling spuds or otherwise helping to prepare for the evening meal which was called 'tea' (never 'dinner' — that was at lunchtime). Where were my sisters? They will be quick to remind me that they did a sight more housework than I, and I know that would be right, but isn't it strange that in my mind I see only Grace and me?

She taught me to iron. She passed on the fundamentals of cooking, for she was always scathing about men who expected women to do 'all the dirty work'. She passed on her opinions about this and that, and always came back to the dreadful realities of war. I guess she was concerned about raising sons who would inevitably, it seemed, fight in wars. War was the only thing that ever made her cry, and she was about to cry again, for in September 1939, only twenty-one years after the Armistice which was to restore peace forever had been signed, the armies began to roll across Europe once more, and we knew, automatically, that it would involve Australia.

I was about to remember things in precise detail.

5

The Boys Enlist

It was to be a long time before I knew anything about the facts of life so I was absolutely amazed when, on New Year's Day, 1939 my brother suddenly came into the world, weighing a massive 7 kilograms (15 pounds). Somebody must have had an inkling of the imminence of his birth, for I had been sent off to Ballarat for the day with an old uncle, J P Williams, along with my sisters. When we returned Grace was sitting up in bed. We had a new brother. As easy as that.

'That's good. Somebody to play footy with,' I said to Grace. 'What's his name?'

'Francis Geoffrey,' she replied, 'he'll be called Geoffrey.' Nobody ever knew where she got the names.

It was a joyful day for all of us, and 1939 was off to a good start, but that soon changed.

It had been a terribly hot summer. Day after day red dust from the Mallee palled the Melbourne skies. The sun was a fiery orange ball behind this ominous filter. Searing north winds blew relentlessly down streets like Higinbotham, which runs north-south. The nights seemed as sticky and as sweltering as the days. I failed to twig to the imminent birth of my brother, but I could sense that some other momentous thing was about to happen.

It did, in the shape of Black Friday, 13 January 1939. Fires raged all over Victoria, New South Wales and South Australia. The bush literally exploded. Seventy-one Victorians were burnt to death, and Melbourne was in a state of shock. My sister Pat had just had her first holidays as a working girl, and she had stayed at a guesthouse named 'The Glen' at Healesville. She was very proud of a framed photograph of herself with all the other guests, posed in front of a lovely old homestead with THE GLEN painted on the roof. When told the guesthouse had been reduced to a few twisted sheets of iron and some charred timbers Pat couldn't believe it. She cried inconsolably.

Indeed, the entire world was in turmoil, with a lot of concern about the antics of this fellow Adolf Hitler. There had also been vague mutterings about the Italian leader, Mussolini, who had invaded a place called 'Albania', but nobody was quite sure where that was: there was confusion with Abyssinia, which the Italians had also invaded. But as we hadn't heard of either place they didn't matter all that much to us. We didn't know how to take 'Musso', as he was invariably called. Was he a fun figure or a fair dinkum rogue? The Pope was Italian, so they were sort of 'on our side' as Catholics, even though we felt free to call Italians (other than the Pope, of course) 'dagoes'. But the Germans were different. We were still sure from the so-called Great War that the Germans were a dangerous bunch. It was fairly obvious they were thumbing their noses at the people who had supposedly vanquished them. They had made a farce of the League of Nations by unilaterally re-arming and looked ready to get aggressive again. Even Dr Mannix, who had probably been correct when he described World War 1 as 'a sordid trade war' which should never have been waged, was now pointing

to the ominous happenings in Europe. At the same time
we knew the Pope was happy that Franco, a friend of his,
but also pally with Hitler, had triumphed in the civil war
in Spain. It was all very confusing.

Nobody was surprised when Germany invaded Poland
on 2 September 1939. Australia declared war on Germany
just 45 minutes after Great Britain. We felt good that,
technically, and because of the International Dateline, we
had actually declared war *before* England. We heard our
new Prime Minister announce on the wireless that
because England had decided to halt German aggression
Australia would support the Mother Country. My Dad was
not too sure about this new bloke, Robert Menzies. He
seemed 'very flash', not like the previous Prime Minister,
Joe Lyons. Lyons had abandoned Labor, but he was a
Catholic, so that made him trustworthy at least. Nobody
demurred, however, when Menzies took us into the war.
Get it over and done with, most said. Good for the
economy, others reckoned.

Grace seemed the only person not excited about the
prospect of another war. She just shook her head and said,
'They'll never learn, will they?' Even her brothers Martin
and Bob seemed to take it stoically, accepting the inevitable. After the horrors they had seen at Gallipoli and on
the Western Front they must have been screaming
inwardly to somehow call a halt to this new madness, but
I guess men ran the risk of being dubbed cowards if they
expressed such sentiments, especially men with 'fine' war
records. To a boy it just seemed stupid to resume the
battle between basically the same exponents on the same
battlegrounds where millions had died to no avail. And
yet, there seemed to be an element of sense to this war
because this fellow Hitler did seem dangerously ambi-
tious, out to conquer the world, we felt.

The boys rushed to enlist. What amazed me was the
speed with which sleepy Australia mobilised. Who made

all those uniforms so quickly? The badges? The buttons? The boots? The hats? The guns? A funny thing about war is that the armorers seem to have it all planned in advance. I had never noticed the Drill Halls in every suburb, but they must have been waiting there since World War 1. Now they were bristling with military personnel again, with boys and men happily, excitedly, lining up to enlist to go to war. They all wore their best suits to enlist and they incongruously marched in their 'civvies', as civilian clothes were now dubbed.

The men stood around in clusters until told to 'come on parade' inside the Drill Hall. There they were lined up to fill out personal details, have a medical examination and await the results. The 'rejects' were sent home. Those fit for active service were assembled, told when to report back for actual admission to the forces and the issue of uniforms (often the next day). Then on a symbolic level the new recruits were put through a minor show of army discipline.

'Squad . . . attention!' Columns of three and a bit of marching. 'By the left, quick march! I said left, soldier! Don't you know your left from your right!' They loved it, the old hands. Good to be back in harness, they said.

The masses were being manipulated again, in the oldest game on earth. All the standard ploys were implemented. The Germans were again called 'Huns'. The baby-bayonetting stories were trotted out. The cartoonists had a great time mixing metaphors as they depicted Hitler as a goose-stepping rat. Almost immediately stories began to circulate about white feathers being handed or posted to boys unwilling to join up. Many people quickly secured jobs at munitions factories, thereby absolving themselves from military service while at the same time securing highly paid employment for 'The Duration', as the unknown length of the war was henceforth called. Banners and bunting flew. Troops marched proudly through the city streets, urged on by their fellow Australians to do to Hitler what their fathers had done to old Kaiser Bill. King George conveniently forgot his German antecedents and gave a stirring, if somewhat stuttery address to the Empire, telling us what was expected in these times of tyranny. We sat watching a photograph of the king as his hesitant, nervous voice crackled across the ether from London to our six-valve Radiola wireless.

It was hard for me to imagine what war was like. There were no films at first, no TV of course, and we had no personal experience to go by, unlike the men who had fought in the Great War and the women and children of Europe who had suffered. Photographs only seemed to show how the countryside was devastated in Europe, not the personal suffering, not the fear in children's eyes. I had never seen a tank, never seen or heard a shot fired — not even at a rabbit — and I had no idea how I would react if the Germans came marching down Higinbotham Street shooting and bayonetting everyone they encountered. Would I be frightened? I tried to pretend I'd be brave, but I knew privately I would probably run and hide.

The most stark reminders to me of the reality of war were the sad old veterans of World War 1 who manned the lifts in all the big city stores and offices in Melbourne. They sat on their stools, with one or no legs, their crutches beside them at all times, announcing the different floor levels.

'Haberdashery, Boys and Mens Wear, Manchester, Fifth Floor Cafeteria,' they would intone. It must have been a devastating, demeaning existence. The round RSL badges on their lapels seemed such an inadequate acknowledgement of their bravery and deprivation, and their obviously (to me anyway) ruined lives. They never smiled.

'What are you thinking now, with a brand new war

for your son to go to?' I wondered. 'You wasted that leg, didn't you? You know that, but you're not allowed to say it, yet I can understand why you have forgotten how to smile.'

Even though we in Victoria were 12,000 miles from the war, Melbourne was buzzing with excitement from the outset. Dance halls and places of entertainment were packed, recreation centres were set up in the city by the ACF (Australian Comforts Fund) where service personnel could meet, eat cheaply, play table tennis and attend dances. Army camps were established at Royal Park and Broadmeadows, close to our home, and at Puckapunyal further north. Sailors from HMAS *Cerberus*, (the naval base) were all over the city, and there were Air Training Schools at Point Cook and Laverton. We hadn't seen air force uniforms before, and more young men wanted to join the air force than the recruiters could handle.

I don't remember Japan being mentioned in the first years at our house, but apparently there was some reluctance to send Australian troops and the ships of the Royal Australian Navy to Europe just in case Japan came into the war on Germany's side.

All we knew was that ordinary Australians were itching to get into things. Again, there was the lure of the great adventure, the uniform, the trip overseas, especially to those familiar countries of the British Empire, comfortingly colored red on the world maps, places like England and Canada for the air force. It must all have been a great enticement to boys from isolationist Australia who would otherwise have no chance to see the world.

Many local Coburg boys joined the forces and began their training. Our cousins Laurie and Joe Egan from Warrnambool were among the very first to enlist. Unlike World War 1 conscription was quietly introduced, although conscripted men only had to train for three months and were not to be sent overseas. They were called 'chockos' or chocolate soldiers.

I began to keep note books and familiarise myself with maps of Europe, for at school there was kudos to be earned by whoever was the most knowledgeable about the war. I was prompted to sit up at night after tea and work on my war books by watching my Dad, who was a prolific letter-writer throughout his life. He began a correspondence which went right through the war with various relations and former work-mates of his who went away to the war. It was fun to sit up together, and I formed a similar life-long habit of writing songs late into the night, just as my Dad wrote his many and wonderful poems.

There was an initial stalemate in the war. After the invasion of Poland, the Germans made no further moves. It began to be thought there had been a false alarm, that peace might yet be negotiated, and the boys wouldn't get their trip overseas. But then we learnt a new German word to go with the *schweinhund* and *dummkopf* already used to pillory Hitler and his mates. Suddenly, there was *blitzkrieg,* lightning war. In a matter of days the Germans had occupied Holland and Belgium, and moved into France. The supposedly impregnable Maginot Line was hurdled and the French defences reeled. Italy came into the war on Germany's side and England itself seemed under imminent threat of invasion. Australia and New Zealand quickly moved to send their assembled troops overseas. The wharves in Melbourne rang out with 'Waltzing Matilda' and 'The Maori Farewell', the ship-to-shore streamers finally broke and dropped into the greasy water, and thousands of 'wild colonial boys' again sailed to war.

Now this Hitler joker would know what fighting was about. Peter Dawson's record 'Australia Will Be There' was revived and sold thousands of copies:

Australia will be there-ere-ere-ere-ere
Australia will be there.

And surprise, surprise, the Depression was over. Not

only was my father in work, so were my teenage sisters. They both got their Merit (Grade 8 Primary) Certificates, and that was generally considered a good enough education for a girl. Peg had in fact gone on to do a year's 'commercial' at St Aloysius' Girls College, something of an indulgence for working-class Coburg people. This enabled Peg to get a secretarial job at the Royal Arcade Hotel in the city. Pat had initially worked in a factory at the Lincoln Knitting Mills, but she too secured a job at the Royal Arcade as a bar attendant (definitely not a barmaid, Grace assured people) serving in the Ladies' Wine Bar. The girls were at The Arcade when war was declared, and they recall asking their superior, Miss Brown, if they could watch the first march in Collins Street. She refused.

'It's too sad,' she told them. So Grace was not the only perceptive one. Was she *Miss* Brown because of a fiancé lost in the Great War? Where is Miss Brown's song?

We felt that Pat was definitely grown up for she had started smoking. At eighteen it was almost compulsory. Not in front of Grace though, for Grace would probably have still been inclined to screw the flesh or at least give The Look for which she was equally famous. (To this day our family have competitions to see who can give the most compelling authoritative Look *a la* Grace, but none of us goes close.) No matter how flash a teenage daughter might think herself, Grace was very definitely still in charge.

'Flash' was what today's jargonists would call the 'buzz word' of the early 1940s. And a definite part of being flash was to smoke cigarettes. The cigarette companies have always been very clever with their advertising. Today they do it through sport, because advertising tobacco products is banned in so many places, and the message has to be indirect, subliminal. When we were kids it was not whether but *when* you began to smoke. The advertising figures, ironically, were singers like Richard Tauber, Richard Crooks, Laurence Tibbett, Jeanette McDonald and Nelson Eddy. They all dressed glamorously and gently caressed their throats with one hand as they held a cigarette with the other, inferring that the smoothness of the cigarettes was probably the reason why they sang so beautifully. And it was important to take on the smoking mannerisms of the famous filmstars. Smoking was permitted in cinemas, and it was fascinating that every time Spencer Tracy lit a cigarette for Katherine Hepburn the audience would all light up and puff and cough in unison. Later the models for cigarette advertising became the soldiers themselves, telling us to pack Black and White smokes in their ACF (Australian Comforts Fund) parcels. Who could resist?

In a couple of years we would have rationing of clothing and food, but in the first euphoric months of the war, before the casualty lists started to appear, people began to dress extravagantly and behave erratically. Men all had sleeked-back hair (Robert Taylor style) and those not in uniform wore good quality double-breasted suits. I remember that my sisters had some lovely floral frocks and that they took a great pride in their appearance as they went off to work in the city. On the weekends they wore their joddies — jodphur trousers, as part of an ensemble with severe but smart little tailored jackets, shirts and ties. Flat-heeled lace-up shoes completed a very flash outfit. They seemed to be very conscious of boys (or 'young men', as they would call them — 'boys' were monsters like me).

There was much talk around the house about who was joining up, and how they looked in their uniforms, and who was flash and who wasn't. Very definitely on the outer were chaps who were fresh or had 'BO' (body odor) or 'halitosis'. It seemed to me that the familiar young blokes of the same age group as Pat and Peg, fellows like Donny Power, 'Curly' O'Meara, and Richie Miles, were being passed over by my sisters for older men, preferably in uniform. I remember Richie Miles and Donny Power trying to get the girls' attention one night by having a 'spelling bee' as they perched up in the gum tree outside our house. Pat and Peg were unimpressed. At 3 a.m. Grace poked her head through the bedroom window and told the boys to 'buzz off'.

The girls spent their leisure time at dances — Peg loved dancing, Pat was not so keen — or at the flicks, or going to picnics or at 'socials' where it was quite common to meet strange young men in uniform without any of the pre-war conservatism about 'being picked–up'. I remember being totally contemptuous of all the talk about men and uniforms. Girls were fairly boring creatures, I thought, whose shallow lives revolved around inconsequential things like combing their hair and sighing over Nelson Eddy, with whom they were totally infatuated. Peg would stand for what seemed like hours in front of the mirror in our hallway, gazing into her own eyes, titivating her hair. She literally wore a bald patch in the carpet she spent so much time on the hair. Thank goodness Sal was still sane.

I was now in Grade 3, enjoying being taught by 'Cocky' Reardon. Our subjects were English, mental arithmetic, social studies, handwriting, craft (or 'handwork' as it was called), drawing, history, drill and singing, and of course, sacred studies (which today is called Religious Instruction). Each period started with prayers and each page of written work was 'offered up' to God or Our Lady by a written heading, ranging from A M D G (*Ad Maioriem Dei Gloriam* — To the Greater Glory of God) or J M J (Jesus Mary and Joseph) or S H J (Sacred Heart of Jesus).

There was a great concentration on English with Cocky, learning to write letters and essays (called 'compositions'), parsing and analysis, and spelling. Handwriting was one of Cocky's great loves and every page of written work was scrutinised as much for the neatness as the content. History was all about England, rattling off the names of Kings and Queens:

Willy, Willy, Harry, Ste [Stephen]
Harry, Dick, John, Harrys Three

learning about the Wars of the Roses, Oliver Cromwell, the Crusades. In my entire schooling there was no mention of Australian history. We didn't have any history, did we? Well, we did, sort of, but anything 'historic' about Australia related only to crime — convicts, bushrangers etc. — and was better left unlearned.

Cocky knew of my detailed interest in the war, and asked me to give a rundown on events each day for the other kids. What a little smart-arse I was becoming! I would use Cocky's pointer to explain things on the map of the world. It was good for me, though, as it forced me to think through from the general to the particular, an approach which has served me well in different forms of writing.

A highlight of the year was that Leo 'Milky' Walsh and I were selected to be on the main school concert. In the fashion of the times we had our faces corked black, like Al Jolson. Milky was dressed as a little black girl, and I was a boy. We sang a duet:

We're two little dusky diamonds
Real gems you know
We're the real picaninnies
Only found in Ohio
Some folk think that we are all black
But that's not so —
You look about, and you will find out
We all are brown in Ohio

Later in the year Milky (his Dad had a dairy) and I were both selected to join the prestigious Bel Canto choir, which was run by a well-known priest, Father

Lanigan, who conducted auditions at every Catholic school in Melbourne. When Grace heard I was to be auditioned for the choir she showed her usual shrewdness and suggested I sing 'The Men of the West', feeling fairly sure a priest with a name like Lanigan would be kindly disposed to the stirring Irish song:

> While ye honor in song and in story
> The names of the patriot men
> Whose valor has covered in glory
> Full many a mountain and glen.
> Forget not the gallant old 'west boys'
> Who rallied their bravest and best
> When Ireland was broken and bleeding
> She looked for revenge to the west.

If I remember correctly, Milky sang 'In the Bushes at the Bottom of the Garden'. So much for patriotic airs! We were both admitted to the choir for the next three years, where we were run-of-the-mill singers among some very beautiful boy soprano voices. Looking back, and comparing things to today, it's quite amazing what we young boys fitted into our lives. Here I was, a racing tipster, war expert, choirboy, girl hater, altar boy, genius at school, budding Bradman at cricket, the next Jack Dyer at footy, and I hadn't even started to be the next Nigger O'Reilly. Tough Ted, I privately called myself. And life was good, especially if you were modest.

6
V . . . —
da da da daaaaaaa

Winston Churchill was unpopular at our place. Hadn't he masterminded Gallipoli and help sacrifice thousands of young Australians, including our Uncle Jack? Wasn't he responsible for the 'Black and Tans' being sent to maraud the Irish? Grace was always scathing about him, calling him 'a bloody warmonger'.

But Chamberlain was pathetic, we felt, letting Hitler tell him all those lies, and then telling the world there would be 'peace in our time'. Something had to be done about him. Suddenly, with the lightning speed of the aptly named *blitzkrieg*, the Germans were about to invade England. It took the Germans no time at all to enter Paris and the French authorities capitulated immediately.

'Typical Frogs,' my Dad said. 'They're only worried about all those flash buildings in Paris.' There was probably a lot of truth in that.

Churchill was appointed the new British prime minister, and immediately had to oversee the withdrawal of the British troops, cut off in occupied France, with the Germans advancing from the east, and the Italians to the south. I forget just when we heard Churchill's famous speech about 'their finest hour', but I know it won him

grudging approval. He seemed the right man for such
desperate times. Not that Dunkirk was any great victory,
but, like Gallipoli, it was a brilliantly executed evacuation,
and the Tommies had the chance to resume the fight.

Mind you, we were puzzled about events in general,
and it didn't help that there was a big strike in the coal
mines of Australia at the same time. People were infuri-
ated about this and blamed 'the Commos'. That helped to
explain Russia's intransigence.

'You just can't trust Commos,' everyone said. Just
when we thought the Russians might be on Britain's side
in the war we found that they had already signed a treaty
with Germany. Russia and Germany carved up Poland.
Poor old Poles, they must be the world's champion suffer-
ers.

The Japanese seemed to be getting away with murder
in China and some very graphic photographs of damage
caused by Japanese air raids appeared in the papers.
Everybody seemed sure it was only a matter of time and
Japan would come into the war on Germany's side, but
when and where?

There were lots of complaints about the Yanks.

'They'll do the same as last time,' people were saying.
My Auntie Cis, Mum's sister, was very forthright. I can
see her now, sitting at our kitchen table, looking at my
father myopically through her thick glasses and smoking
her cigarette, which she held in a hair clip so she would
not get nicotine on her fingers.

'The bloody Yanks, Joe,' she pontificated, 'they'll sit on
the fence and sell arms to everybody, you watch, and then
they'll come in on the side of whoever's going to win.' I
thought she was a bit unfair to Roosevelt, who seemed to
want to come in on our side, but he was having problems
talking the other Americans into it.

I was beginning to realise just how devious war was.

The Australian 6th Division had gone to the Middle

East, and very early in the piece we had a letter from our
cousin Laurie Egan. Laurie was always a larrikin. His
letter was literally cut to shreds, and the censor had
written on the envelope, 'Tell the writer to watch his step.'
Honestly, the letter was like the paper friezes we used to
cut out with scissors when we did handwork at school.
About the only news we gleaned from Laurie's letter was
that he had written it, and he was in high spirits.

That would soon change, for Italy, who owned Libya
and Abyssinia at the time, invaded Egypt, and the African
campaign, in which the Australian boys would cover themselves with glory, was under way. They were playing for
high stakes in that desolate region, as it was all about
control of the Mediterranean and the Suez Canal and
access to the oil of the Middle East. We were never sure
of the status of Egypt. It was always colored red on the
world's maps, but we knew it wasn't part of the Empire
as we were. I took great interest in the African campaign
because of the Australian involvement, and it was fascinating to scan the maps (I still spend hours doing this),
learning all the new place names, reviving some names
familiar to our parents from World War I days.

We were aware, too, of incredible and devastating
activity in the Mediterranean itself. Malta was being
bombarded, and the Australian fleet was well-represented
in naval battles against the powerful Italian navy, which
was made even more formidable through the backup of
the Italian air force. We felt that the Italians were jokes
as soldiers (as my Italian friend Vince Scali subsequently
said to me: 'We're lovers, not fighters') but they were very
powerful on the sea and in the air. The most exciting early
news of the war came when we heard that HMAS *Sydney*
had sunk the Italian cruiser *Bartolomeo Colleoni*. Uncle
Martin reminded us that this was a good omen, for *Sydney*
had sunk the German ship *Emden* early in the Great War.
But at the same time we were jolted when told that some

Australian merchant ships had been sunk in Australian waters by mines and through attacks from armed German merchant ships flying false colors. We did not get detail of things like this at the time, just the general picture, for censorship reasons. We got absolute chapter and verse about the Battle of Britain, being fought relentlessly in the skies over England.

Little newsreel theatrettes began to open up in the city. Pop loved to go to these and took us occasionally. We came to know the names of many famous airmen who took part in the Battle of Britain, like the Australian, 'Killer' Caldwell, and the Irishman, Paddy Finucane, and we really admired the courage of the British women and kids who were putting on such a brave front in adversity. We marvelled that the London underground stations could take so many people who sought shelter from the bombs, and the cameras always showed the women with their thermos flasks and blankets, cheerful, laughing and singing, joshing with the London bobbies. Then we would be shown the devastation of the bombing. This was when we began to rethink Churchill, as he strode defiantly through the wreckage, smoking his huge cigar and giving his V for Victory sign. That was good tactics, we felt, and soon we kids were all doing it, puffing on imaginary Havana cigars and going *da da da daaaaaa* to the tune of Beethoven's Fifth, for dot, dot, dot, dash (. . . —) was V in morse code.

The morale of the British civilians and their plucky air raid Wardens had a salutary effect on Australians — in our part of the country anyway — and people really began to get behind what was called 'The War Effort'. Food parcels were organised and sent to Britain as well as to our troops overseas. Some of the packaging of these parcels was a treat to behold, with people having great discussions about how best to pack custard powder, fruit cake, cigarettes and dried fruit into one parcel without it

Saving became a patriotic duty and the *Heralds* I sold reminded civilians of this

finishing up an unholy mess. People began to collect paper, rags and scrap metal for the munitions factories. Everybody saved to buy War Savings Certificates. Petrol rationing started and we saw the first cumbersome gas producers on cars, stoked up by all sorts of fodder.

Of course The War Effort was used by people to justify their own eccentricities and minor obsessions. Grace told us a yarn when she returned home after spending some time with her sister Cis, who was having a baby at Koroit in Victoria's Western District. Cis was married to a man named Mick Dwyer. Like a lot of people in the Western District, Micky spoke with a real Irish brogue, even though born in Australia. Grace was travelling somewhere with Mick in his little car, which he used in his work as a milk inspector. He came to a downhill stretch, and she was surprised when he switched off the ignition.

'Save the benzine, Grace, save the benzine,' said Mick. Grace wasn't sure whether patriotism or tight-fistedness had prompted Micky's actions, as they silently rolled down the hill.

I had several school holidays in the Western District myself around this time, and I loved it. We had lots of relations. There were the Dwyers at Koroit, there was Uncle Pat Egan and Auntie Dolly who lived at Warrnambool, as did Uncle Bill Brennan and Auntie Bess, who had a *cake shop*!

There were older cousins at all these households, but the family I loved to visit were the Dennington Brennans. This was Uncle Bob, Grace's brother, and his wife Aunty Rita. They had nine kids, and I got on famously with all of them. Uncle Bob and Aunty Rita spoilt me absolutely, and yet their own kids didn't seem to mind or even notice. If there is such a thing as a saint it was my Aunty Rita. I never heard her say a harsh word about anybody, nor did anyone else. She knew I was a healthy eater with two favorite dishes — mashed potatoes done in lots of milk and butter, and sultana slice cake, which we called 'chester cake'. When I visited them I travelled 250 kilometres (alone, would you believe at age 9-12?) to Warrnambool by steam train from Melbourne, and Uncle Bob would meet me in his car, which would be full of laughing kids. As a farmer Bob always had a car, which was used for all sorts of things as well as carrying people. When we arrived at the farm there would be Aunty Rita saying, 'Let me have a look at you. Goodness, haven't you grown.' Then she'd say, 'Come inside. I've got something special for you, Teddy.' I would be pointed straight at a huge dish of mashed potatoes, followed by a whole tray of chester cake. I would be over the moon, and would insist that the other kids share, but they seemed prepared to let me eat the entire food mountain, so much did they enjoy seeing somebody with such an appetite. I guess it was like going to the circus for them: 'Roll up, roll up, they're feeding him now. Tickets at the ticket box. Muldoon the Glutton, the man who ate his mate. Roll up.'

My greatest favorite cousin was Kathy, who was a little older than me. She was not very healthy but had, like her mother, a lovely soft nature and seemed to derive enjoyment from being with me. That's what I thought anyway, but on reflection I'll bet she made everybody feel good. Kathy was certainly the first girl I was ever polite to or courteous towards. I simply loved her. Yet I also got on very well with her sisters: Margaret, about my age; Judy, a year younger; and Betty, a couple of years younger. They seemed to know such good games. The oldest girl, Eileen, was already a nurse, so I didn't see much of her. Arthur, or Artie as we called him, was the oldest boy, and he had joined the army, although he, too, was never very robust. Leo, the next boy, was a great mate, and an incredible worker for a boy of about 16. Frank was the scholar of the family, always with his nose in a book and talking about politics. He eventually became a lawyer and the writer of some very scholarly books. And then there was poor little Peter, the baby, the same age as my brother Geoffrey. Peter used to get hell from the rest of the family. They teased him mercilessly and called him 'Peemite', which Frank assured us meant 'a confounded pest'.

Dennington is in rich, volcanic country about 250 kilometres west of Melbourne, between Warrnambool and Port Fairy. The railway line went right through Bob's farm. The kids either walked or rode bikes to school about a mile from the farm. It was mainly a dairying area, but farmers also grew potatoes and onions — usually highly productive crops. With a good vegetable garden and some chooks, the Brennans were self-supporting, except for meat and basic items like bread, tea and sugar.

There was so much to do on a farm. I'd spend most of the time with Leo, for I genuinely wanted to learn about life in the country, which seemed just so much more exciting than the city. Leo taught me to milk cows by hand — they had no milking machines — and I had some rides on their little pony Dolly, a cantankerous little bugger, although Leo had her measure. But one day when I urged Dolly into a gallop, intending to ride her as far as 'Toots' McCosh's farm, further down Yangary Road, Dolly decided she wanted to visit O'Keefes, on the farm next door to Bob. Dolly did a fast left turn without telling me. I kept heading for Toots's farm. I lost about a square foot of skin as I skidded into a patch of stinging nettles.

Leo taught me how to dig spuds and onions, how to bag the spuds and sew the full bags. He let me help harness the draught horses, and he used to plough and harrow the paddocks on their rich 40-acre farm with these wonderful animals. Leo had to take the two big cans of milk to the Nestle's factory each morning, and it was a delight for a city boy to be allowed to drive the horse, and to wave with Leo to every single person we passed. Leo was a very tough kid and when he in turn visited us in

Melbourne, he would put on a real cocky front and sidle up to city kids twice his size.

'Hey, mug, you want a fight?' he'd challenge. But always with a grin on his face. He's never changed, and we have remained great mates. Leo would have played the role of Crocodile Dundee with as much flair as Hoges did.

After tea we would settle in for the night, with the Aladdin mantle lamps, fuelled by lighting kerosene, softly burning in their big kitchen. The Brennans weren't into singing like we were, and Auntie Rita would get me to sing as we did the dishes. Of course, I'd take a lot of prompting. We might listen to the wireless for a bit, to hear *Dad and Dave*, and then get ready for bed. Somebody would inevitably want to go to the dunny, which was a tin-can job, way out in the backyard, so we'd all go, with a hurricane light. It would be pitch-black outside, and the wind always seemed to be moaning in the big pine trees which so typify Victoria's Western District. We'd urge on whoever was inside, and roar with laughter at any sounds from within. Invariably someone blew out the light, or Leo would hide behind a tree, wrapped in a sheet to scare us, or somebody would start on the ghost yarns.We always started with the chant:

> Between the hours of twelve and one
> The ghost will come and strike you dumb.

Back we'd run to the house, half-scared, half-excited, and pile into bed. Three or four kids in a three-quarter bed was the norm, and there'd be more ghost yarns or a story, punctuated by the odd fart, and shrieks of laughter.

I have never forgotten one night. I lay holding Kathy's hand, with Judy and Betty topping-and-tailing with us in the three-quarter bed. I felt so secure, so happy being among such a harmonious family. We were lucky kids to have such good parents, and I remember thinking to myself, Who'd be an only child?

In later years I would learn about relationships from Aboriginals. They taught me the importance of mother's brother and father's sister, who should have a vital role in your upbringing.

Uncle Bob was a great man in that he had the knack of making you feel you were the most important person in the world, and that your opinions were worth the asking. He was the first adult who plied me with questions. What did I think about this or that? As though what I had to say really mattered. It was true Socratic teaching, for here was a man of vast experience himself. Bob had travelled all over Australia and New Zealand as a young man, shearing, contracting, and generally, as a politically -minded young man, caught up in the euphoria of early Labor politics. He went to the war in 1915 to spend the next three disillusioning years in the hell of the front lines in France. He was gassed and was eventually repatriated home. But the ship was torpedoed not far from the British Isles, two days out. Bob spent hours in the water and lost all his belongings.

My Aunt Mary, Grace's elder sister, was in England during World War 1, and she met Bob when he arrived in London on leave from the Western Front. She said Bob looked dreadful, and had aged ten years in two. She thought she would cheer him up, so she took him to see a show in London's West End. But Bob was appalled at the opulence of the crowd, who seemed indifferent to the fact that a bloody war was being waged on their behalf in France. He embarrassed Mary by standing up in the theatre to shout at the crowd:

'Here you are in all your fancy clothes. Don't you know there's hundreds of young Australian boys dead and not even buried on the Somme?'

Mary took him out of the theatre, and later they went

to the beautiful West Country of England where he broke
down and cried, for it all seemed so peaceful compared to
the carnage of France to which he had to return.

'This country's so beautiful it's enough to make a man
cry,' he said of Devon.

After the war Bob took up a soldier-settler block at
Hawkesdale, and then he moved to the farm at
Dennington. He was a solidly-built man, nicknamed
'Nugget', or 'Nuggy' as Grace called him, and he was a
great favorite with all of us. He had the bluest of blue
eyes, which were often sad, but would occasionally light
up at a joke or a good political point. Bob and my Dad
were great friends. Grace told us that Nuggy was very
quick tempered as a boy and that he used to bite his own
arm in frustration or anger. I saw in him a combination
of his three sons. He displayed the quiet humour of Artie,
the erudite quest for knowledge of Frank and the cocky
competence of Leo. I never once heard Bob complain, yet
his health must have been dreadfully impaired by his
wartime experiences. He certainly did not seek sympathy
or praise for his part in the war, being more interested
in others than talking about himself. He was a great man.

A much sadder figure was Grace's other surviving
brother from the war, Martin, who went to Gallipoli with
the 7th Light Horse and fought in the Middle East after
he got off the Peninsula. Martin had been taken prisoner
by the Turks after his horse was shot dead in a cavalry
exercise. The Turks forced him and other prisoners up
into the Palestine hills without boots or provisions and
left them to perish. Martin told me he survived by eating
grass. He came back from the war very disturbed, 'shell-
shocked' as people would say. He was in and out of
Bundoora Military Hospital for the rest of his life. Martin
would often visit us, and he always brought us sweets, so
we liked him a lot, although he was very hard to predict.
He always called me 'Ned'. Later, in the second war,

Martin went north to work with the CCC (Civil Construction Corps) and helped build the road from Alice Springs to Darwin. Apparently he was very aggressive if he'd taken a drink, but as there was never any liquor at our house we never had any bad experiences with him. And his visits were usually on Sunday when the pubs were shut in any case.

Grace and Pop were very good with Martin, and they called him 'The Lad'. Pop and Martin would yarn and have a game of chess, although Martin found it hard to concentrate, and Grace would urge us to be solicitous towards him.

'Poor chap,' Grace said, 'that's the reward he gets for fighting for his country. And who cares?' Grace certainly did care. I guess she felt especially sad at seeing this fine-looking young man come shuffling back from the war, yet another wrecked life. When Martin left us after a Sunday visit he would have to return to the loneliness of the hospital or a room in some men's hostel or other, while we had a family to share life with. What a rotten life for him! Martin had been married but his wife left him during the war. We understood that there was a son somewhere, but subsequent searches after Martin's death were in vain.

As for father's sister there was the wonderful 'Nornie'. Nora Egan had never married. She owned a house in Neill Street, Carlton, one of the delightful old terrace houses criminally knocked down to allow the construction of those Housing Commission monstrosities. Originally, Nora had shared the house with her sisters Maggie and Mary, also unmarried, and for a time before I was born our parents had lived in the house also. It was a large, two-storey home, beautifully furnished. When our family moved to Coburg another of Pop's sisters, Sara, came with her husband Jim Wilkinson and their family to share the house with Nora.

Pat and Peg were special favorites of the maiden aunts. They had given my sisters a piano, which they proceeded to learn to play by ear — and very well indeed. Pop and Nora were very close. Grace, who usually kept her emotions to herself, obviously liked Nornie very much too, so it was not surprising that Nornie spent a lot of time at Coburg with us. She just seemed to like being around us, and she would come to visit most Sundays.

Pop had a brother, Jim Egan, who lived in Higinbotham Street also, at No. 12. Without fail, each Saturday in winter, regardless of the weather, Jim, his wife Kit, and Nora would go to the football to watch Richmond play. They were club members, so if Richmond played 'at home' at the Punt Road oval, they would sit in the front row of the main grandstand. Talk about one-eyed supporters! Woe betide anybody who dared utter a word against Richmond in general or Jacky Dyer in particular. It was the only aberration in their lives; normally they were three quiet gentle people. On Sundays Nornie would give us a post-mortem on the footy (occasionally we were allowed to go with them) and it was amazing to see the transformation in this gentle maiden aunt if Richmond had lost the match. There would be the most violent diatribe, usually against the umpire — she particularly hated Hawkins.

' Grace, as soon as I saw that robber Hawkins was the umpire I knew we had no chance.'

'That stinking Essendon mob, Joe, they should gaol the lot of them.'

'That filthy Jack Mueller. He's only a dirty Hun.'

After she'd got it out of her system she would revert to being quiet demure little Nornie again. But we didn't dare laugh at the time.

We would laugh later. We all loved Nornie dearly, despite her one eccentricity. She would usually stay for Sunday night tea, generally the cold meat left from the hot roast at lunch time, followed by a fruit salad which Nornie and Pop would make together on a ritual basis. They would chat away while they cut the fruit, very precisely and slowly, occasionally popping pieces into their mouths. 'The Egans are great fruit lovers,' Grace always said. Nornie and Pop were a bit like us kids doing the dishes, we felt, prolonging cutting the fruit salad in order to sustain the moment. They would share their experiences of the previous week, and Grace would quietly leave them, for the exchange seemed very precious. After tea the girls would do a few numbers for Nornie on the piano, we'd all sing for her, and then it would be time to take her to the tram.

There was intense competition for this job. Usually it went to Pat and Peg, but as they got older and went to work Sal and I would do the walk. We'd have a great old chat as we strolled slowly up to the corner of Sydney Road and O'Hea's Road, where we'd put Nornie on the No. 19 tram. She would change to a St Kilda tram at Moreland Road. Always the last thing was a quick kiss. I didn't dodge this kiss, although I was not much into kissing, because we knew that at the same time she would press sixpence each into our palms. The sixpence would normally be in the form of two threepenny bits. Nornie had obviously anticipated Grace's shrewdness with her own. We would pocket one threepence in the knowledge that Grace would say, 'Did Nornie give you any money?' when we returned home. We knew that she would follow up with the suggestion that we could contribute to 'the housekeeping' by dropping the threepence into her little jar. Because we were aware that Grace had a hard time making ends meet we did not complain about this, especially as we still had the other threepence. It was a nice little game, played skilfully by all.

When the Wilkinsons, who had a large family, came to live at Neill Street, Carlton, Nora, typically, gave up her own home and took a job as companion to a wealthy family who lived in a mansion on the beach at St Kilda. She had Sundays off and invariably visited us. We knew she was very special in our lives and later, much later, all of this would take on an intriguing new dimension.

In 1972 my Dad retired from work. He was 74. When he went to apply for the old-age pension he was told he must produce a birth certificate. In the State of Victoria you can establish your date of birth by two means, a simple Entry of Birth which simply gives your name and date and place of birth, or there is a much more detailed Birth Certificate which gives all sorts of other detail. It seems that throughout his life whenever my father had to prove his date of birth he had simply obtained an Entry of Birth. But in 1972 he was required to get the more comprehensive certificate. When he did so he found that his beloved 'sister' Nora was in fact his mother. He was understandably shocked rigid, particularly as Nora had died a few years previously, her sad secret going to the grave with her.

We children rejoiced, for Nornie, who had always been very special to us became even more so as our grandmother. At the same time we were aware of the profound shock to our Dad, who (I think, anyway) developed a nervous shake, which was diagnosed as Parkinson's Disease, almost immediately.

I tried to recapture the circumstances of my father's conception and birth. Probably a one-off juvenile roll-in-the-hay for 17 year-old-Nora (with a chap named Michael Scanlon, so I guess, by rights, my name should be Ted Scanlon?) Then the agonising pregnancy of a girl who almost certainly would not have been instructed in the facts of life. Discovery by her Irish-Catholic parents. The recriminations. Off to confession you go, my girl. Abortion is out of the question, so what do they do? You will stay on the farm, out of sight, and when this baby is born it will be presented to the world as your mother's 'change-of-life' baby. And you will take a sacred oath never to reveal the secret. Nor will you ever have anything to do with any man, ever again.

It was probably something like that. All the little memories of Nornie and her foibles came back to us all, and had new, special meanings, for in discussing her foibles we were considering ourselves.

We thought of all the times when Nornie and Joe had been able to be together as brother and sister, a gentle, loving relationship. We pondered the power of the oath she must have been required to take, which prevented her from revealing her secret to any of us, even on her deathbed, with Sal's kids (Nornie's great-grandchildren) playing around her bed. You can bet your life that somebody would have remembered to throw the good old Catholic guilt-prompter 'under pain of mortal sin' into the act. We shared an anger against the system which had kept mother and son apart and denied us the knowledge that she was our grandmother. Poor Nornie, another sad life.

7

Timoshenko And The Cofinitions

The film *Forty Thousand Horsemen* was shot mainly in the sandhills at Cronulla Beach, Sydney, and our cousin Artie Brennan was one of the two hundred Light Horsemen who kept riding past the camera to make it appear they were the forty thousand Australians who played such an important role in the Middle East in World War 1.

The film opened in early 1941 in Melbourne and the timing was impeccable. Anzac Day was coming up and the Middle East campaign in a new war was getting under way, with the 6th Division in the thick of things. The film, starring Chips Rafferty, immediately attracted packed houses, and if I remember correctly over a million people attended in the first month. We all saw it, loved it, and many people went two and three times.

While it was a thrill to see the film our family was in for some sad news. The Australian 6th Division captured Bardia—taking 40,000 Italian prisoners, Tobruk and then Benghazi. Everybody was very proud of them, but then the word came through that our cousin Joe Egan was listed as 'Missing, Believed Killed in Action' during the assault on Tobruk. In a few weeks Joe's death was confirmed.

Forty Thousand Horsemen stirred patriotic impulses in Melbourne in 1941

About eighteen months later, when some of the 6th boys returned to Australia, it was whispered that Laurie Egan, Joe's brother, had deserted as soon as he arrived home. Only then did we learn that Laurie had been alongside his brother when Joe was blown to pieces by a shell. Poor Laurie never recovered from the shock, and was to spend years on the run, even after the war, before finally being exonerated.

There was a great burst of patriotism when the 9th Division was formed in Australia. I saw them march in the city and they looked magnificent. The highly-trained 9th was sent to the Middle East to be immortalised at Tobruk and other places. They would eventually be dubbed 'the Rats of Tobruk' by the Nazi broadcaster 'Lord Haw Haw' when they withstood the might of Rommel's onslaught. We were a little irreverent about His Lordship and we took delight in chanting:

> Lord Haw Haw, the humbug from Hamburg
> The hee-hawing, high-browing Hun

The 9th Division would later change their colour patch to a T to signify Tobruk and whenever people spoke of them we would form our hands into a T just as one signals 'time out' in basketball. It was a bit like Churchill's V for victory, and equally good for morale.

The 6th Divvy boys were sent from North Africa to Greece. When they only had the Italians to contend with, the Allies (Greek, British, Australian and New Zealand soldiers) did very well. But when Germany sent an overwhelming force into Greece there was terribly fierce fighting in which the outnumbered Allies defended gallantly but were forced to retreat, then finally evacuate to Crete where the fighting continued.

Anzac casualties were heavy and many were taken prisoner, to the point where there were vague rumblings that the British had defended Greece 'to the last Anzac'.

The inference was that, as in World War 1, Dominion soldiers were **often** put into the front lines of battle to the point of absolute expendability. Our boys and the New Zealanders were praised to the skies in the press and it was agreed the bravery shown in Greece and Crete was the highest level ever of Anzac valor. I don't know what the old diggers would have thought of that, but that's the problem with war, isn't it? You have to keep troops under that sort of pressure, so that eventually only fanatical acts will bring the plaudits. Where does it end? Kamikaze?

I kept busy studying the maps, tracing the different campaigns, learning the names of the participant generals. My brother Geoffrey, who was very bright — he had seemed like a three-month-old baby at birth — was always wanting to climb up to have a look at the maps. To this day my brother loves the use of words. He will almost salivate as he looks for the right word to make a precise point and he is a great lover of wordsmiths like Gilbert and Sullivan — so am I. For some reason he decided a map was called a 'cofinition'. So it became an after-tea ritual to study the 'cofinition'.

At about this time Germany made its biggest single mistake of the war: it invaded Russia. My Dad's glee knew no bounds.

'That's the end of them,' he declared. 'Remember Napoleon.' However, for a few months, on the Russian front, and, indeed, all fronts, the Germans seemed invincible. They had pushed us out of Greece and were poised to invade Crete. They were pushing us back eastward in Africa, where their amazing new general, Rommel, swept all before him. Rommel put Tobruk under siege and used tanks like they had never been deployed before. The German Luftwaffe was blowing hell out of England with their air attacks, particularly on London, although they still couldn't beat the Allied Air Force to the point of being able to contemplate invasion of Britain. And then they captured Leningrad. It seemed nothing would stop them.

Suddenly the 'Commos', who had been vilified as the people responsible for all the strikes in Australia, the people who had treacherously signed a pact with Germany when we expected them to come into the war on our side, the ones we prayed for at Mass because they had forsaken Christ, the ones who sent you to the salt mines in Siberia if you weren't careful, were our friends, our allies. 'Curl the mo, Uncle Joe,' became a greeting, as people twirled imaginary Stalin moustaches. In those days graffiti was virtually unknown in Melbourne (don't things change!) but alongside the occasional FOO WAS HERE and the Mr Chads peering over brick walls saying WOT, NO BEER? we now saw the hammer-and-sickle emblem on walls everywhere. A film session at the cinema would end with 'God Save The King' for which we would all stand, but then there would inevitably be a loud shout — 'What about Joe?' — and everyone would have a good laugh. Josef Stalin was certainly popular in Melbourne in 1941.

And there was no Robert Menzies around to warn us about 'reds under our beds', as he would later in his career. Our prime minister was in England (crawling to the Poms we thought) as an adviser to the Imperial War Cabinet. Menzies came to be criticised often in our house, probably unfairly, but the only news we ever seemed to get of him was that he had been given yet another honorary university degree.

Mr Fadden was the acting prime minister and he and Mr Curtin, Leader of the Labor Opposition, issued a joint statement over the wireless (we hadn't started calling it the 'radio') telling us that Australia and the Free World were in real danger. We must save, we must put all our resources into the war effort and we must observe the new blackout regulations. It was incongruous, if exciting, we thought, that the blackout was so stringent in a place like Melbourne. Street lights were hooded, shop windows were boarded up, all domestic windows had to have blinds. Cars had their headlights painted or hooded, except for a thin strip of light about three centimetres wide. People were advised to wear white if they must go out at night and we had ARP (Air Raid Precautions) wardens to enforce the regulations. It was all part of a move to convince people the Germans were a real threat any- where, everywhere, at all times.

The casualty lists confirmed this. They were the first things we read in the newspapers, especially when so many previously listed under the ominous heading MISS- ING were now confirmed as KILLED IN ACTION, WOUNDED, or PRISONERS OF WAR. We were aghast at how many of our boys had been killed or taken prisoner in Greece.

It was about this time I broke Mr Phelan's window and started to sell papers. There was quite an excited buzz to life on the streets, despite the depressing news from the war. Essendon was looking good in the football, Harold Badger and Scobie Breasley were the leading jockeys, and the races were still being run each Saturday. Jitterbugging was the new dance craze, and there were competitions everywhere. Melbourne had three flourishing ice-skating rinks, St Moritz, Wirth's and The Glaciarum. The Glaciarum was called 'The Glaci'. Vaudeville at the King's and the Tivoli featured Fred Tupper's Variety Show; Hal Percy; Mal Verco, the ventriloquist with Ginger; and the much-loved Mrs 'Olmes and Mrs Hentwhistle. Walter Lindrum had just made his world record break of 3735 at billiards. Jack Davey had a new show on 3AW called *It Beats the Band* although the only shows we were allowed to 'watch' on the wireless were *Dad and Dave* and *Martin's Corner*. Once or twice I remember being allowed to 'watch' *Fu Man Chu* but generally such shows were deemed not suitable for our family. 'Watching' the wireless was precisely what families did. You sat around, close to the set, in absolute silence, unless it was a funny show when you felt free to laugh and generally join in, lustily singing classics like:

My Mabel waits for me
Underneath the bright blue sky
Where the dog sits on the tuckerbox
Five miles from Gundagai

And right through 1941 *Forty Thousand Horsemen* kept breaking records.

But there were still no Yanks in the war. In fact, we thought we might never see them involved, for the Germans and Japanese seemed to be doing such provocative things, yet Roosevelt seemed the only American prepared to retaliate. He had a meeting with Churchill and he warned Germany about sinking American merchant ships in the Atlantic. He even formed a War Cabinet, but that was as far as it went. Auntie Cis's view, that the Americans would wait and see, was looking prophetic.

My Dad was proved to be a good prophet of history. The European winter set in. The Russians put up an almighty struggle and we marvelled at their heroism. Despite his armed might it became obvious that the only way Hitler would enter Stalingrad and Moscow was over the dead body of every single Russian. That would have been an almost impossible task even without the winter, but the weather was to be the final determinant. When we saw the newsreels we shuddered: hundreds of German soldiers frozen to death in the snow, their fingers welded to their rifles, their eyes propped open in icy disbelief. Hitler should have read Victor Hugo's *L'Expiation* to learn what the Russian winter had done to the last foreigner who thought he might conquer Russia:

Il neigait
L'Empereur revenait lentement

My brother Geoffrey's time had come. The great hero of the Russian resolution was Marshal Simeon Konstantinovich Timoshenko, reputed to down a bottle of vodka at one pull as he strode up and down the barricades at Stalingrad. His name rolled off everybody's lips. He became the most admired single person in the war up to that point. So it was only natural that my brother Geoffrey would latch onto such a wonderful name with unmitigated glee. Every time we unrolled the cofinition he would now say, 'Timoshenko! Timoshenko!' It became his nickname, to the point where only my mother, his godmother Mary Reid and occasionally my sisters would call him Geoff or Geoffrey thereafter. He was Timoshenko, Tim for short.

It was fascinating to me that the war shifted to another and unexpected front at about this time, largely because oil-rich Irak (as Iraq was spelt then) came into the war on Germany's side. The British thought this was terribly ungrateful, for they had supplied considerable aid to Irak (which Uncle Martin was quick to tell us had been called 'Mesopotamia' when the Australians fought there in World War 1) through the agency of King Feisal, the friend of Lawrence of Arabia. But the Nazi fifth column had infiltrated various Iraki rebel organisations, which had now taken over the country. This meant that the Axis now had control of the huge oil pipeline which took oil to the refinery at Haifa in Palestine (now Israel) on the Mediterranean.

So British troops invaded Irak, the RAF bombed and strafed the pipeline and the Australian 7th Division invaded Syria. The 7th had been fighting in North Africa previously. Syria was aligned to France, and the Vichy French Government (always referred to as 'the traitors') had control of the Syrian airfields and their outposts were manned by crack units of the French Foreign Legion. The Aussies would soon fix that.

Rommel was giving the Allies a real pounding in North Africa but he was held in high esteem by all of us from the outset. He was obviously a great tactician and a straight soldier despite his nickname 'The Desert Fox'. He had recaptured Derna, Benghazi and Bardia and the only deterrent to a clean sweep of Libya were the Rats of Tobruk. The 9th Division was writing its way into the history books and at school we honored with prayers a young Corporal J H Edmondson, who won Australia's first Victoria Cross of the war. Sadly, posthumously.

What we saw as Bob Menzies' Anglophilia (although we hadn't learnt posh words like that yet: we just called it 'crawling') was to be his undoing. By the time he returned to Australia full of pomp and big ideas in May 1941 he had already run foul of his own party, let alone the Labor opposition, which was led by a powerful trio in Curtin, Chifley and Evatt. His own party forced Menzies to resign as prime minister and Arthur Fadden, the leader of the Country Party briefly took over. Labor was able to force an early election, however, and John Curtin was appointed the new prime minister.

That election was to prove to be a fortunate event, certainly in the opinion of those in Higinbotham Street, for the principal complaint from all quarters in Australia was that the total war effort was not being used to maximum advantage and we seemed to be doing whatever Whitehall commanded us to do at all times, without the security of the Australian continent being given proper consideration.

Despite the political turmoil there was still plenty of sport being played and I followed it all very closely. Typically, towards the end of 1941, as the first Tuesday in November approached, then as now, the Melbourne Cup dominated discussion. In 1941 the talk was particularly about the emergence of a brilliant three-year-old, Skipton, who won the VRC Derby. Skipton went on to win the

T.G. 42 Y.   COMMONWEALTH OF AUSTRALIA–POSTMASTER-GENERAL'S DEPARTMENT   Office Date Stamp

THIS TELEGRAM HAS BEEN RECEIVED SUBJECT TO THE POST AND TELEGRAPH ACT AND REGULATIONS. THE TIME RECEIVED AT THIS OFFICE IS SHOWN AT THE END OF THE MESSAGE.

TELEGRAM

THE DATE STAMP INDICATES THE DATE OF RECEPTION AND LODGMENT ALSO, UNLESS AN EARLIER DATE IS SHOWN AFTER THE TIME OF LODGMENT.

Office of Origin	No. of Words	Time of Lodgment	No.
Melbourne 1	67.	9.17	Copy only.

Postal Acknowledgement Delivery Personnell

Mr P J Egan
242 Leibeg St
Warrnambool

It is with deep regret that I have to inform you that VX 42964 Egan J.J. previously reported missing believed killed in now reported killed in action on 17th May & desire to convey to you the profound sympathy of the Minister for the Army and Military board

Minister for the Army

Telegram received 24 February 1942 by my uncle Pat, advising him
of the death of his son, Joe, at Tobruk

H.M.A.S. SYDNEY'S COMPLEMENT

FULL LIST OF NAMES

645 OFFICERS AND MEN BELIEVED LOST

The complement of H.M.A.S. Sydney, which the Prime Minister, Mr. Curtin, has announced is missing and must be assumed lost, is 645.

She carried 41 naval officers, one R.A.A.F. officer, 594 ratings, five Air Force men, and a canteen staff of four.

The list of names is:

OFFICERS

ANDERSON, William T. Engr.-Lieut. (Pl.) R.A.N.R. (S), N.S.W.
BACON, Jack C., Lieut.-Com. (O.), R.N., N.S.W.
BARBEY, Stephen R., Flying-Officer, R.A.A.F. S.A.
BATCHELOR, William O., Warrant Engineer, R.A.N., Vic.
BIGGS, Alexander E., Warrant En-

BUCKLEY, Daniel S. Ordinary Seaman, Vic.
BUDDEN, Keith E. A./Yeoman of Signals (T.), N.S.W.
BUNDY, Frederick P. K., Petty-officer, N.S.W.
BUNTING, James, Able Seaman, Qld.
BURGESS, William R., Signalman, N.S.W.
BURGOYNE, Maxwell A., Leading Steward, N.S.W.
BURKE,

FINLAYSON, Harry, Mech. I., N.S.W.
FISHER, John W., Ldg. Cook (S.), N.S.W.
FITZGERALD, Augustine P., Blacksmith IV., Vic.
FITZGERALD, Lloyd O., A/S.P.O., N.S.W.
FLEMING, Wilfred S., Able Seaman, N.S.W.
FOOTE, Reginald E. Cook (S.), S.A.
FORBES, Robert O. S., Ordinary Seaman, N.S.W.
FORSYTH, Glenbervie E. E.A. IV. Vic.
FORTH, Herbert, Able Seaman, Vic.
FOSTER, Norman D., E.R.A. IV., N.S.W.
FOSTER, Roy E. Leading Aircraftman, Qld.
FOULKES, Robert E., Teleg., N.S.W.
FRANKLIN, Edward W. Leading Seaman, N.S.W.
FRASER, Noel J., Ordinary Seaman, S.A.
FREER, Walter E. A., Able Seaman, S.A.
FRIAR, Jack A., E.R.A.III., N.S.W.
FRISCH, Ernest D. Able Seaman, Q'ld.
FRITH, William R. O., P.O., R.N. London.
FRY, Robert A., Stoker, Vic.
FISHER, Kenneth J. Ordinary Teleg., N.S.W.
GAMBLE, Frank R., P.O. Teleg., Vic
GAMBLE, Ronald F., A/P.O. Telce (T.), N.S.W.
GARDINER, Heathcote D., Ordinary

LILLYWHITE, Harry E., Shpt. I., N.S.W.
LOCKARD, Terence G., A Signalman, Tas.
LOVE, Snowden E., Stoker, W.A.
LOWENSTEIN, W. Stoker, Tas.
LOWRY, Frederick W., Able Seaman, Q'ld.
LYNCH, Stephen M., Able Seaman, Tas.
LYNE, Raymond V., Ordinary Seaman, Vic.
MACKINNON, Murdo, P.O., W.A.
MAIES, Trevor, Shipwright IV., Tas.
MANN, Keith A. Ordinary Seaman, Vic.
MANNING, Maurice Leading Cook (S.), N.S.W.
MARLEY, Sidney, Sergeant, R.A.A.F., N.S.W.
MARSON, Albert R., Mech. II., Vic.
MARTIN, Alan D., Ordinary Seaman, S.A.
MARTIN, James H., Able Seaman, N.S.W.
MARTIN, Leslie F., Steward, Vic.
MARTIN, Leslie J. F., Ordinary Seaman, N.S.W.
MATHESON, Edward A. J. Ordinary Seaman, N.S.W.
MATHEWS, John W., Able Seaman, Vic.
MAXWELL, Ian M. Ordinary Signalman, Tas.
MEDLEN, Lindsay J., S.B.A., S.A.
MELANDRI, Percy E. V., Bandsman N.S.W.
MENZIES, William, Able Seaman,

RICHTER, Arthur J., A/S. P.O., N.S.W.
RILEY, Edwin M., Ord. Seaman, Qld.
RIPPEN, Adolph H. G., Telegraphist, W.A.
RITERS, Edward, Able Seaman, N.S.W.
ROBERTS, Lyndon I., Stoker, W.A.
ROBERTS, Ronald C., Assist. Cook (S), Vic.
ROBERTSON, Michael J., Leading S.man, N.S.W.
ROBERTSON, Thomas H. A. Stoker P.O. N.S.W.
ROBERTSON, William J., Leading Cook, Vic.
ROGERS, Charles A., Able Seaman, N.S.W.
ROGERS, Ralph C., Signalman, Tas.
ROLFE, Edmund S., Able Seaman, be
ROLLEY, Ernest D. Steward, Qld.
ROSEVEAR, Geoffrey, Able Seaman, N.S.W.
ROSEVEAR, Lance, Able Seaman, Tas
ROSS, Donald, P.O. Std., N.S.W.
ROSS, James T., Sy. P.O., N.S.W.
ROTHBAUM, Lionel, Asst. Std., W.A.
ROWE, Allan L., Able Seaman, W.A.
ROWE, James R. J., Telegraphist, W.A.
ROWE, Lindsay T., Stoker II, Vic.
ROWLANDS, Harold E., Sy. C.P.O. N.S.W.
RUDALL, Peter E. Ord. Seaman, S.A.
SALMON, John, Able Seaman, N.S.W.
SAMPSON, Louis N., Sy., C.P.O.,

The *Herald* carried casualty lists. The issue of 1 December 1941 was a
particulary sad one, as the names of the dead from HMAS *Sydney* were
published that day

Melbourne Cup. We were smugly able to point out that our family had some knowledge of the owners, through some vague Western District connection, and we knew that the name of the horse, Skipton, was an anagram of the name of the owner's husband, P Kitson.

Football never seemed to have been played at a better level, despite the fact that Richmond didn't reach the Grand Final. Melbourne won their third successive VFL (Victorian Football League) premiership at the Melbourne Cricket Ground before 80,000 spectators, beating Essendon. The following week another Melbourne club won the VFA (Victorian Football Association) premiership, also played at the MCG, attracting 40,000 spectators. It had been a fascinating year for the VFA, which had lured many VFL stars to the lesser Association game via lucrative fees despite the VFL outlawed the move. There was a payment scheme (the Coulter Law) which said that VFL players could not be paid more than three pounds for a match. So champions like Ron Todd, Des Fothergill and Lance Collins had defected to the VFA, along with waning stars like Laurie Nash and Bob Pratt. Just to show he wasn't quite a has-been Pratt kicked 183 goals in the 1941 season, playing for our hometown VFA team Coburg. But Coburg went down to Port Melbourne in the Grand Final.

This would be the last premiership played at the MCG for a few years, as it was then barricaded and turned into very basic shelter for the armed forces being trained in Melbourne. The football finals were to be played for the next few years at Carlton and St Kilda. Cricket at Sheffield Shield level had been postponed For The Duration and Test cricket was, of course, out of the question.

Any euphoria we might have felt over sport was quickly dispelled. HMAS *Sydney* was sunk in the Indian Ocean by a disguised German raider KORMORAN and in the same week HMAS *Parramatta* was sunk in the Mediterranean near Tobruk. Australia mourned the loss of over

1000 young men. Mr Curtin urged everybody not to give Christmas presents, but rather to use any savings to buy War Bonds which would go towards replacing *Sydney*.

And if all that wasn't bad enough we were chilled by news that Japan had attacked Pearl Harbour on 8 December 1941. The war was about to take on a frightening new meaning. The waiting time was over and America could sit on the fence no longer. But what about us? Australia seemed suddenly quite vulnerable, with most of our best forces overseas.

LONG-DISTANCE THINKING

The rift between Churchill and Curtain was closely followed and debated

8

I Swear Off the Grog

There was another great flurry to reinforce The War Effort when Pearl Harbor was attacked. Munitions factories in Australia doubled and redoubled their output. Aeroplanes (although not very fast or effective ones) were built. Men and women joined up in thousands and it became a common sight to see women in uniform driving in the streets of Melbourne. I don't remember seeing a woman drive a car before that time. And some women were smoking in public!

Not Pat and Peg though. They wouldn't dare smoke in front of Grace, despite the fact that they both had left the Royal Arcade Hotel and gone to work in Navy Records at Victoria Barracks by 1942. They were sworn to absolute secrecy about their work.

Our various relations and their friends were coming from and going to the war and our house was bursting at the seams. We had been able to get a little sleep-out which we called The Bungalow built in the backyard and on weekends it would be jammed full of bodies.

One Sunday morning we counted ten blokes in the bungalow which was about three metres by two in area. My cousin Frank Brennan and a mate of his were sleeping blissfully in my brother Tim's cot. The many gay (in the old sense of the term) young servicemen really had my Mum fooled. She thought they were all such happy, laughing young fellows. I knew that part of the reason for the gaiety was the grog they had hidden under various hedges, fully aware that Grace barred alcohol. My paper-selling experiences were making me a bit more astute.

We had met Western Australian cousins Frank Brennan and his brother Len for the first time in 1942. Len was in the air force. Frank had been in the army in the Middle East and had now transferred to the air force. I pricked up my ears when they told me of their brother Bill who had run away from home, aged fifteen, and had joined the merchant navy. Goodness, I thought, he's only seven years older than I am, and I guess that was the first stirring of Celtic restlessness within me. While I didn't want to get hurt or anything like that, I could see how glamorous the various uniforms were, changing pimply-faced youths into film stars overnight, as well as providing a wonderful opportunity to see the world. Despite all that Grace had drummed into me about war, I hoped it might keep going long enough for me to be in uniform.

Although the Japanese had taken the Americans by surprise at Pearl Harbor and delivered a crushing blow to the US Navy, we found it hard at the outset to take them very seriously. We were still being told they were a very inferior species, all short-sighted to the point where they couldn't do things like fly aeroplanes. (After Pearl Harbor we had to rationalise *that* opinion.) We had been led to believe that the Japanese could be beaten very easily once Japan was invaded, for they lived in paper houses. Cocky Reardon told me about this one day: 'We don't even need bombs. We could just fly over them and drop big rocks on their houses.' Thank you, Cocky!

Australia's 8th Division had been sent to Singapore

early in 1941. Fifty years later I came across an article
in the *Herald*, ominously dated 19 February 1941, one
year to the day before Japan bombed Darwin. The article
was written by Clive Turnbull, Special Correspondent,
who accompanied the 8th Division troops when they
landed at Singapore under the command of Major-General
Gordon Bennett. Mr Turnbull wrote:

> 'They are thousands strong, and as magnificent a body
> of men as ever left Australian shores . . . . . It will be
> God help any enemy who sets foot on Malayan soil now
> that the country's material fortifications have been rein-
> forced by regiments of first-class fighting men.'

A year later we were overwhelmed by the speed and the
ferocity of the Japanese onslaught. New and indictingly
unfamiliar maps of a region called 'Oceania' made us
realise *for the first time* just where Australia *was*. The
map showed, too, the extent of the threat to Australia
and just how far we were from Britain.

During January 1942, and before America began to
mobilise, Japan had invaded the Dutch East Indies (now
Indonesia) and, incredibly, New Guinea.

That was bad enough, but we could not bring ourselves
to believe the next news shock: the Japanese conquered
and captured Singapore, with 15,000 Australians taken
prisoner. It couldn't happen, we said, stunned. We quickly
looked for a whipping boy and, typically Australian,
decided that the Poms and particularly Churchill were to
blame. What can you expect, we said, when the guns faced
the sea and couldn't be swung round to stop the Japanese
who seemed to have just ridden in on bicycles from French
Indo-China and said, 'Boo! Hands up! You're all our prisoners!' It was as unreal as a game of cops-and-robbers at
school. Our entire security had always been based on the
knowledge that Britannia ruled the waves and that any
threat to us would be countered immediately by the

British Navy deploying its might to blast the enemy out of the water, for this was the only direction from which Singapore could be attacked, or so we thought. Potential attackers could only be European powers — the Germans, Dutch, French or Russians. No Asians could ever mobilise sufficiently to pose a threat. Not a chance. Asians challenging England? Never!

It was a bit late for post-mortems, but even a 10-year-old boy could see exactly what Japan had been planning for years, and was in the process of achieving, right under our noses. I am convinced that the main reason why we allowed them to get away with it was the superiority factor. Australians, Britons and Americans thought of the Japanese and all the other people not 'like us' as biologically incapable of posing a threat. We knew the Japanese were industrious, but we felt they simply copied everyone else's patents and made inferior goods. Anything pre-war bearing a MADE IN JAPAN label was bound to break. What else could you expect from myopic sub-humans who lived in paper houses? How could you take them seriously?

This upstart Tojo was to blame. Previously the Japanese had been obsequious towards the Yanks because they got most of their oil from America. So, for a few years while the Japanese were doing confrontationist things in China, their diplomats had been bowing and scraping to the Americans who accepted such pandering as their due from 'monkeys in formal dress'. But Tojo, the new prime minister, and the other Tokyo imperialists could see that with the support of Vichy France in French Indo-China and Portugal in Timor they could easily get access to oil in places like Borneo. They probably realised — as we did not — that the Dutch, who had been very cruel rulers in Indonesia, would not get great support from the 'natives', as the indigenous people were called. The only impediment to a quick annexation of Oceania was Singapore. Everyone had been told of the might of the British Empire and its naval supremacy and that Singapore could not be captured from the sea. Of course it couldn't, so why bother trying? Send in the bicycles. Nobody will take bespectacled caricatures of soldiers on bicycles very seriously, will they?

Unfortunately for Australian morale, we were not told at the time of the fierce opposition mounted against the Japanese on the Malay Peninsula by members of the 8th Division and the Australian air force before the capture of Singapore. On the face of things it seemed that the British commander, Percival, had simply waved the white flag and thereby committed 15,000 Australians to the horror of Japanese prisoner-of-war camps for the next four years. To add to the confusion the senior Australian officer, General Bennett, escaped. We were told much later that it was all part of a plan to enable Bennett to live to fight another day, but hang on, said the ordinary people, doesn't the captain stay on the sinking ship until all the others have been evacuated first?

While the impact of Pearl Harbor left the Americans reeling, the Japanese moved with lightning speed to a tightly co-ordinated plan which would enable them to get various strongholds and then go on the defensive. Australia didn't matter; it could easily be isolated.

We faced the prospect, as even Grace now warned us, of 'eating rice in slave camps to the end of our days'. Frightening stuff. I had some grim exchanges of news and opinions with the women in the Ladies' Lounge at Brown's Pub as I sold them their CITY FINAL edition of the *Herald*. They puffed their fags. They sipped reflectively on their fourpenny darks and five-ounce beers. Not even a tip for Saturday's races cheered them all that much.

And I did a lot of private praying. Praying came easily to me in those days. My faith in God was immutable, although I didn't really expect any miracles like Hitler and Tojo being struck dead, which was the logical divine way of ending the war. I accepted that the war was part of God putting us to the test. It was vital to keep up the faith — keep on praying and doing one's best — because the heaven to which we eventually aspired would make any earthly struggles worth while. Heaven would be that wonderful, never-ending state where we would float on in eternal happiness, meeting the Blessed Virgin, being on first-name terms with Julius Caesar and Napoleon — meeting everybody really — and best of all, knowing what was going to happen on earth next week. There we'd be, we Catholics especially, looking down on those stupid creatures dithering around on earth as we had once done, making their mistakes, committing their sins. Hey Julius, just look at those boys down there playing with themselves! Don't they know that not only God, but everyone in eternity is watching them? So why don't they take the silly smirks off their faces?

I had not yet started to ask Why? about anything, for we were constantly told it wasn't necessary to question. We were told at home, at school, at Church, that we were privileged, being Catholics, as we had the run on the rails. Just do what Mother Church tells you and you are assured of eternal life in Heaven. The Protestants had only a marginal chance, probably none at all if one was brutally frank. As for the misguided Jews, well, they'd had their big opportunity and they'd blown it. And the poor old pagans who hadn't been baptised — they were better off than misguided Jews and Protestants, because they didn't know any better, but it didn't matter how good they might be in life, they could only aspire to Limbo. At least in Limbo they would meet all those lovely little babies, the Holy Innocents, who should have been Catholics but had died or been aborted before they could be baptised. Yes children, the nuns constantly told us, baptism is vital. Rather than being taught First Aid at school, the principal thing impressed on us about accidents was to make sure you poured some water on the head of

✠

Promise Made at Confirmation

In honour of the sacred thirst of Jesus on the Cross and in reparation for my own sins, I promise to abstain from all intoxicating liquor until my twenty fifth year.

Name *J Egan*

Date *9-10-4C*

"O Jesus, through Thy sacred thirst on the Cross, have mercy on us."

Jesus mercy; Mary, help.

The pledge I signed when I was confirmed

anyone about to die, saying 'I baptise you in the name of the Father and of the Son and of the Holy Ghost.' You might thereby be changing history for someone otherwise destined for Purgatory or Limbo. Hell was another matter. If you died in the state of mortal sin you were gone, finished, and you too might meet Julius Caesar or Napoleon and know what was going to happen next week, but it wouldn't do you any good because you would be burning in hell-fire for ever! Think about it, girls and boys. Try to imagine eternity. It never ends.

I was confirmed in September 1941 and it was a great occasion, although the ceremony was a bit long-winded. Grace suggested I take 'John' as my Confirmation name. She explained that many of her relations thought I should have been named John originally, after her brother Jack who was killed at Gallipoli. But four of her brothers had named their sons 'Jack' to the point where the new generation of Jack Brennans were referred to as Mick's

Jack, Peter's Jack, Jim's Jack and Bill's Jack. Later there would be Gus's Jack. As my surname was going to be Egan Grace hadn't seen much point in calling her boy John. But she felt my confirmation name should be Jack (John) and I was happy to comply because I knew from our talks how close she had been to her brother.

The nuns prepared us for The Great Day for weeks. I particularly loved learning the difficult Gregorian singing, which I could handle better than most of the other boys (said he, smugly).

Grace was very happy I would be signing the pledge, thereby promising to abstain from alcoholic liquor until I was 25. By that time, she felt, I would presumably be intelligent enough to know that booze was bad for me anyway. Grace had a real set on alcohol, but she was not absolutely wowserish about it. Her brothers all took a drink. My Dad didn't drink, mainly because he had the responsibility of bringing up a large family on low or no wages for so long. So I was quite happy to sign. Not that I had too many options, mind.

I was confirmed by Doctor Mannix and that was the closest I ever came to the awe-inspiring 'Dinky Dan' who did so much to dominate our lives. Like all Catholic ritual it was great theatre if nothing else. The packed church, the knowledge that you were 'centre stage', the singing, the candles, the thuribles and the incense. Presiding over this, suitably aloof, was old Dan in his rich vestments, his mitre on his head making him look ten feet tall, sitting on his throne and vaguely waving his right hand so that at all times we could see the symbol of his Apostolic succession, the heavily jewelled gold ring which we would soon and in total deference kiss. Eventually, one by one, we filed into the sanctuary. Girls had been told that they were especially privileged on Confirmation Day, for they were not normally allowed into the sanctuary of the church. At last I was kneeling in front of the great man,

aware that a priest assisting was translating all of our
names into Latin, so there'd be no likelihood of being told
to 'take your chance, anyhow, wid Maginnis'. A deft rub
of the Holy Oils on my forehead, the awareness of now
being Joannis, a whiff of incense as he waved the thurible
over me, and with a warm inner glow I knew I was a
fully-indoctrinated Catholic.

The next Sacrament would be the priesthood, a few
years down the track. Knowledge of the life and exploits
of my cousin Bill Brennan on the ocean wave had caused
me to think a bit, but perhaps I could be a ship's chaplain?

As preparation for my ordination I was always watching the priests, checking their mannerisms as they said
Mass, analysing who performed to best effect.

It was little wonder I was hooked, for we had over the
years a variety of priests in our local parish who were
quite impressive in their different ways. There were the
fun-loving, card-playing Irishmen, Fathers Lynch and
Duggan. There was angelic Father Hunter, who had a
beaut little Ford car, registration number BU604, into
which he would cram six or seven altar boys for some
great picnics at Mordialloc. There was the incredibly
handsome Father McCarthy (privately called 'Justin' by
all the women of the parish as they fluttered their eye-
lashes) who always just happened to be wearing his tennis
creams and looking ever-so-slightly awry as he burst with
an 'Oh! Sorry girls, didn't know you were meeting today,'
into the Parish Hall, to wreck absolutely the contempla-
tive mood of the teenage girls who were members of the
Children of Mary Society. There was swashbuckling
Father Keogh of the broken nose, who looked as though
he had just cleaned up Ambrose Palmer, and who always
seemed to be seen laying big bets at either the dogs or
the horse races. Hmm, yes, a bit of a lad that one, mused
Grace. But you must have respect for the cloth, she would
hasten to add. There was old Peter McGee who, although

mental, still had that awareness that he was the boss. That was the thing I liked best about the priesthood: the priests were always 'in charge'. I could never get over the level of humility displayed by the cleverest nun in the presence of the stupidest priest. Yes, Father, they'd say demurely. No, Father, thank you very much Father, God bless you Father. I was impressed.

And the Redemptorists! Every second year there would be a Mission run by the Redemptorists and for a fortnight the entire parish would be required to make all sorts of special efforts. Daily Mass and Communion, a Mission confession, and attendance at church every night for Benediction and then *the sermon*. That was the format. We altar boys had to learn to serve Mass slightly differently. The Redemptorists were inevitably very impressive fellows and their sermons at night were absolute masterpieces. Into the sanctuary they would sweep in their black cassocks over which they wore a huge cloaks. The church would be jammed full of people sitting up in anticipation. Talk about hell-fire and brimstone! Up and down their beautifully modulated voices would go, first a joke or two, then an earnest piece of absolute and undeniable logic, weaving you into their spell. And then the arms would hold the cape to its widest extremes and there would be this almighty roar: 'And where will you go when you die?' We would cower in the pews. Oh, were they good!

I took my career as an altar boy very seriously, treated it like an apprenticeship. Pete was the only one who ever lectured or gave you a box on the ears. Most of the priests were terrific to the altar boys, sometimes more frivolous about things than I would have liked, but generally good. I learned that you had to adjust your style to suit the occasion, to present different moods in fact.

Altar boys didn't often get to 'serve' at funerals, unless the school was asked to make an altar boy available. But when I was rostered for a funeral I was solemnity itself and would often have to wipe away an involuntary tear. Weddings were different. I would start off in almost beatific mode, then swap gradually to joyful as the bride and groom relaxed after the priest pronounced them man and wife. Weddings were great, too, in that somebody invariably pressed a ten-shilling note into your palm as you feigned surprise at the end of the service. As I earned about six shillings a week selling papers, ten bob was a fortune. Occasionally Grace would need the money for housekeeping, but mostly she would encourage me to put the money from weddings into my State Savings account (the now-defunct State Bank of Victoria was in those days called The State Savings Bank).

St Paul's Church was right next to Pentridge Gaol, an unbelievably severe bluestone fortress in Coburg. I went to Pentridge on a few occasions to serve Mass for Father Hunter. I was scared stiff, I can tell you, and firmly expected to be attacked from behind while kneeling in the sanctuary of the prison chapel. Fancy having your back turned to all these criminals, I thought (for these were the days before the priest faced the congregation to say Mass). I never had the charity to think that most of them were probably deriving more from the Mass than I was, because they didn't *have* to attend at church. But I didn't try to fool those blokes with any fancy emotional turns. No fear. Heads down, fast game's a good game, Ted. Let's get out of here.

I particularly liked serving at Benediction, for which I might be rostered once or twice a month. It meant going to the church at night and there was an eerie atmosphere in the almost empty building with the stained-glass windows turned black. I was never quite sure *why* it was necessary to have Benediction, but I loved what happened: the Blessed Eucharist was displayed in the Monstrance and held up for Adoration while the Latin hymns were sung. We knew, from our training by the nuns, that the

Body of Christ, the Blessed Sacrament, was at all times
present in the Tabernacle, as the little red sanctuary lamp
testified. You didn't have to *see* God, did you, because you
only saw the substance of the bread in any case? The
nuns had always encouraged us to 'make visits' to the
Blessed Sacrament where you knelt or sat in adoration
and contemplation. We were always urged to be 'simple':

> Jesus, meek and humble of Heart
> Make my heart like unto Thine

One nun urged us to have 'the piety of a French peasant
woman' — however pious that might be. I remember
being impressed when Sister Mary Josepha told me she
had once asked an old man why he paid such long visits
to the church, for she had never seen him kneel and
pray. He just sat with his eyes fixed on the Tabernacle:
  'Oh,' he replied, 'I just look at Him. And He just looks
at me.'
  Benediction provided an opportunity for a bit of adventure as well. There were quite a few altar boys from the
O'Hea's Road end of Coburg, and we would usually be
rostered for Benediction together. Coming home in the
dark at about 9 p.m. we angelic altar boys would invariably play cats on the roof which meant, simply, that we
would throw handfuls of yonnies (Irish confetti, that is,
rocks) on someone's tin roof, and yell out 'Cats on the roof'
as the shower of stones cascaded down the roof slope and
into the guttering. Then we'd race off. It was all very
daring. One night Tommy Way, Lynn Miller and I had
been serving Benediction and on the way home decided
we would give a few houses in Service Street the treatment. Bang! Bang! Bang! went the stones as we flew away
shouting 'Cats on the roof! Cats on the roof!' We turned
into O'Hea's Road and ran straight into the substantial
presence of a policeman, standing just around the corner
with his bicycle.

'What are you up to?' he demanded to know, as if he didn't already.

'Just . . . er . . . muckin' round,' I stammered.

He started to take our names and addresses, and our parents' names, assuring us we'd be hearing more about this. We were petrified. Then it happened. The bobby grabbed Tommy Way by the lapel and Tommy farted in fear. In my opinion a fart is usually good for a laugh, particularly if it is sonorous rather than odorous, and Tommy's was a good one. I couldn't contain myself. I started to laugh, but knew I musn't, so I bit my lip and finished up spluttering apoplectically. The policeman should have been amused, but wasn't and he began to shake Tommy, who immediately let off a spurt of farts like a Gatling gun firing at random. It was too much, and the three of us began to laugh so much the policeman thrust us from him in disgust. We never heard any more of the incident, for I reckon the policeman probably had a good laugh himself when we were out of earshot.

Another great bit of Catholic theatre was the ceremony called Tenebrae, which means *darkness* in Latin. Sister Sal and I have never forgotten the night Pop took us to St Patrick's Cathedral to see this mediaeval ritual, which was part of the Easter Vigil. St Patrick's is a sepulchral place at the best of times, so it was the perfect setting for Tenebrae which is conducted at night and consists of lots of Gregorian chanting by priests and the choir, a procession in candlelight, and then the gradual extinguishing of every single light and candle in the Cathedral. We were left in silent darkness for a moment, until slowly the priests began banging their missals together. The noise was deafening. Then a single candle was lit, the singing started again and gradually normal lighting was restored. The Catholic Church certainly blew it when they stopped having wonderful ritual like this. People need drama in their lives.

St Patrick's Cathedral had inherited a wonderful, ready-made choir as a result of the war. The Vienna Boys' Choir was on tour in Melbourne when war broke out, and were automatically scheduled for internment as enemy aliens, even though some of the boys were only aged about 10. The wily Dr Mannix was quick to suggest that he should be made their guardian. He placed them in foster homes and enrolled them for schooling at St Patrick's College, East Melbourne. They were truly magnificent singers and I eventually became a classmate of the youngest, Kurt Schuster, who was a great bloke. Another, Stefan Haag, became very prominent in art circles in Australia. I often wonder why a book and perhaps a film have not been made around the Vienna Boys' Choir experience in Australia.

It was going to be a couple of months before we actually saw any American service personnel in Melbourne, but we were immediately aware of the seriousness of the situation, because on the same day they attacked Pearl Harbor the Japanese bombed Guam, The Philippines, Singapore, Hong Kong and Nauru. Their army surged into Malaya. They seemed to have troops and ships everywhere, and it was obvious that, like the Germans, they had been thumbing their noses at the rest of the world for years, while everybody else was content to hope they might never be totally provocative. It was time for Mr Curtin to pre-empt Gough Whitlam:

> Men and women of Australia, the stern truth is that Japan has begun a war in the Pacific in which our security and our interests are at stake. I ask the people of Australia to give the best that they can in the service of their country. The fighting forces are at battle stations. Every other man and woman should be in some place of usefulness.

It was a grim Christmas. All leave for Australian service

personnel was cancelled. Churchill and Roosevelt met
in the United States to co-ordinate strategy. I'll bet
Churchill was cheering. At last he must have seen a
glimmer of light, for he knew the might of America was
essential if the war was to be won. He had been warning
Roosevelt about the Germans and Japanese since the
early 1930s. He might have been a bloody warmonger
but he had read things right this time.

STEPPING STONES

The Japanese threat brought a new geographic perspective to us all.
The cartoon appeared on 19 February 1941.

The silky-voiced crooners of the cigarette advertisements gave way to the digger model in the 1940s

9
Just a Few Tin Sheds

We had to admit Japanese strategy was brilliant. They put all their plans in place right under the noses of the Allies, who soon would include America. It's not that our side was in no position to take the initiative, or at least be prepared for the moment when Japan chose to strike. Australia, Britain and India all had troops and aircraft in Malaya (now part of Malaysia). The Dutch had a long-established presence in the East Indies (now part of Indonesia). America had troops and aircraft like Flying Fortresses in The Philippines and a huge naval base at Pearl Harbor in Hawaii. The Flying Fortresses had already set up a circuit whereby they could 'control' the South Pacific, landing at Hawaii, Midway Island, Wake Island, Port Moresby, Darwin, Guam and Luzon in The Philippines. They had established a huge airbase at Luzon three months before the first Japanese attacks, and General Douglas MacArthur was there as Commander of all the United States Forces in the Far East. But I found it — and still find it mystifying — that our side allowed the Japanese to make the first move. I guess we thought it 'civilised' to wait, rather than be 'treacherous' and attack.

For their part Japan knew the first move had better be a good one, and Pearl Harbor certainly was.

We accepted at the time that the attack on Pearl Harbor was the first Japanese aggression in Allied territory. But in terms of actual time they landed at Kota Bharu in Malaya before they attacked Pearl Harbor.

My cousin Len Brennan was a flight engineer with No. 1 Squadron RAAF, flying in Hudson bombers. They flew out to bomb the Japanese troops landing at Kota Bharu and sank a Japanese ship, and Indian soldiers inflicted heavy casualties on the Japanese who nonetheless effected a landing. With the International Dateline running through the middle of the Pacific it is recorded that the attack on Pearl Harbor took place at 6.45 am on 7 December 1941 and the Kota landing occurred in the early hours of 8 December. But if you convert the timing of both actions to Greenwich Mean Time the landing in Malaya was at 4.55 pm and the bombing of Pearl Harbor 6.25 p.m. on 7 December. So the Hudsons sank the Japanese ship before Australia had officially declared war on Japan.

We found all this out a few months later when cousin Len turned up in Melbourne, looking as skinny as a whippet. He and others escaped from Malaya after the surrender and got to Colombo via Sumatra and Java on a tramp steamer. From Colombo they were brought to Australia on the *Stirling Castle*.

It is not widely known, either, that an American destroyer sank a Japanese midget submarine close to Pearl Harbor an hour before the bombing started, but news of this was not transmitted to American headquarters in time to put everyone on alert. The films *The Best Years of our Lives* and *Tora Tora Tora* subsequently demonstrated how Japan's pilots attacked Pearl Harbor from the east, coming from the sun at daybreak, with many US personnel probably suffering the effects of a boisterous

The *Herald* 19 February 1942 played down the bombing of Darwin: air power equal to that used at Pearl Harbor was involved, 243 were killed and 300 injured

Saturday night in balmy Hawaii. The Japanese were certainly aware that it was normal practice for the American fleet to be in port for the weekend. They only needed to listen to the hit parade:

> The fleet's in port again
> Back home, in port again
> Yo ho, yo ho,
> And we'll have a jolly good
> Really wonderful
> Mighty marvellous time

There was another calamity for America in The Philippines the same day. When news of the attack on Pearl Harbor was relayed to General MacArthur the order was given to bomb the Japanese-held island of Formosa (Taiwan) in reply. There was some delay in implementing the order. The Flying Fortresses at Luzon were eventually being loaded with bombs when suddenly the Japanese attacked and knocked out half the entire

American air strength on the ground. The remaining
Flying Fortresses were sent to Darwin and then rede-
ployed, although no one in Coburg was told that at the
time.

It was to be another six months before we added the
Flying Fortresses to our silhouette charts, which in the
first days of the Pacific War showed only Wirraways,
Boomerangs, Hudsons, Blenheims, Buffaloes and Tiger
Moths on our side and the Zeros and Mitsubishis of the
Japanese. We had long since familiarised ourselves, with-
out ever seeing the aircraft, with Spitfires, Focke-Wulfs,
Dornier Do 17s, Heinkel He 111s, Hurricanes, Messer-
schmitt Me 109 and so on, involved in the Battle of
Britain. But my recollection to 1942 is that we saw more
Tiger Moths than any other aircraft in the skies over
Melbourne. Soon there would be Kittyhawks, Beauforts,
Beaufighters, Mosquitoes, Liberators and then the amaz-
ing twin-tailed Lockheed Lightnings. 'Aeroplanes will
never be the same again,' said Biggles, the comic-strip
hero, to his faithful navigator, Algy.

When Pearl Harbor was bombed and Singapore fell
shortly after, Mr Curtin announced on the wireless that
this was 'our gravest hour' so I was surprised how casual
people were about the bombing of Darwin on 19 February
1942.

I recall selling papers on the day of the bombing but
nobody in Brown's Hotel seemed very concerned. There
was the most casual mention of casualties ('some
casualties') and the general consensus was: 'So what?
There's nothing in Darwin anyway. Just a few tin sheds.'

It was not revealed until a few days later, and then
only on page 3 of the *Herald*, that 243 people had been
killed and a lot of ships sunk.

Nobody was aware that the decision had been taken
for Australia to concentrate on preparing to defend the
eastern coastline, particularly around Sydney, Newcastle

and Port Kembla, where the coal, steelworks and major naval base were located.

It wasn't that the rest of the continent was to be forsaken. On the contrary, Darwin was held to be a vitally important base, not so much for repelling invaders, but as a launching point for troop movements and bombing attacks by the Flying Fortresses. And Darwin had huge, recently-installed oil tanks along the foreshore, so the Japanese attack concentrated on Darwin harbor, the oil tanks and the airfields, both the civil airstrip at Fannie Bay and the new RAAF airstrip. It is highly likely that Japanese Intelligence had gleaned accurate information about Darwin and the northern coastline through its pearling fleet, which had worked in north Australian waters for many years when Japan was held to be a friendly nation. When I went to Darwin a few years after the war I saw the evidence of the many bombing attacks on the town.

But in 1942 the pummelling Darwin took was not as traumatic to me as blowing up our new gas stove.

One Saturday I was at home, listening to the football, while Grace was ironing on the kitchen table. She asked me to cook the lamb chops we were having for tea that night. We had had the new gas stove for a few months. I hadn't lit a gas stove previously and she told me to turn on the knob and light the griller. I turned on the oven switch, but was holding the match near the griller.

'It won't light,' I said.

'Have you turned the gas on?'

'Yeah,' I said, and pointed to a knob to show that it was indeed in the on position. She was unfamiliar with the new stove as well.

'It must be switched off at the meter,' she said. I went out to check.

'No, it's on at the meter,' I reported when I returned.

'Try again,' she said, so I lit a match. When the griller

still would not light I opened the oven door. There was a flash, an almighty blast and I was half-blown and I half-ran out the kitchen door. I stood outside shaking with fear and shock.

Then slowly I ventured back inside. The door was blown off the stove. There was Grace, sort of laughing. She was unhurt — but she had no eyebrows. I began to laugh, almost hysterically, and she told me to go into the bathroom to look at my own face. It was as black as Nigger O'Reilly's and I too had no eyebrows. But the biggest laugh came when we discovered a lamb chop stuck to the kitchen ceiling.

We had cold meat and salad for tea.

Grace was always ironing, not only our clothes, but she took in ironing for other people. She was a beautiful ironer, never using an ironing board, just the kitchen table on which she'd place a blanket, then a sheet. She said she liked ironing and she would even iron banknotes if anybody had any crumpled ones. She taught me, and later Tim, to iron. I am good; he is terrific. Sal and I had been given a secondhand bike as a joint Christmas present, but as it was a boy's bike with a crossbar, Sal didn't use it as much as I did. Grace would pack the contracted ironing neatly into a cardboard box, which I had to deliver on the bike, which had a carrier on the handlebars. I bailed up when first told I had to deliver the ironing, not on physical grounds, but I hated having to acknowledge that my mother was so poor she felt she had to take in ironing. I was and remain something of a snob in this respect for I still prefer to pretend I have money rather than acknowledge I haven't.

'What do I say if someone asks me what's in the box?' I demanded the first time.

'Tell them they're not allowed to look, because your mother is a canary breeder and you are delivering prize canaries which might escape,' she replied. That took some of the pain away, so delivering 'canaries' became a part of the routine of a Saturday afternoon. Only many years later did I become reconciled to the fact that there was no disgrace in being poor as kids and, in retrospect, I admire tremendously the sacrifices my parents made so that we kids could enjoy a better lifestyle than they had. Grace saw the ironing as a pleasant way of boosting her housekeeping money so that she could give us plenty of good, plain food and keep us in clothes that were 'clean and well paid for and don't you forget it'.

Grace had another way of augmenting the housekeeping. We had a big plum tree in the back yard and, each summer, when the tree was loaded, we would be given the job of picking the plums which she then sold to us at four a penny. Amazingly, we didn't cheat on this exercise. I guess we realised it was a good sort of a game, really, a bit like Nornie's threepences.

Daylight saving was introduced in 1942 and the younger Egans loved the long summer nights, although many parents immediately began to deplore the fact that they couldn't get their children to bed at a reasonable hour. Not our parents, though. They liked to sit on the front verandah and watch our games which would go on in the twilight until 9.30 or 10 p.m. Hidey and Kick the Tin were the night-time favorites. Kick the Tin is a bit like Hidey except that an empty jam tin is upended and placed to make a home base or safe area. The person who is He or In is required to count to 100 while the others hide. Then, as the hiders are discovered, they are brought to the base where they have to sit. They are allowed to signal to another hider that there is an opportunity to come out of hiding without being caught and release those at the base by kicking the tin. The person who is He has to return to base, retrieve the tin and start again. The released prisoners are permitted to hide again. It was a great game of cat and mouse.

My brother Tim was walking and talking by this time, but occasionally Sal and I would be told to take him for a ride in his pram, which meant wheeling him up and down O'Hea's Road while Grace was busy getting tea ready. This was a bit dull, we felt, so we devised this game of running full bore with the pram, which we'd then allow to speed off down a slope on its own, while we stopped. We'd count to ten and then race to see who caught the pram first. One evening we set the pram going, with Tim sitting up gleefully as he sped at what probably seemed to him like a hundred miles an hour, past Wilson's grocer shop, heading for Molesworth Street. Round the corner of Fraser Street, on his way home from work came Pop, serenely walking along, his Gladstone bag in his hand. All he saw of course was Tim, sitting up solo as he hurtled along in the pram, for we hadn't yet started to give chase. Pop dropped his bag, sprinted like Jesse Owens and reached the pram at the same time Sal and I hove into his view. To our mortification our father, gentle Joe Egan, who wouldn't even raise his voice in anger, gave us one good whack on the arse each, right there and then. It seems funny: Grace used to give me 'a hiding' with a strap regularly , but it never hurt as much as that one smack from Pop did. Sal has never forgotten it either, for it was the only time Pop ever smacked or even had to remonstrate with her — I am fairly sure she was his favorite child. Pop did hit me one other time when I spitefully tore up a project book of Sal's.

The family laughs about another time when Grace had given up on reforming me (my principal crime was that I always came home late from anywhere) and she said, 'I've had enough of him, Pop. It's your turn to belt him.' So into the wash-house I went with Pop who winked as he instructed me, 'Right, start yelling,' as he whacked the razor strop against a chair. I should have been awarded an Oscar the way I carried on, but I don't think we fooled anyone, especially Grace.

Mind you, Grace owed me one at the time. A couple of weeks earlier she had laid me out, cold. I was playing footy in the back yard, when she called me in for my tea. I ignored her call, and went back for one last kick. Bang! Straight through the window of the bungalow went the football. She came out into the yard, a broom in her hand, and took a swing at my back side with the broom. I ducked, and she whacked me over the eye. Down I went for the count, blood pouring from the injured eye. The next thing I remember is Grace pouring water over me, but not forgetting her usual admonition, 'Don't you dare tell your father about this.' I kept quiet over the incident.

You had to get up early in the morning to put one over Grace. I remember one time I had been given a hefty tip selling papers. I had enough money to buy a chocolate malted milk at McKay's Dairy in Sutherland Street on the way home. As I walked in the door Grace, who always insisted she had the best sense of smell in the world, asked me from ten feet away, 'And where did you get the money for a chocolate malted milk?'

One of the great joys of getting a tip selling papers was to buy a dim-sim from an old Chinese chap we called 'Dim Sim Charlie'. He used to come to Brown's pub every evening with a gleaming steel pot jammed full of the most wonderful steamed dim-sims I have ever tasted. 'Dim Sim. Tuppy each,' he would call as he walked briskly through the noisy crowd of drinkers. He always seemed to be wary in the pub, probably a bit apprehensive about ridicule. But he did a roaring trade and most nights, especially in the cold winter, I would buy a dim sim. Charlie always dug out a big one for me with his fork, placed it neatly on a small square of tissue paper and swapped it for my proferred two pennies. I suppose I romanticise but I can still remember the joy of savoring every morsel as I nibbled away, prolonging the pleasure. Charlie smiled as he watched my enjoyment. 'Dim Sim, good tucker,' he would say, then squat on his knees and rest his back against the pub wall, patiently waiting for six o'clock when the drinkers would spill out of the pub and he'd make a few sales. Then he would disappear.

Unfortunately my taste for dim-sims exposed some of the blind prejudice my parents had inherited in the isolationist Australia of those days. Although they never laid eyes on Dim Sim Charlie I was told 'He makes those dim-sims out of stray cats' and 'Make sure you wash your hands after you've given him money.' It didn't worry me though, and I am thankful for Charlie's introduction to Asian food, which I still love. My parents had not travelled around much, so their attitudes were perhaps understandable.

My Mum's mother had apparently always been terrified of Chinese since the goldrush days when as a child she lived at Dunkeld, near the Grampians of Western Victoria, and the Chinese jogged past her homestead in thousands on their way to Bendigo and Ballarat. They had been denied entry to Victoria so their ships berthed at Robe in South Australia and they would walk, then jog, then walk, to cover the distance as quickly as possible.

My Dad had gone briefly to Barcaldine in Central Queensland as a young man, but had mainly been in Victoria. My parents were neither more nor less xenophobic than the average Australian, guided by publications like the influential and popular *Bulletin* which still had its slogan 'Australia for the White Man' emblazoned on Page 1. It was just that they had no experience of foreigners and, to their credit, when I eventually introduced them to my great mate Ron 'The Flying Chinaman' Chin they thought he was a 'lovely young man'.

Uncle Bob, Mum's brother, and Aunty Mary, Mum's sister, were good examples of how travel broadens one's attitudes. Bob had been all over Australia, to New Zealand as a shearer and then to World War 1. Mary had been born in Gippsland, third child in Mum's large family, the only girl among seven boys — Michael, Robert, Peter, Jack, Martin, Joe and Jim. Then Cis came along, ahead of Bill, Grace and Gus. Exhausted after being mother's help for so many years, Mary took the decision in her late teens to go to Western Australia where she worked around the mining towns as a waitress and housekeeper. When World War 1 started she decided to go to England, where she worked in munitions factories and then joined the Land Army, an organised female agricultural workforce. She and Bob could not only talk articulately about their own experiences but seemed to have a level of understanding and tolerance other Australians rarely possessed. It wasn't just my parents. Everybody was indoctrinated with the belief that only those people exactly like you were any good. Not only did that create crude racial stereotyping — Chows, Dagoes, Huns and so on — but it also turned all religious and political activity into war.

I had my first disenchantment with religion around this time. Grace thought it would be good 'discipline' for me to take one end-of-term holiday at Rupertswood, a huge mansion and farm inherited by the Catholic Church and run by the Salesian Fathers. There were about 100 boarders and they took in other boys at holiday time for 'an adventure on a farm'. Rupertswood, formerly the home of Sir Rupert Clarke, is just to the north of Melbourne, near Sunbury. The priests were mainly Italians, who had not been interned strangely, and they ranged in nature through fat and jolly to ascetic to humorless. The Salesian brothers were mainly Australian-born fellows training for the priesthood, and what a bunch of sadists they were. They would cane the boys with seeming delight as they supervised farm and school work. Their specialty was in the dormitory at night, where the slightest noise brought

the order: 'Out of bed, son. Drop those pyjamas.' They
would administer six good whacks on the bare bum with
a large clothes brush. As well as being cruel, it seemed
like absolute voyeurism to me even then. I only got one
six and kept out of their reach for the remainder of my
stay, but I still had bruises on my backside when I got
home. Parents would sue today.

I said to Grace, 'They're just a bunch of perves.'

Disappointingly, Grace replied:

'Nonetheless, Teddy, you've got to have respect for the
cloth. And don't you let me catch you using filthy words
like that again.'

Thereafter, I could understand some of the anti-Cath-
olic prejudice I heard expressed.

10

Overpaid, Over-sexed and Over Here

We saw our first Americans in March 1942. General MacArthur arrived, after a slow trip by road, air and train from Darwin, where he had fled from The Philippines. We were told of his soon-to-be famous statement 'I shall return.' His corncob pipe and his Cherokee nose were meant to give us instant assurance that this was a man who meant business. He set up headquarters in Melbourne and overnight it seemed the Yanks had taken over all the toffier parts of the city. On our side of town all the prestigious homes and flats in Royal Parade, Parkville, seemed to have American officers installed. A huge camp of conical tents, Camp Pell, sprang up in the Royal Park Reserve near the Melbourne Zoo. Americans crowded our trams, for they had taken over the recently-completed Royal Melbourne Hospital in Parkville as their main office and communications base.

They showed us the real meaning of the word 'flash'. American uniforms were superior, cut from the best cloth. Australian uniforms looked like hessian bags. The newcomers had exuberant manners, excellent teeth and they sported flash rings which we were informed were 'fraternity rings' as they uttered incomprehensible jargon about 'college' and 'graduation' and 'Phi Beta Kappa'. Their badges and insignia looked smart, and they were usually prepared to part with these if asked, unlike Aussie service personnel, who could be prosecuted for such largesse. Most kids in Melbourne quickly sported either a brass US or a Marine Corps badge and every second teenage girl acquired a sailor's 'gob' hat.

The women and kids loved their accents. Immediately you could sense that Australian men were bristling with resentment at these latecomers to the war who were going to take all the credit for winning it. It would take most of us a while to sort out the difference between American fact and American bullshit, and to realise that glibness was obviously a vital part of the American education system. Kids were won over quickly and we all began to say 'Hi, buddy' to one another and reply, 'Sure' (which came out as *Shooer*) to any question requiring an affirmative.

Food and clothing were either in short supply or officially rationed in Australia and beer and cigarettes were hard to get. Not so for the Americans though. They handed out Lucky Strikes, Camels and Chesterfields to adults, and 'candy' and chewing gum to kids with the indulgence of dipsomaniacs in a brewery. Their pockets bulged with cash and they were prodigious tippers. On a few occasions I was given a two-bob piece for a twopenny *Herald*, enough to buy twelve newspapers, and told, 'Keep the change, boy.'

And some of them were black! The thought of black men in uniform had never occurred to us in Melbourne, not realising that hundreds of Aboriginal men had enlisted to fight for Australia even though they couldn't vote at elections and were not even counted in the census as people. But here were these black Americans, drinking in pubs, dancing with white girls and always seeming to be laughing uproariously as they slapped one another on the back and said, 'Right on, man.' Various half-serious admonitions were made to Australian girls like 'Don't go out with the black Yanks on a dark night. If they close their mouths you'll think they've gone home.'

We all had a good laugh coming home from Mass one Sunday morning. We always walked slowly, usually a couple of families together, the adults chatting, the kids playing. This particular Sunday we were walking with the Brasher family, who lived in Webb Street, three streets further on than us. Behind us about ten yards, walking at the same pace and within our hearing came Cocky Reardon and her sister, also a teacher, and a couple of other families. Someone in the rear group mentioned the black Americans. Cocky, who was about sixty, a tall gangly spinster, said with her characteristically squeaky voice: 'There's no way in the wide world you'd find me going out with one of them.'

We quickly discovered that within the American ranks blacks were treated differently. There were reports of absolute brutality by the American Provost Corps, military police, who apparently took great delight in beating up the black servicemen at dances, singling them out for savage treatment with batons the size of baseball bats. But the American blacks were very popular among Australians in Melbourne because they were always scrupulously clean, they always seemed to be laughing and everyone admired their skill at things like jitterbugging and sport. And the enigmatic Australians really do often support the underdog.

There was reluctant but fairly general agreement that without the Americans we would be done over by the Japanese. Mr Curtin was at loggerheads with Churchill, insisting that our 6th and 7th Divisions should come home immediately, but Churchill was anxious to beat Hitler first. There was no way the 9th Division could come home.

They were crucially involved in Africa and would soon go
to Syria.

HMAS *Perth* and *Yarra* were sunk in waters near Java
in a gallant but unsuccessful attempt to stop the invasion
of that huge and vital island, which we suddenly realised
was one step away from the Australian mainland.While
not condoning the actions of the Japanese we had to admit
their planning and execution was superb. Their equipment (especially things like landing craft) was infinitely
superior to anything the Allies possessed. Their ships and
aircraft were fast and powerfully armed. Their soldiers,
sailors and airmen had been trained, hardened (often by
battle) and were generally dedicated, often at a fanatical
level for their allotted task of securing a perimeter around
the Pacific.

Back in Coburg, air-raid shelters were dug in the
grounds of St Paul's School. Evacuation papers were filled
out by many families authorising their children to be sent
to country areas in an emergency. Uncle Bob put his age
down and joined the army once more in this latest war
to end war. His son Frank put his age up and also joined
the army. Uncle Bob was furious: 'You're supposed to have
your father's permission,' said Bob.

'I told them you were dead,' replied Frank.

'Well, remember that when you want to get out. I won't
be around to help you. I'm dead,' snorted Bob.

My dad had flat feet and was not considered fit to join
the army, but he was in a Reserved Occupation working
on the wharves, so was not required to enlist in any case.
But everybody was now either conscripted into the forces
or required to enrol with the Manpower Department
which would then place people in work considered vital
to the war effort.

General MacArthur was promoted to Supreme Commander of All Allied Forces in the South-West Pacific Area
after Churchill and Roosevelt divided the world into three

war zones and agreed that the United States should control all Allied action in the Pacific Zone. Supported by MacArthur (whose political background made him suspicious of England) Curtin really dug in his heels and insisted that the 6th and 7th Divisions be brought back to defend Australia rather than be sent to Burma and India. Churchill finally consented.

That decision was fortunate. The Japanese had invaded the New Guinea mainland at Lae and Salamaua.

In Britain the German air attacks continued. In return the Allies gave as good as they got, blasting German ports and industrial cities. We were very proud of the thousands of Australians who manned the aircraft and staffed the airfields of Britain along with the British, Canadian, New Zealand, Free French and Polish airmen. We considered the Poles to be particularly heroic, for they had escaped from their homeland to fight on our side.

While the air struggle was intense there was a stalemate as far as troop movements were concerned. Germany could not subjugate the Allied air forces to the point where invasion of the British Isles was feasible. And while Germany controlled all of mainland western Europe, Britain had only been able to contemplate an invasion of Europe after America entered the war. But while well-equipped materially, America's forces were woefully ill-prepared for the realities of war.

The irresistible German force had met the immovable Russian people at Stalingrad and Moscow, and the Russians slowly began to gain the ascendancy on their front, despite shocking losses of military and civilian lives.

The Germans were doing well in Africa, however, as Rommel swept all before him, and looked set to capture Alexandria and the Suez Canal. Australia's 9th Division had been withdrawn from Tobruk after the historic siege. They had been sent to Syria, and Rommel was able to recapture Tobruk. We war watchers of Coburg didn't know yet, nobody did, but Rommel's dream run was to come to an end as another of the great names of the war appeared. General Montgomery, the English general better known as 'Monty', was given the command of all the Allied forces and told not just to stop Rommel but to regain control of the entire North African coastline. As part of the operation the crack 9th Division was returned to fight with 'Monty'.

In the Pacific the Japanese were looking unstoppable. They surged through Burma, and incredibly, at the time, seemed poised to invade and capture India, with its millions of people and vast resources. They had almost completely occupied the East Indies, although an amazingly successful Australian force in Timor proved to be a great frustration. The Japanese had firm footholds in New Britain, New Ireland, the Solomons and on the New Guinea mainland at Lae and Salamaua. They continued to bomb Darwin, although we were not told the number of these raids, nor just how much damage Japanese bombers inflicted. There were air raids on Broome, Wyndham and Townsville. We refused to believe it at first when told on 31 March 1943 that large Japanese submarines outside Sydney Heads had launched three midget submarines which entered the harbor. All three were subsequently sunk but not before one of them had torpedoed the old Sydney ferry *Kuttabul*, which had been taken over by the Royal Australian Navy for use as a depot ship. Nineteen men were killed on *Kuttabul*, but the result could have been even worse, for the torpedo which hit *Kuttabul* was meant for the American aircraft carrier *Chicago*.

It wasn't all bad news though. The 6th and 7th Divisions came home to absolutely rapturous receptions wherever they appeared, and the nonchalance and confidence of these seasoned veterans was infectious. Melbourne was bursting at the seams and everybody seemed to acquire some sort of souvenir of the fighting in the Middle East. At school kids turned up with Italian buttons and coins, German water bottles and 'eagle' badges and one kid had a German helmet. We began to feel a bit confident, even buoyant after the Coral Sea battle was fought in waters not far east of Townsville. Even though then and later it was played up to be a more decisive victory than it was in fact, the engagement none-theless deterred the Japanese from their plan to invade Port Moresby. They would almost certainly have suc-ceeded and that would have placed Australia in great peril. They were close enough as it was.

Another name that captured the Australian imagina-tion was that of Lieutenant-Colonel James Doolittle, who led a daring raid by sixteen American Mitchell bombers on the Japanese mainland. The bombers were transported from Pearl Harbor on the carrier *Hornet* to a point 650 miles (1000km) south of Japan. They flew on, discharged their bombs and scurried to China where most of the fourteen surviving bombers had to crash land as they ran out of fuel. It must have been the first indicator to the Japanese that they just might not be invincible. From our point of view there was that element of madness to Doolittle's attack which inspired people and made them cheer. High morale creates heroes and heroes create high morale.

Songs are as necessary a part of the wartime propa-ganda machine as heroes are. Vera Lynn was belting them out in Britain, reassuring us that we would meet again, although she didn't know when or where. But she felt certain there would be:

> . . . blue birds over
> The white cliffs of Dover
> Tomorrow, when the world is free

In Australia the lyrics were not as memorable but we did our best with 'The Aussies and the Yanks':

We're all together now
Like we've never been before
The Aussies and the Yanks
And we're gonna win the war
And now throughout the ranks
Everyone can give their thanks
For the Aussies and the Yanks are here

The song was a gentle reminder that the Yanks had
started late — again:

We will show 'em all
Something they have never seen
We're gonna fight again
Like we did in '17

Some thought all would be well when:

A boy from Alabama
Meets a girl from Gundagai . . .

Already there were scores of marriages between Australian girls and American servicemen, and the general
consensus was that these girls were fabulously lucky.
They would go to the life of luxury we knew all Americans enjoyed. Hadn't we seen it on the films? Americans
were so affluent they made many Australians feel quite
inferior. But those not quite so enchanted with the
Yanks took delight in parodying the official Marines
battle hymn, so:

From the halls of Montezuma
To the shores of Tripoli . . .

became:

From the streets of Melbourne city
To St Kilda by the sea
The Aussie girls are showing us
Just how stupid they can be
In the good old days before the war

All the Aussie girls were gay
But now they've gone completely mad
On the twerps from the USA.
With their dashing Yankee accents
And the money flowing free
They have captured all the hearts but those
Who have open eyes to see
And when this war is over
And the Yanks no more are seen
They'll prefer an Aussie dustman
To a United States Marine.

One day when selling papers I swung on to the city-bound tram from North Coburg, a No.19.

'Heroodagetyapaper,' I intoned, then I heard something that shut me up at once.

Standing in the middle of the crowded tram were two New Zealand soldiers. They were both happily tipsy, but they looked magnificent in their lemon-squeezer, hats and their uniforms which were my first experience of 'jungle greens'. One was a Maori, the other a Pakeha (a white New Zealander) and they were singing in the Maori language, harmonising beautifully. They were obviously so proud of who they were. The crowd on the tram was spellbound. So was I, instantly. I forgot about selling papers and stood directly in front of them, taking in their performance in great draughts. The Kiwis were immensely popular in those days, before programmed slanging was introduced to sour relationships between our two countries. At the end of each song the crowd roared its applause, and I clapped hardest of them all.

It was some of the most important singing I ever heard. I had never seen anything quite like it before, and haven't since. I stayed on the tram for about three miles until Park Street, Brunswick, where they got off, still singing and staggered into the Sarah Sands pub to have another drink.

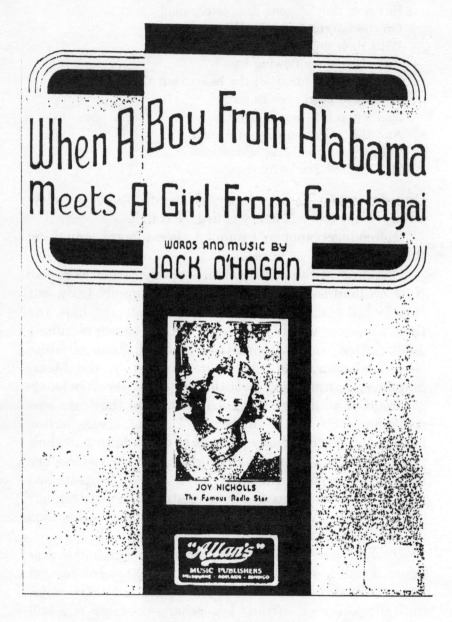

The cover of the sheet music of the song that, more than any other, celebrated the Yanks' arrival in Australia

Above My mother's parents. Peter Brennan from County Galway, Ireland, and Martha Williams, born in Victoria to Robert and Honorah Williams.

Left: My maternal great grandparents. Robert Williams, a sailor from Mousehole, Cornwall, jumped ship at Portland, Victoria, and worked for the Henty Brothers, pioneer Victorian settlers. Later, he was arrested for severing his indentures as a sailor and was the first prisoner, for three months, in the Portland Gaol. Honorah Corcoran was from County Cork, Ireland, and came to Australia as one of Caroline Chisholm's emigrant girls, the so-called 'God's Police'.

Left: Nora Egan, the much loved 'Nornie', photographed about 1915. We were led to believe she was my father's elder sister.

Above: My parents. In 1922, at Camperdown, about 100km west of Geelong, Grace Brennan married a farm boy, Joe Egan. This is their wedding photograph.

Left: Grace and Joe with my sisters, Pat *(left)* and Peg, born in 1923 and 1924 respectively.

At the wedding of my uncle Bob Brennan, mum's brother, to Rita
Toogood in 1921. *From left:* my mum and dad; Bob; Rita; Lil
Toogood, Rita's sister; and Bill Brennan, mum's brother. I loved
visiting Uncle Bob and Auntie Rita and their kids at their farm in
the Western District.

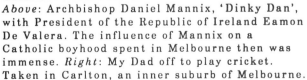

Above: Archbishop Daniel Mannix, 'Dinky Dan',
with President of the Republic of Ireland Eamon
De Valera. The influence of Mannix on a
Catholic boyhood spent in Melbourne then was
immense. *Right*: My Dad off to play cricket.
Taken in Carlton, an inner suburb of Melbourne.

Grace's 'Great' War, subject of my 'Song for Grace'. Her brother Jack *(left)* joined the 9th Light Horse. He was blinded, lost a leg and died of his wounds at Gallipoli, aged 27. Martin *(above left)* survived Gallipoli, but was captured by Turks in the Middle East, and endured terrible privations. Shell shock scarred the rest of his life. Bob *(above right)* spent three years as an artilleryman on the Western Front and was badly gassed.

Altar boy Ted Egan aged 10. I always fancied that I looked just like St Aloysius Gonzaga.

Pat *(left)* and Peg, Confirmation Day, 1935.

In this photograph taken in 1972 at my parents' Golden Wedding Anniversary, Peg, Pat and Sal are trying - unsuccessfully - to capture Grace's 'look'.

Above: The WA Brennans.
(Standing, from left) Frank, Bill
and Bob. *(Seated)* Cec, Len,
Aunty Isobel, Uncle Mick.
Right: Family photo 1933. Pat
(left) and Peg flank Grace holding me. Sal in front, Pop behind. *Below*: Miss Coburg 1940.
Pat, aged 18, looking very flash
in her 'joddies'. *Below right:*
Peg *(right),*Sal and me in front
of the bungalow at Coburg, 1940.

Aged 18 months, in the vogue Sunday best of the day.

Two-year-old or so, with sister Sal (Shirley) as passenger.

Flying solo - 'Look Mum, no feet.'

Peg, me holding Geoffrey (Tim) and Shirley (Sal) with Roger, the dog.

Bradman executing one of his back cuts at the MCG. He once said to a bowler: 'Bowl faster, bowl faster. When you play Test Cricket you don't give Englishmen an inch. Play it tough, all the way. Grind them into the dust.'

Bill 'Tiger' O'Reilly
*A wrong'un that you'd
never pick
And if that's not enough
The type of killer
instinct
That would call the
devil's bluff*

I was at St Kilda oval in 1944 when this photo of Jack 'Captain Blood' Dyer was taken. Dyer kicked 9 goals against Essendon.

The Dennington Brennans. *From left, seated*: Eileen, the wonderful Aunty Rita, Judy, Peter on Uncle Bob's knee, Betty and Margaret. *Standing:* Kathy, my favourite cousin; Leo; Artie; and Frank. Kathy died when she was 14, shortly after this photograph was taken. Artie died aged 22, two years later. Uncle Bob joined up - again - in 1942.

Coburg Central bandsman Teddy Egan, aged around 14, photographed at 4 Higinbotham Street, Coburg, with kettle drum.

The Egan sisters at Ivanhoe for the wedding of Shirley. *From left*: Pat Toone, Shirley and Peg Gleeson.

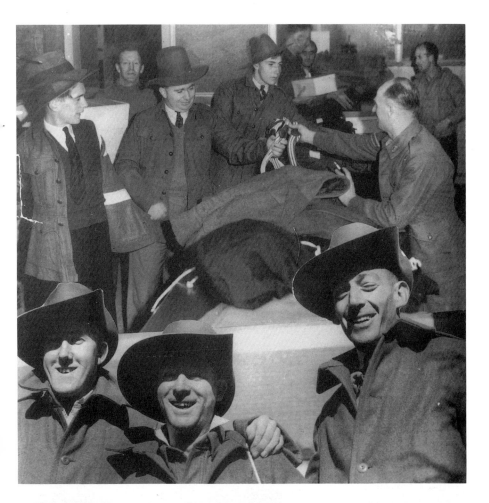

In 1940, the *Herald* carried a lot of patriotic enlistment propaganda, like this one showing the transformation from civilian into soldier, average bloke to digger. I wanted to wear one of those uniforms too. My three cousins, *(from left)* Laurie (Lawrence), Joe and Gus (Augustus) Egan were quick to volunteer for the army.

Above left: A comforting sight in 1942 . The Yanks arrive at last. The caption read '...these pictures taken "somewhere in Australia" ... it's a long way to Tokio, but the Americans know where they're going.' *Above*: Black Americans were very popular in Melbourne, particularly after it became evident they were treated unfairly by their own military police.

Above: A friendly game of football (footbrawl) at the MCG.

Photographs like this in the *Herald* of American GIs with Australian dates on Princes Bridge may have been meant to cement good community relations with our allies, but helped, too, to reaffirm the opinion of diggers that the Americans were 'over-sexed, overpaid and over here'.

General Douglas MacArthur with Australian Prime Minister John Curtin at a meeting of the War Council in Melbourne. None of us Coburg experts was invited.

Soviet leader Josef Stalin takes his seat beside US President Franklin D Roosevelt and British Prime Minister Winston Churchill at Teheran, the capital of then-Persia, to discuss the future of the world. Again, no Coburg representation.

'Let's count Pegs boyfriends - starting with the Bobs'. Peg was what was known as a 'gay flapper' in those more innocent times. Aged about 19.

The first grandchild, Michael Toone, Pat's son, sits on Grandma Grace's knee, Tim beside them. *(Left to right)* Sal, Peg and proud mother, Pat. Me and Joe take up the rear.

Below left: With my niece Ann Gleeson at St Pauls Presbytery, just before I left to go 'up north'.

Below: Grace and Tim at his admission to Flinders Naval College, 1953.

Pat's wedding day, 1945. *From left*: Merle Mattei, Peg, 'Twin', Pat and Terry, St Paul's, Coburg.

Pat (left), and Peg, with Peg's future husband Jack Gleeson. Taken on the front verandah of 4 Higinbotham Street, 1944.

Surely one of the sweetest pictures that the *Herald* ever carried. After six years of war, VP (Victory in the Pacific) Day was celebrated. *Caption:* 'This amazing scene took place on The Block on Collins-st. Dancers swayed back and forth across the road in the glistening wet streets...' I went to the shindig at the Brunswick Town Hall and got kissed a lot.

Travelling man. Me aged 17, Barmerah, SA, 1949. I sent this photograph to my mother just before going to Darwin and The World.

Fruit picking at Red Cliffs, near Mildura, March 1949.

Ruefully, I boarded the next north-bound tram to Coburg and had to appear to be selling *Heralds* to appease the 'conny'. But I wasn't concentrating. My life was influenced forever.

It was the awakening in me that Australia, too, had a dual heritage, and I know the importance of that day to an eleven-year-old boy reared on the notion that singing was something one did naturally and spontaneously, because as soon as I got to Darwin as a seventeen year old I would start to learn to speak Australian (Aboriginal) and learn to sing in the many languages available to me in the cosmopolitan north. I have always liked New Zealand and New Zealanders ever since, and I am saddened as I see signs that the Maori-Pakeha relationship is not as strong as it once was. When I went to New Zealand for their National Folk Festival in 1981 there were no Maoris present and everybody was either singing *rol-de-fiddle-di-day* English songs with exaggerated Pommy voices, or the Australian songs popularised by the Bushwackers.

MacArthur appointed General Blamey 'Commander of All Allied Land Forces' to appease Prime Minister Curtin, who felt that Australia was always good enough to provide troops for the front line of the toughest campaigns, but not allowed to have a say in their dispersement. But there was to be no doubt who was going to be the boss of the total operation, nor who would be required to do the dirtier jobs. It was fairly obvious, too, that Blamey's authority would really cover Australian forces only, and this left something of a sour taste in people's mouths of a different kind. Blamey was not universally popular in his native Melbourne. Among other things he had been Commissioner of Police in Victoria between wars.

Our soldiers were hastily sent into the jungle areas of Papua and New Guinea. Straight away they engaged in bloody hand-to-hand combat with the Japanese. Condi-

tions were deplorable. Living on bully beef and biscuits
for months on end, sweating all day and freezing at night
in malaria-ridden jungle, these young men, some of them
militia — the 'chockoes' who were not expected to serve
outside Australia — and all of them totally inexperienced
until the return of the troops from the Middle East, were
about to display the ultimate in courage.

Denied sea entry to Port Moresby the Japanese, who
were firmly in control at Rabaul and Lae, planned to cross
from New Guinea into Papua and Port Moresby via the
only track available through that impossible terrain, the
Kokoda Trail, over the Owen Stanley Ranges. They landed
at Gona and Buna and advanced to Kokoda itself. At that
point the Australian soldiers, assisted by planters, Papua
and New Guinea Administration officers and the local
Papuans who came to be called 'the fuzzy-wuzzy angels'
halted the Japanese attack and valiantly began the task
of repulsing the invaders. At about the same time the
Americans landed at Guadalcanal and began to blast the
Japanese into subjection. American morale was high
because in June 1942 they had a decisive victory over the
Japanese navy at Midway. But for the next few months,
little progress was made in this new region of war. The
Australians were engaged in brutal one-on-one jungle
fighting, going two steps forward, one back, while the
Americans relied on saturation bombing and sheer
gunpower to achieve progress northward through the Sol-
omon Islands.

The two different approaches to war caused lots of
discussion in Melbourne. Everybody acknowledged that
the Americans had wonderful equipment, particularly
aeroplanes, and they never seemed to suffer any shortage
of material or equipment in combat areas. The Australian
boys were ill-equipped. Despite the heroic efforts of our
air force, for the Japanese Zeros were just too fast for our
fighters, Australian troops were badly protected in the air.

On the ground they were subject to all kinds of sickness and disease, largely because drugs and medicines were in short supply. Given the nature of the fighting and terrain it was difficult to provide and maintain adequate medical care. There was, too, the sheer privation of even being in such harsh conditions. Jack Gleeson, the young man who eventually became my brother-in-law when he married Peg fought through the entire New Guinea mainland campaign, and went on to Bougainville. He never ate one solid meal in his life after the war.

So while there was grudging admiration for the Americans and a feeling of relief that they were in the war on our side, particularly as Britain didn't seem to have us too high on its priority list for care and attention, Australian servicemen felt free to consider the Americans to be not much good individually in a crisis. 'Not worth two bob in the hand-to-hand stuff,' said one digger on leave from New Guinea in Brown's pub. Another felt that 'if the bastards run out of Coca Cola and icecream they reckon it's time to go home'.

In late 1942 and early 1943 relationships between American servicemen and Australians, soldiers especially and some sections of Australia's civilian population became strained. It wasn't universal by any means, but there were a few factors about which most Australians agreed. The Americans were just too affluent. It was sheer envy on our part, but they looked too polished altogether in their flash uniforms. They could and did talk and our laconic fellows seemed almost Neanderthal as conversationists in comparison. They were either beautifully mannered or glib, or both, and women and children could not resist them. Most Australian men could not stand them. The joke question was:

'What's wrong with the Yanks?'

The answer, 'They're overpaid, over-sexed, and over here,' became a Melbourne cliche.

And then along came Leonski to justify everybody's prejudices. 'I told you so,' people said, grimly. In mid 1942 a young girl was found strangled, and the word went around that she had probably just been grabbed outside a dance hall and killed for no reason. Police felt sure the killer would strike again; they were right. Two more girls were killed in similar circumstances. There was abject fear in Melbourne, for the police warned that this was the work of a psychopath — we'd never heard the word before. Women were told to take no risks, not to go out alone, and to avoid dark lonely places. Pat and Peg were working at Victoria Barracks and had to work overtime each Monday night, with no pay, on what was called their 'war effort' night. This necessitated travel by train to Coburg late at night. Fortunately they worked and travelled together, but with the trains blacked-out in any case they were very apprehensive, so Pop used to meet them at the Coburg railway station.

Suspicion began to centre on the American personnel at Camp Pell in Royal Park and that made things worse, because the girls' train passed through Royal Park. Eventually an American, Edward J (same first name and initial as I had, everyone quickly reminded me) Leonski was arrested, brought to trial and quickly convicted. He was hanged at Pentridge Gaol, and I can remember shivering in contemplation of the grim execution as I passed Pentridge on my way to school the morning Leonski died.

Then there was the 'Battle of Brisbane'. General MacArthur moved from Melbourne to Brisbane, where he took over Lennon's Hotel as his headquarters. The American presence in the Solomons and the Australians in New Guinea meant large numbers of Australian and American troops were quartered at various centres along the Queensland coast. There were several brawls between Australians and Americans, and in November 1942 there was a real donnybrook in Brisbane during which American military police shot dead an Australian soldier. It was hushed up officially but the word passed through the grapevine quickly and did nothing to enhance relationships.

But life went on. I really enjoyed Grade Six at St Paul's because I had the best teacher of my school career, Sister Mary Josepha. Goodness, she was pretty, and, come to think of it, she was probably only about twenty-one. Females were slightly more tolerable presences in my life by 1942 and, according to my family, I was 'keen' on Theresa Fitzgerald. Peg used to insist that I 'did cartwheels' every time I saw Theresa. That was an exaggeration, although I acknowledge that I was a profound show-off as I flew for imaginary high marks in the style of the inimitable Jacky Dyer and delighted at showing that I could leap up and touch shop verandahs.

I made a profound mistake one day though. The Fitzgerald girls, Theresa and her sister Kathy, were going to Mass before school and I walked to church with them from Stock Street, taking a few high marks to impress them on the way. It seemed fairly natural that I would sit with them for Mass, and I was so busy impressing them I wasn't careful where I put my lunch, two banana sandwiches in a paper bag. I put the bag on the seat and didn't notice the arrival of Mrs Clune, the fattest woman in the parish. She must have weighed twenty stone. She grunted her way into the pew and sat down with a huge sigh of relief and a splat — right on my lunch. What a catastrophe! What a laugh! Fortunately, Lynn Miller shared his lunch with me that day.

Sister Josepha didn't seem to mind that I was a smart-arse, and she was the only teacher who ever got the best out of me. Grace used to say of me, 'He's a stubborn boy that Teddy Egan. You can lead him but you'll never push him'. Sister Josepha seemed to have worked that out too. I was just so anxious to please her.

School was good for Sal at that time, too, as she now attended St Aloysius' College in North Melbourne, which was usually shortened to Snal's. We used to say 'Sal's at Snal's'. Sal always liked school, and was good at it. She formed lifelong friendships with some of her teachers, particularly Sister Mildred, who taught her at St Paul's and again at St Anne's Scholarship School, which she attended to gain entrance to St Aloysius'.

With Sister Josepha's encouragement I began to read a few of Henry Lawson's short stories, like 'The Drover's Wife' and 'The Loaded Dog', but that was the extent of my Aust. Lit. at that time. There were lots of other books though. I loved the William books despite their English orientation for we seemed to accept that England was the only real base for literature and history, Lawson's stories being an aberration. We all considered Australia to be a fairly dull place, even though we liked it as a home. Most comics and magazines had either been discontinued or reduced drastically in size due to paper shortages, but one comic which remained available throughout the war was The *Champion*. It was probably deemed of sufficient pro- paganda value to justify its continuance. I couldn't wait to get it each month, particularly as it was published in England and had lots of precise references to the detail of the war, through the exploits of Rockfist Rogan RAF, and Fireworks Flynn and His Freebooters. An intriguing mystery was solved each month by Colwyn Dane,'Tec (which we *Champion* readers knew was short for 'detective'). Sherlock Holmes had nothing on Colwyn Dane.

Sister Mary Josepha was probably aware she was pretty, but knew she must subdue all such worldly non- sense behind the veil and her vows of poverty, chastity and obedience. She nonetheless used to blush outra- geously when anything 'naughty' or funny was said in class. My hunch was that she was from a big family where laughter was prevalent. But being a nun was very serious business, particularly when she was surrounded by tyros like Sister Mary Placidia and the formidable Sister Mary Enda. In Placidia and Enda I was again seeing the power and control of 'the cloth'. It seemed to pervade all areas of life: the church through the capes and mitres and vestments; the school through the habits the nuns wore; and the war through the military uniforms and insignia. Yes, definitely Ted, get into a uniform. Be a priest and be in charge. Or join the navy.

Rationing was strictly enforced, but I couldn't see all that much point to it. It certainly didn't affect our house unduly. Sugar, butter, tea, meat and clothing were all rationed and storekeepers had to go through the task of cutting out the ration coupons (which many people insisted on pronouncing as *kew-pons* to the delight of our family) from the various ration books and tediously filling out endless returns for the rationing authorities. It entailed a lot of red tape, and we daily heard stories of where you could get things 'on the black', the black market. Many luxury items like sweets disappeared from shelves altogether, but that was easily solved if you knew some Yanks. Cigarettes and tobacco were in short supply but that could be sorted out by enrolling with a regular supplier who allocated you a 'ration' even though you didn't need coupons. There was the implied obligation to buy other commodities at the same shop to keep you in the shopkeeper's good books. I remember that people rolled thinner cigarettes, called 'racehorses' or 'whippets', but otherwise I don't recall anyone desperately short of tobacco or anybody other than derelicts having to resort to 'butt-stooping' where you picked up other people's butts and re-rolled the tobacco. Tailor-made cigarettes were hard to get, but that, too, was easily fixed if you knew some Americans. I had my first smoke at about twelve. It was a standard part of growing up to be given a cigarette, told to 'do the drawback' and thus provide a good laugh for your elders as you coughed and spluttered. 'You'll get used to it,' they would all say, prophetically, and you did. Heavy smokers used to court the few non-smokers in the hopes of purloining an extra ration.

Biscuits and cakes were either hard to get or made from dripping instead of butter so they tasted awful anyway. Anybody with the ingredients for a good cake usually had it baked for a food parcel to send to the boys up north. Parents cajoling their children to eat their vegetables began to tell them that 'the boys up north would love that cabbage'. Previously it had been 'the starving children in China'. Our response to our Mum was to ask why she didn't send it straight to the boys up north — and to China — instead of trying to make us enjoy blooming cabbage.

Petrol was strictly rationed. Most cars were restricted to enough petrol to take them fifty miles (80km) in a given month. Some petrol could be obtained 'on the black' it was rumored. Gas producers and charcoal burners were fitted to some cars, but these were cumbersome devices, difficult to operate and regulate. In any case travel was restricted by shortages of other commodities like tyres and batteries.

Mr and Mrs Baxter had a grocery shop on the corner of Higinbotham Street and O'Hea's Road. It would be called a 'deli' today. They had a beautifully maintained maroon and black saloon car and would occasionally take some of our family for a drive on a Sunday afternoon. It was such a thrill. We, of course, never had a car. My parents — and Pat and Peg — never learned to drive even in later life, when cars were much more common. Driving, except for the girls in uniform, was definitely considered to be men's business. It was all very formal, driving with the Baxters, best clothes and all that. As they were shopkeepers we considered them to be slightly above us in status. Not that we felt inferior or they acted superior, but their whole economic situation seemed unattainable to us at the time. Grace used to do a couple of days a week housekeeping, washing and ironing for Mrs Baxter and they enjoyed each other's company, being both very formal, reserved women who did not gossip. Mr Baxter was a 'thorough gentleman' and that, coming from Grace, was the ultimate praise. They had no children of their own and I know they genuinely liked us, for we kids were always on our best behavior in public. Otherwise the flesh might be screwed, mightn't it? Yes it *is* a lovely day, Mrs Baxter. Why is that child in agony, you ask? Naturally, we kids called them 'Mr and Mrs Baxter', never dreaming of referring to them as Gordon and Hilda, but they and our parents were also on a 'Mr' and 'Mrs' basis. Nowadays, even my grandchildren call me Ted, but it was considered very rude when we were children to refer to adults by their first names.

Baxter's shop was a sheer delight. They had a great young bloke named Les Munday working for them, until he joined the army. Les was a very funny fellow, although he never overstepped the mark. The Baxters and Les wore starched white uniforms and aprons, and, because everything came 'in bulk' in those days, the shop was always full of the delightful smells of bacon, ham or fritz (German sausage) being sliced, or butter being cut with a wire and then 'patted' into different shapes, or tea being put into jars from a newly-opened chest. We always 'booked up' things against Dad's payday each Friday, but occasionally there would be a minor cash transaction when I or one of us would order 'a ha'porth of broken biscuits please, Les'. Les would invariably slip us a wink and include a couple of whole biscuits among the broken ones he handed us.

One day Grace, who was getting to be fairly hefty at this time, dropped a spare elastic garter on the floor in Baxter's shop as she opened her purse. Les, gallant but nonetheless a dag, quickly picked it up for her and asked, tongue-in-cheek.

'Is this what you use to keep your banknotes in their roll, Mrs Egan?' He had picked the wrong person. Grace snatched the garter from him, gave him 'the look' and spat out a withering, 'Don't you try to be smart with me, young man.' She couldn't help laughing at home when she recounted the incident and we haven't stopped laughing about it since.

Another shop I remember with affection was Eddy Gannon's butcher shop. Poor old Eddy finished up doing a short stretch in Pentridge Gaol for some minor offence and lost his shop as a result.

'There you are, got in with the wrong crowd,' said Grace. 'Show me your companions and I'll tell you what you are.' And she thought it might be 'the death of his saintly mother' when Eddy was convicted. I remember Eddy as a beaut quiet bloke. He would let me help him in the shop, spreading out the sawdust on the floor, cleaning the chopping block with a wire brush, feeding the sausage machine and doing simple little bits of butchery. I have been fascinated with butchery and butcher's shops ever since and later became a good butcher myself in the bush, where on different Aboriginal reserves we had to slaughter and butcher our own beef. In return for helping him Eddy took me a few times to the Flemington abbatoirs at 5 a.m. on Saturday mornings. I was fascinated at the hustle and bustle, especially around the killing pens. Bullocks were poleaxed in those days. Up a race they would go, bewildered, passing underneath a man with a huge pointed pole. He would hit them with deadly accuracy and they would be dead, throats cut, bled, and be skinned and quartered in minutes. Eddy would bring home — on the back of his utility, mind — the offal: brains, liver, lambs fry, tripe, sweetbread and kidneys. And before leaving the abbatoirs he would select the quarters of beef and lambs to be delivered to him during the week. The slaughtermen always gave me a bullock's eye as a present. I didn't think it was ghoulish, but Grace would tell me to 'get that damn thing out of here' whenever I tried to show her what a sad look the animal had at the time of its death.

Relationships towards the Americans improved, particularly when they began to return to Melbourne on leave after being 'blooded' by active service. It seemed to knock some of the brashness out of them. Pat and Peg struck up a friendship with an American named Ted L Carver — they all seemed to have flash names like this. Ted was in the US Navy based at Victoria Barracks where he worked in a secret area called 'The Coding Centre'. He was a very polished chap, an officer, and my parents deemed him a 'thorough gentleman' too. Another chap who came courting Peg was a marine, Charles Hiram Parker who insisted that we called him 'Chuck'. We thought the name was hilarious as 'chucking' had recently become slang for vomiting, but we never told him outright. We used to say, 'How yer going, Chuck?' with a simulated hurl on saying his name, but he thought that was how those 'damn cute' Aussie kids talked. He was a nice bloke and he used to stay weekends at our place. He never wanted to do anything spectacular, and seemed to be happy just sitting around. He liked to play chess with Pop. He would sit for an hour polishing his shoes, spitting on a rag which he then used to bring the shoes to a mirror finish. We had never seen shoes like Chuck's. They had no laces, only buckles, and he called them 'Oxfords'. We called them 'Arksfords' as we imitated his Toledo, Ohio accent. Whenever there were servicemen staying over they either slept on the floor of the lounge room, or on the couch, or out in the bungalow if there were a few of them, which was often.

The boys of Coburg were very impressed with Chuck

Parker. We played football with paper or sock 'footies' made either from newspapers rolled tightly together and tied with string, or old socks rolled tightly together. Even if real footballs had been available we would not have been able to afford them. But Chuck Parker brought us an American football and showed us how they threw the ball in their game. He was a great thrower or 'chucker' as we punned with him, and not even Jimmy Hughes from Molesworth Street, our very best kicker, could out-distance Chuck's throwing.

It became quite a point of discussion in Melbourne as to whether an Australian Rules footballer could kick a ball further than an American quarterback could throw, particularly after American teams put on an exhibition match of American football which, we felt, was called 'gridiron'. (Nowadays most Americans seem perplexed when Australians refer to their game as gridiron.)

Eventually it was decided to have a big charity day at Punt Road Oval, Richmond, the home of the beloved Tigers. I was allowed to attend, and what a day it was. There was an exhibition of American football which we thought was absolute madness. We were very scornful of all the padding. And they wore helmets! Two teams put on a display of Aussie Rules football and there was a tug-of-war between the Melbourne Fire Brigade and the Americans. The fire brigade won. There were displays of jitterbugging and all sorts of other activities to raise money. And then came the big contest.

Fred Hughson, the Fitzroy fullback, took on Bill Jost, a famous American quarterback. It was a thrilling contest, five kicks or throws each, and Fred Hughson eventually won. His best kick, the longest dropkick in history, went 83 yards 11 inches (76m) to beat Bill Jost's magnificent throw of 76 yards 3 inches (69.6m). Another highlight of the day was an accuracy contest whereby Australians and Americans tried to land a football into a baby's bathtub from fifty yards. To my delight Jack 'Skinny' Titus, the old Richmond (and later Coburg) full forward, stabkicked the football into the tub three times from five shots. The crowd went wild, for 'Skinny' was a very popular fellow, especially at Punt Road. He was only 5 feet 8 inches (1.72m) tall but he kicked almost a thousand goals in his illustrious League football career. He was famous for his toothless grin and he was flashing it that day. He was the only full forward I ever saw who consistently drop-kicked a set shot at goal and he was deadly accurate as he again showed us.

Sister Mary Josepha really blushed when I took her a big bunch of flowers (roses which my Auntie Kit allowed me to pick from her garden) at the end of my grade six year. It wasn't my idea, it was Grace's and I thought it was all a bit stupid, but I enjoyed the experience none-theless. Sister served us tea in the huge tiled parlor at the convent and I devored about ten delicious rock cakes as we chatted about life in general and what we would be doing over the holidays. She said she would spend some time on retreat and also visit her family in the country. It wasn't like it is today for nuns. They still had to wear their habits, even when they went home to their families. They had to take another nun with them, for nuns always had to travel in pairs. I guess it helped cut down on things like 'temptation' if you had somebody to keep you in check all the time. And they were not allowed to engage in any activity unless they had specific approval from Reverend Mother beforehand. I'll never forget one day, years later, when we took my cousin Molly Carroll (a nun) for a drive. We pulled up to get fish and chips all round for the drive home. Molly declined, saying,

'I'd better not. I didn't ask Mother if I could have fish and chips.'

Sister Mary Josepha, as always, was very interested in what I proposed doing over the holidays. Not much, I told her. I was still selling papers, although I had long-since paid off old Phelan. He used to subtract 2/- each week and sign his name in a little book I presented him as I made each payment. He never once smiled about the incident. I suppose he felt he was letting me off lightly, taking so long to pay the debt, and without interest. I wasn't looking for any charity from him. In addition to selling papers I was doing a bit of work at Baxter's shop, helping to get the deliveries ready.

But a fair bit of time and thinking would go into preparation for a big change in my life. I was going to St Joseph's College, North Melbourne, the next year, leaving the nuns and going to the brothers.

The *Champion*, top comic of my youth

11

To the Brothers

When I started at the Brothers I was still in short pants and treated accordingly. It was like tribal initiation. You could have kids six feet tall still in short pants and little squirts knee-high to a grasshopper wearing long 'uns. Going into long pants was a recognition by the boy, or parents, or both, that he was approaching puberty, and for most boys it became the point where they started to wear underpants. The only kids in short trousers who wore underpants were the rich or the 'cissies' — Mum's boys — and I was certainly neither. I was still very much a kid, still a boy soprano in the Bel Canto choir, not to be taken very seriously by anyone other than myself.

In my adult life I frequently use the expression 'It's only what you deserve' said either to myself or to somebody who expresses pleasure if I buy them a drink or shout them a slap-up feed. I privately think 'Ted, it's only what you deserve' as I open a good bottle of wine, or sit reflectively sipping a piercingly-cold Foster's. I feel that I have worked hard in various commercial areas and deserve the rewards. As I prepared myself to go to the Brothers I was also saying 'It's only what you deserve' but I have to acknowledge that a different kind of smugness

143

pervaded my attitudes then. No gratitude to the parents who had worked overtime and taken in ironing to give me chances they never had. No, just that insecure little smart-arse looking back at me from the mirror silently saying, 'Yes, you are a cut above the others, so all these things being done for you are *only what you deserve.*'

At the same time I knew my parents saw the opportunity for me to have a secondary education as part of the fulfilment of the dream that their children would not suffer the same indignities they had, of being poor and uneducated in the formal sense through no fault of their own. They, too, felt it was only what I deserved to go to the Brothers. They saw it as their responsibility to the kids they had brought into the world.

Not every boy got such a chance. Many left school at the end of primary, which was Grade Eight. They went into factories, apprenticeships or became laborers. In those days every kid just naturally got some sort of job at the end of school. Only the 'brighter' kids — which merely meant 'better suited academically', not 'brighter' in any real sense of the term — went on to high school, so it was deemed a privilege. Nowadays I am envious of people who have technical or trade training for I am useless with tools and have no handyman skills. I think it's silly to have compulsory academic-style schooling to age sixteen or whatever. A lot of kids would be better off being upended into the big bad world rather than wanking around at school pretending it's beneficial for them. But then, if I was The Dictator I wouldn't have compulsory education for any child of any age, but I'd make school such an attractive exciting place that children would queue up pleading to attend. But that's another story.

In my parents' view, going to the Brothers would be the means whereby I would acquire the piece of paper to make me immune from Depressions, class discrimination or any level of insecurity. There was a play-it-safe attitude

involved with all of this, for a clerical career in a bank
or the Commonwealth or State public service was considered the ultimate attainment. Everybody knew you
couldn't be sacked from these jobs, and getting the sack
for whatever reason was *the* great fear in the minds of
the survivors of the Depression. Security above all things.

The Christian Brothers were fairly happy to go along
with this approach and boys were encouraged to pass their
exams, get secure jobs, lead uncomplicated lives, not ask
too many questions, do what the Church told, and be good
Catholics. All very straightforward. They were the Christian Brothers of Ireland, *Fratres Christiani de Hibernia*
as I would quickly learn, founded by Edmund Ignatius
Rice and charged with the responsibility of raising good
Catholic boys who had been strengthened by a good
classical education. Although the headquarters of the
Christian Brothers was at Strathfield, New South Wales,
they were very much subject to the authority of the bishop
of whichever diocese they served. In Melbourne this meant
you know who — Doctor Mannix — who was constantly
antagonising politicians on the question of State Aid. The
State Government took the stance that it had the consti-
tutional responsibility to provide educational services and
was doing this through state primary, high and technical
schools. The Catholic church was in the forefront of a
movement which sought to have private schools subsidised
by the government, as long as academic standards were
maintained to the state's satisfaction. Doctor Mannix's
campaign stressed the need for Victorian Catholic schools
to get better academic results so he could demonstrate
that it could not be said Catholic children were not
properly educated in the formal or academic sense, even
though the church at the same time insisted on its right
to have its religious teachings pervasive in every aspect
of a child's education. Mannix wanted to be able to say:
'Look at the exam results.'

There was also the implied threat that the state would never be able to handle the volume if the Catholic kids suddenly sought hundreds of thousands of places at state schools. (Many years later, at Goulburn, New South Wales, when a Catholic bishop looked like taking this threat further, he had to back off when the state government geared up to accept the challenge and build sufficient schools to take in the Catholic kids.)

The State Aid battle was still being fought in 1943, when I went for my interview to see whether I was suitable for enrolment at St Joseph's College, in Queensberry Street, North Melbourne. I was quite nervous. My parents attended the interview and I was annoyed at their obsequious (so I thought) attitude to the Principal, Brother King. It seemed to me they were grovelling in his presence as they answered 'Yes, Brother King,' 'No, Brother King' and 'Oh, he'll do his very best, Brother King'. Brother King seemed to me to be a fairly ordinary bloke, and he was. No great eloquence or inspiration to him, but nice enough. He shocked me a bit by calling me 'Egan' but said that my track record at St Paul's (top of my class every year) indicated that I was just what St Joseph's was looking for — a good Catholic boy to pass his exams while his hard-working parents paid the fees. So we left with a copy of the *Cynosura* ('Star of the North' the annual college publication) a list of books, uniform requirements and an unnecessary number of 'Thank you, Brother Kings'. The pandering was part of respect for the cloth, I guess. The fees were £4 10s 0d a term, which was very reasonable, and Brother King intimated that there were scholarships available for boys who got good academic results, so we felt a bit confident there.

The war was on, clothing was rationed, and luxury items were not available. I looked with envy at pre-war photographs of St Joseph's boys in fancy striped blazers, caps with ornate badges, beaut footy jerseys, and the

athletics team wearing silk shorts and fancy, mono-
grammed shirts with tiny sleeves which Americans had
recently taught us were called 'T-shirts'. The photographs
included many famous men in sporting and academic
circles. There was Alan La Fontaine, the Melbourne football club champion, and Kevin Dynon, who had just
started playing with the Shinboners, which was what
North Melbourne Football Club was called then. There
was Bat Curran, the professional runner. Two other boys,
already familiar as adults, had each been dux of the
college — B A Santamaria and A A Calwell — an unlikely
'double' I would think, a few years hence. There were lots
of old-boy priests and a couple of bishops.

It was made clear that blazers, embroidered pockets
and fancy caps were not available due to war restrictions,
but boys were nonetheless required to wear basic college
uniform at all times. This meant black shoes, a navy-blue
suit, white shirt, tie (purple with white stripes) and a
plain navy-blue cap. Plain navy long socks were accept-
able, but college socks — navy with purple and white
band- were preferred when available.

My books were purchased and Pop did a beautiful job
of printing, Old English style, 'E J Egan', in the front of
the most expensive book, *Latin for Today: First Course*. I
discovered on my first day at school the title of this book
had to be inked over to become *Eating for Today: First
Course — Bacon and Eggs*. I spent hours 'covering' my
books, but this was no hardship as I had done the same
for years with my *Record of the War* books, which I still
kept up-to-date even though I had to stop selling papers,
as I could not get back to Coburg early enough from North
Melbourne.

I was to inherit Pop's old Gladstone bag, as these were
the standard schoolbags for high school boys. Very clever
bags they were, too, durable, capacious, easy to carry and

we could put them on the running boards of crowded trams if the conny wasn't watching.

Grace took me to Mr Chubb, the boys' specialist at Walker's Stores in Sydney Road, Coburg, to have me fitted out for my suit. Just one suit, mind; it would be pressed every weekend and dry-cleaned at the end of term. And two white shirts, socks and shoes.

'All a little on the large side, Mr Chubb. You know how they grow, these boys.'

'Yes, Mrs Egan.'

And I had to get my 'Scholars Cocks'. I would be required to travel by tram to school, boarding the tram at Bell Street, right at the spot where I sold papers. The No. 20 tram took me to the Haymarket at North Melbourne, where the big roundabout is nowadays, the junction of Flemington and Sydney Roads. It was normally a twopenny fare for children, but the Tramways Board issued books of Scholar's Concession Tickets — 100 in a book, which allowed school children to travel to and from school at reduced rates. I think it cost five shillings per book, which meant you travelled at around half-price, but they were very strict. You could only get one book per term, they could not be used for other than travel to and from school, they were not to be traded or sold, kids using these tickets had to be in uniform and holders were not allowed to occupy seats. When you got on the tram the conny would take one of your tickets and issue a new one, also marked Scholar's Concession Ticket in return. On your first day some kid would explain that they were called 'Scholars Cocks' because if you folded the ticket, concertina style, you could cover letters until the caption read 'Scholar's Co ck '. We also played poker or crib to see whose ticket had the serial number representing the best 'hand' at cards.

In one of my *Record of the War* books I kept track of the many servicemen who passed through our home. And there were plenty of these, because Melbourne was a wonderfully hospitable place during the war. My mate Bill 'Wallaby' Waudby recently told me that when he was in the air force, on leave in Melbourne, it was not uncommon to be invited home by complete strangers. In one instance he was on a tram and got talking to the conny, undoubtedly an attractive girl if I know Bill. She told him she was going off shift at the end of the journey and asked if he would like to come home and meet her family. He thereby made some lifelong friends.

Our home was like that. Quite often relatives would bring friends home, and that was fine. There always seemed to be enough to eat and there was the added attraction at our place that we had two good-looking teenage girls, a third who was getting to be that way, and a family which loved to have parties. What more could you ask? Pat and Peg both played the piano very well by ear. Sal was learning music, so could do selected pieces. Pop played the accordion and we could all sing. The girls had what Grace called 'the repertoire', a list of hundreds of songs they could accompany. Once again I guess I am romanticising a little, but Pat and Peg only seemed to hear a song once on the wireless and they could remember the words and play the tune on the piano.

There were lots of boys, Aussies and Yanks. Two more regular presences came to be Joe 'Flyer' Flynn and Jack 'Terry' Toone. Pop had given them their nicknames. They both worked with him at F H Stephens as drivers. 'Flyer' was nicknamed thus because he was a very fast driver, 'Terry' after the film cartoonist Terry Toon. When Pat's eighteenth Birthday was coming up he invited Terry and Flyer to 'my daughter's twelfth birthday'. They fronted up, complete with a tin of toffies for some snotty-nosed kid, only to be greeted by Miss Patricia, very sophisticated and flash in her joddies and furious with Pop — not really, she wouldn't know how. Typical Pop. Pat and Terry became a steady twosome and eventually got married.

No permanent twosomes for Peg though. Peg was out to play the field like it had never been played before. She had about ten blokes 'on a string' as we used to say, manipulating them all beautifully (as only Peg can do — ask her kids) as they went to and from the war. Flyer was a front runner for a while, but when he and Terry joined the army that meant 'Flyer' was often in camp, so Peg had plenty of other suitors, as well as attractive cousins always happy to go to dances, picnics and parties with a dasher like Peg when they were on precious leave. It was a joy to watch.

My brother Tim was very alert. At about four years of age he began to see the possibility of getting his share of the limelight by becoming a great conversationalist, which he is to this day. He used to sit in his high chair at the end of the table while we had meals, taking everything in and wherever possible participating in the conversation. You had to be fast to grab attention at our house, for we were all motor mouths and there were usually visitors as well, so Tim would bide his time and then come in with what he thought would be some big attention-grabber. One day there was a momentary lapse in talk as we concentrated on food, so he asked, *apropos* of sweet bugger-all: 'Have you ever seen Mum on a tram?' We had a good laugh at that, but it encouraged him. A week or so later we choked on our food from laughing and spluttering when he came out with (in the presence of a couple of Peg's new suitors), 'Let's count Peg's boyfriends, starting with the Bobs. There's Bob Heathcote and Bob Hogan and Bob Casey . . . '

Our parties were augmented by the Sheehan and Norris families, who were great friends. The Sheehans came from the Western District and Margaret 'Nana' Sheehan had gone to school with Grace. She was a magnificent woman, a great laugher, and must have been a stunning looker in her day. She was married to Joe ('Poppa' as we all called him) an ugly, pugnacious-looking bloke after the style of Lou Richards. Like Lou, Joe was a very funny fellow and could screw his face into all sorts of expressions as he told his famous jokes, complete with hilarious facial grimaces, which become set party pieces we never tired of hearing. We used to feed him a line to get him going. One of our favorites was about a drunk, and our way of getting Poppa to tell the yarn was to say, 'Poppa, tell us the one about the drunk and the poor box.' He would smile, and stand, for this was his moment. He'd screw up his face in concentration. We'd smile in anticipation.

> Well, there was this old fellow at Koroit, and he was always getting on the grog. One Sunday at Mass the priest talked about devotion to the Blessed Virgin.' The priest said, 'Dear people, if you pray to Our Lady, she can intercede for you in Heaven, for she is the Mother of God.' Well, the drunk heard this and the next time he staggered past the Church, drunk and late at night, he thought, 'I'll go in and pray to the Blessed Virgin. Well, he prayed and prayed, and then he said, 'Dear Mother of God, I pray for sixpence to buy a pot of beer.' As he walked from the church, he noticed the poor box where people left donations. There was fourpence in the box, so the drunk pocketed it, and began to walk home. On the way he had to pass through the cemetery, and on this particular night he was not aware that his wife had asked the priest to give him a fright, as she was getting tired of him coming home drunk every night. He walked into the cemetery, which was very dark, and a thin shaft of moonlight outlined the white tombstones. The drunk was a bit frightened, but became terrified when, suddenly, the priest jumped from behind a tombstone, wrapped in a white sheet.

'Stop and repent, you sinner,' roared the priest.
The drunk stopped in his tracks, shivering with fright.
'Who . . . Who are you?' asked the drunk, quaking.
'I am Almighty God,' roared the priest.
'Well, you're just the bloke I want to see,' said the
drunk. 'Your bloody mother owes me tuppence.'

The Sheehans lived at the Bell Street railway crossing
and their job was to open and close the gates to allow
the trains to cross the road with safety. We used to often
go and sit in the warm little cabin, heated by a lovely
fire, with whichever member of the family was 'on shift'.
We all called them 'Nana' and 'Poppa' because they had
reared their own children and then two of their lovely
grand-daughters Enid and Val. Everybody was out to
match me with Enid, but we were just good friends.
Enid and Val went to school with us. The Sheehans all
loved music and dancing and they did not constitute any
sort of threat: they were happy to sing choruses to our
solos.

The Norris family consisted of Gert and Chris, and
their four daughters Kay, Maisie, Jean and Melva. Pat
and Peg had met Kay who was an AAMWA, a nurse in
the Australian Army Medical Womens Auxiliary. When
Kay mentioned to our girls that her parents wanted to
move from Tasmania to Melbourne it was quickly pointed
out that 1 Higinbotham St was for sale. They bought it.
The Norrises were great assets at a party too, for they
loved cooking and food. Gert would always bake a chocolate fudge cake. Melva was into small cakes and Chris
had been a pastrycook, so they were always very welcome.
Supper was always the feature of an evening's entertainment. Cups of tea, cakes, sandwiches all round and,

usually, some sort of competition to see who prepared the supper. It was a lot of fun. There was singing. We knew the intricate steps of all the old time dances and it was amazing how many people could be on the floor dancing in a lounge room about four metres square. Peg would call The Lancers or The Alberts. There would be the Pride of Erin, the Charmaine, the Lucille, the Dorothea, and of course the progressive Barndance. The girls would vie to dance with Poppa Sheehan. He was a superb dancer. He always wore his dancing pumps to our place, because he knew we loved to watch him, just so light on his feet, swirl the girls around. He could waltz and pivot on a threepenny bit.

We would do our set pieces. The girls played the piano for community singing. Pop played the sqeezebox for the dancing. Between solos we'd have 'a breather'. Gert Norris invariably sang 'Banks of the Wabash' in her slightly quavery but distinctively lovely soprano, half a world away from Indiana:

> Oh, the moonlight shines tonight along the river
> From the fields there comes the scent of new-mown hay
> Through the sycamore the candle lights are gleaming
> On the banks of the Wabash far away . . .

I usually sang 'The Mermaid':

> On Friday morn, when we set sail
> And our ship not far from the land
> We did espy a pretty, pretty maid
> With a comb and a glass in her hand, her hand,   her hand
> A comb and a glass in her hand . . .

and all would join in the chorus:

> While the raging sea did roar
> And the stormy wind did blow

> We jolly sailor-boys were up, were up aloft
> And the landlubbers lying down below, below, below
> The landlubbers lying down below

Three of Grace's favourite songs would be sung every
night without fail. At the end of the night we sang 'The
Maori Farewell' and then we'd link hands and sing 'Auld
Lang Syne', after the style of New Year's Eve. Come to
think of it, every night at our house was as happy as
the best New Year's Eve party you ever attended. But
sometime before that we always sang 'Two Little Boys'.
Grace had learnt this song as a girl in Western Victoria,
and fortunately she had memorised the entire song,
word for word, note for note. We didn't know who had
written the song, but everybody who came in contact
with us considered it to be the Egan family's song, a
kind of signature tune:

> Two little boys had two little toys
> Each had a wooden horse
> Gaily they'd play, each summer's day
> Warriors both of course

Years later I taught the song to Rolf Harris, who went
on to make it world-famous. Many million record sales
later Rolf thinks I'm a beaut bloke. It was interesting
that when Rolf recorded the song he tried to register it
for copyright in my name, classified as 'Traditional:
Arranged Ted Egan' — a style used when an old song
is revived. At that point it was established that the song
was written by two Americans, Madden and Morse,
during the American Civil War. The song was apparently
based on the true story of two brothers who fought on
opposite sides in that dreadful war. We still think of it
as our family's song, and sing it whenever we get
together. Rolf never fails to acknowledge where he
learnt the song and it was his 'biggest-ever' hit. It's

interesting, though, that you rarely meet an American who has heard of the song, let alone knows the words or tune, so the world can be thankful to Grace, I reckon.

I was very introspective on my first day at St Joe's, commonly known as 'North'. It was immediately obvious that I was a very small drone in this beehive of activity, hundreds of boys and almost all of them older and bigger than me. New boys stood around nervously, trying to take in the detail of the games being played everywhere by the old hands, the dunnies, the tuckshop, the general geography of the place, and not knowing what was expected of them. Old boys greeted one another profusely. Too profusely — a born show-off like me could spot that many of them were bunging it on in front of the new kids. The bell rang and Brother King took the first assembly, welcoming us all and trying to instil in us the importance of performing well and being good Catholic boys. 'Right, to your assigned class groups.'

Brother J S Nash was to be my first teacher, and he seemed fairly awesome to me after Sister Mary Josepha. He was a tall, dark, handsome man, always completely in control of himself and his pupils. You never took liberties with Brother Nash. Unfortunately, I quickly formed the opinion that he had his established favorites and I never tried to do anything other than stay out of trouble with him. That was a pity: without doubt he was a most intelligent man and a good teacher who would probably have responded had I been more positive.

But I had a major handicap: I was the youngest in my class right through school, by eighteen months in most cases. Brother Nash (or 'Sir' as we were expected to call him at all times) placed great stress on a 'mature' approach. I could not compare with his favorites, Brian Doyle, who went on to become an Olympic rower, and Peter McLaughlin, a nice but very serious bloke who usually topped the class — and that didn't please me either. Rock McGlock as we called Peter, went on to be a doctor. So I stayed in the background, passed my exams and basically did the minimum. Brother Nash obviously spotted that, for he commented on my school report, 'If this boy applied himself he could be a real achiever'.

I loved the introduction to sport on a competitive basis, although, again, the war prevented us from getting anything like the opportunities kids get today. There was no sporting equipment due to the war, St Joe's didn't have a sporting oval or a gymnasium or anything other than a handball court and a vaulting horse. Cricket was hardly played at all in Melbourne during the war, and certainly was not played at competitive level at school. That was a shame, for I know I would have become a really good cricketer if coached and encouraged. Footy was played at House level for we were (or I was anyway) a bit young for the inter-collegiate games which started in the Under-15 bracket. I was captain of one of the House teams, but that did not say much about my or anyone else's ability. The kid I considered the very worst player in my team was Brian 'Skinny' Martyn. He was a tall, gangly, very likeable bloke — but he was hopeless at football. I used to say to him: 'I'll put you on the wing, Skin. Just stay near the boundary and keep out of everyone's road.' Ten years later 'Skinny' was playing in the ruck for North Melbourne — just a slow developer.

I was introduced to *the* great love of my school life — forget the lessons — the game of handball. Not the pathetic nonsense called handball they have in the Olympics, but Irish handball, which is played on a big three (or four) walled court. It's like playing squash, except that you use your hands rather than a racquet to hit the ball. The ball is very bouncy. Straight away I was hooked. I mentioned this fact to Terry Toone, who had also been a pupil at St Joe's. Terry said he'd teach me to play, and indeed we did have a few games at Coburg, playing up against the brick wall at the Lincoln Mills. I still let Terry get away with thinking he taught me all I knew, and taking the credit when I eventually won the All-Schools Championship in 1947. Handball is a grand game, one of the best activities to co-ordinate eye and body movement ever invented.

It was fascinating to get the interstate perspective that the Christian Brothers imparted, because they were from all parts of Australia and Ireland. The order had colleges in all States. It was not just that many of them talked affectionately about rugby, which was foreign to us Melbourne boys, but all sorts of other things were strange. Their handwriting was different, and fairly dreadful in most cases — Cocky Reardon would have been appalled — so my (and everyone else's) handwriting skill diminished immediately. They used different terms for things. Suitcases were called 'ports'. Boundary umpires were called 'touch judges' or 'line umpires'. Brother Nash had a few expressions of his own. If he adjudged you eligible for 'the cuts' — generally no more than six good whacks on the hand with the thick strap which he kept up his sleeve — he wouldn't do it then and there, but would tell you to be 'on deck' at an appointed time. He said this was to enable him to 'cool down' and not be angry as he administered the strap, for he wanted it to be accepted as 'character-building' rather than punishment. I felt it was to enable him to be colder, more efficient, and more satisfied that the punishment had been delivered to best hurt the recipient. Maybe I'm unfair. Maybe he was annoyed at the fact that from the first time I got the cuts I was determined that he could beat me to death but I would never give him the satisfaction of knowing he hurt me. (He's a stubborn boy that Teddy Egan, you can lead him but you can't drive him.)

There were some new subjects, Latin, French, some very elementary science and commercial principles, where

Brother Nash was a very thorough teacher. He also taught accountancy at night-school, as well as attending at Melbourne University himself, doing a Master's Degree, so we could not complain that our teachers lacked qualifications. But there didn't seem to be any real purpose to our schooling other than to pass exams and get a secure job. What we were doing at school had no relationship to the real world outside. I began then to be very critical of teaching, teachers and the educational system, and generally remain so.

School is still not practical enough. The reason why Australian Chinese kids do well at school is that many of them do practical business things for their parents, so they understand mathematics, economics, catering and so on. We used to do immaculate Profit and Loss Accounts, Ledger and Journal entries and Trial Balances for fictitious businesses, and I invariably got top marks, but I have no understanding whatsoever about the practical application of these things. With great satisfaction I know that when I became a teacher, I imparted good money sense among my pupils at Groote Eylandt. I set up a real shop with real money and I used to sit behind a table and I'd say to my Aboriginal pupils, 'O K, I'm Chin Gong, the Chinese shopkeeper, and I'm here to trick you simple blackfellows. What would you like to buy?' I used to try to cheat them in transactions, and they would get furious with me, but no way were they going to allow any Chinese shopkeeper to beat them. And I used to do science experiments without ever talking to them, pretending I was even dumber than I was in fact. They would finish up shouting at me and my ineptitude as they forced me, by pure logic and reasoning, to take things to a satisfactory conclusion, after which I'd allow them to explain how they worked it out. If it was good enough for Socrates to teach Meno's slave thus, it was good enough for me, but that, too is another story.

I enjoyed Latin and French, for I love all language study, and I feel sorry for kids who don't study Latin these days. How else can you understand English? The French we learnt was all a bit impractical though. I can read French reasonably well, but I found when I went to France that I had problems in the simplest talking, and, more important, listening situations. I had been taught all the declensions of verbs and could say *La plume de ma tante* in a style that would have impressed Peter Sellers' Inspector Clouseau. I won a gold medal at the Melbourne Eisteddfod reciting Victor Hugo's *L'Expiation*. But I'd have preferred something more like the experience of my cousin Judy Brennan, who had nothing like my formal education but went to France and worked as a waitress for a few years. Judy learnt to speak French colloquially, to the point where, in 1956, she got a job as an interpreter at the Melbourne Olympics. She still teaches at Alliance Française.

Science was not applied to any possible work or life experience, but was merely a subject where one parroted off things like valencies and chemical equations without any clue to the application of such knowledge. What's K $_9$ P and all that stuff? I'll never forget that we once had to draw (on graph paper) a hydraulic jack. We had no car at home and I had no idea what a hydraulic jack was. So we, meticulously copied, into our science books this drawing which had arrows pointing out the fact that if pressure was applied at point A this pressure, being 'exerted in all directions' in space B, would cause the hydraulic jack to work. Nobody ever thought of putting a hydraulic jack under a car, lifting the car, and asking us to work out why this was possible. About ten years later in Darwin, when I bought my first bomb car, someone said: 'Oh you've got a hydraulic jack, that's good.'

Elocution was something the brothers were very keen about, and this introduced us to Miss Eleanor 'Elly' Sul-

livan. She was related to Peter Sullivan, one of the boys
in my class. 'Sully' was held somewhat in awe for his
father had been a member of Essendon Football Club's
famous mosquito fleet in the 1920s. Miss Sullivan was a
great character, a big voluptuous bottle-blonde who wore,
as my father observed 'enough paint to paint a battleship
and enough powder to blow it up'. She would sweep into
the room for elocution lessons, which we enjoyed, because
it was a relaxation from the discipline imposed by Brother
Nash.

'Take out your *In Fealties* boys,' she would say with a
relieved gasp as she slumped into a chair, for she was
fairly hefty. We had this poetry book entitled *In Fealty to
Apollo* — to this day I haven't the faintest idea what the
title meant - and she would name boys to read selected
verses, while she snapped open her powder compact and
checked her warpaint in the mirror. At the end of the
reading she would analyse the speech of the reader. She
had her favorites, especially Jim Inglis who was one of
her private pupils as well. Somewhat tongue-in-cheek I
became one of her 'boys', although it took me a long time
to become 'Ted' rather than 'Egan'. First names meant
that you were likely to participate in the play presented
at Speech Night. I used to bung on this toffy voice and
she particularly liked the way I did one of her speech
exercises:

> I love to hear the horses' hard, iron hooves
> Go hammer, hammer, hammer on the hard highway

She was unaware that the show-off in me was only
looking for a laugh from my classmates: the penalty of
being the youngest in the class again. She wrote on my
school report 'this boy has a beautifully modulated voice'
and my family never let me forget it.

Travelling to school by tram gave me a daily look at
'Nigger' O'Reilly who was still selling newspapers at More-

land Road with his consummate style. I used to greet him
with great deference, for he was an absolute idol to a mere
mortal (and now ex-) paper boy. He took my adulation
calmly. 'Gooday Tiger,' he'd grunt to acknowledge my,
'Hello Nig. How are yer?' trying to sound as though I did
not have a beautifully modulated voice. I guess he hardly
even noticed me as he glanced around, ever-ready for a
sale: 'Getyerpaperrrrr.' And he'd be gone.

Usually seven or eight North boys caught the 8.10 a.m.
tram from Bell Street, and we'd talk sport or school or
the war as we stood in a group in the middle of the tram,
but well away from the entrances. 'Come on you kids,
right away from the doorway.' We had to be fairly well-
behaved on trams, for we were wearing school uniforms
and thus were identifiable. The brothers made it very
clear that the biggest offence possible was 'disgracing the
school uniform'. Travelling on Scholars Cocks we always
had to submit to every whim of every conny. I always had
my homework done, usually correct too, so it became a
practice for a few of the lads to copy my homework on
the tram if they had not done it at home or couldn't
understand it. This was the practice right through my
time at North for there was no way Grace would ever let
me dodge homework and I didn't mind sharing my work
with the other kids.

It backfired badly once, however, when I made a couple
of stupid mistakes in my Latin homework. Brother Nash
used to collect the homework books and correct, mark and
redistribute the books while we were engaged in some
written work during the morning. We were into some
sums one morning and he was correcting the homework,
when he suddenly called us to attention:

'Hands up the boys who copied Egan's Latin homework.' About six of my tram companions plus about four
others who had copied from *their* books after we arrived
at school, sheepishly raised their hands.

'Right, you're all on deck at 12 o'clock. And that includes you, Egan.'

The copiers got four cuts each, I got six for my generosity.

'It's not fair,' I told Grace.

'Serves you damn well right.'

12

Swinging Along the Road to Victory

Nornie came to our place early on the Sunday morning after the victory. She was exultation itself, and in celebratory mood:

'I'll bake ye a cake,' she announced. (A lot of people of Irish descent said *ye* instead of *you*.) She was ecstatic, as she mixed the cake, typically licking her finger to sample the icing; she didn't have a single shot at the umpire. Her Richmond favorite after Jack Dyer was 'Dicky' Harris, and Dick had set a record of seven personal goals in the Grand Final.

'Seven goals Teddy, in spite of that filthy Duffy Plummer hitting him with everything except the goal posts. I'd have given that Plummer a good poke with my umbrella if I'd got hold of him, that's for sure.'

'Yeah, it was a great game, Norn', I joined in, 'and how about Jacky Dyer when he went through Buttsworth like a packet of salts?' I was equally joyful, for the Tigers had won the 1943 premiership the day before at Princes Park, Carlton, defeating Essendon in their red and black guernseys.

'Were you there?' She looked up surprised. I nodded.

'Why didn't you sit with us? I could have got you into the grandstand?'

I didn't want to tell her that I wanted to go alone, for she, Aunty Kit and Uncle Jim were just too one-eyed even for a devoted Tiger fan like me. I tipped my dad a wink, and said to Norn,

'What did you think of the umpire?' If ever there was a loaded question this was it. The umpire had been none other than the ogre Hawkins, normally a subject of her Sunday morning footy post-mortems, and the object of many a vitriolic attack. But this time the Tigers had won. She could only damn him with faint praise:

'Oh, he was . . . fair . . . for a change. He must have been to the eye specialist during the week to have the red and black stripes removed from his vision.' She quickly changed the subject. 'Pass the butter Grace, or I'll never get this blooming cake cooked.'

But wartime premiership was something of a hollow victory, said the other teams inferring that all the best footballers were away at the war, and that Richmond must be full of draft-dodgers. Footballers still playing were often heckled:

'Why don't you join up? What are you, a squib or something?' Geelong was so depleted of players they withdrew from the competition, although many of their players turned out for other clubs. Their champion full-forward, Lindsay White, played for South Melbourne. There was an open permit system in operation to allow servicemen to play for a club without a clearance if the military authorities transferred them interstate. So Melbourne saw players of the calibre of the mighty West Australian, Jack Sheedy, who was in the air force. He was one of the greatest players I ever saw, able to handball forty yards and stab kick fifty yards to the chest of a team mate, and as tough as old boots, as the Victorians discovered when they tried to ruffle him.

It was certainly the year in which the war turned around. As early as January, Churchill and Roosevelt met at Casablanca to discuss not *if*, but *when* the invasion of Europe would take place. We ABC listeners and *Herald* readers were not privy to their discussions of course, but there were photographs in all the newspapers showing them to be ever so chummy and confident.

We know now, of course, that they decided an invasion of Europe could not be contemplated until the spring of 1944 and this probably prompted Churchill to be more kindly disposed to the defence of Australia and beating Japan. Nevertheless, he refused to allow the 9th Division to come home, on the grounds that they were going to be an integral part of the North African campaign. And what a part the 9th played.

Once Montgomery was appointed Commander-in-Chief of the 8th Army the colonial troops assigned to him — Australians, New Zealanders, Indians and South Africans — regained confidence that British artillery would support their various infantry efforts. The New Zealanders especially had often been left without support and had suffered inordinately high casualties. It did not happen with 'Monty' though. El Alamein proved to be the showdown of the entire North African campaign. It was said at the time that there had never been a more awesome display of gunpower, tank and air warfare in the history of war. Veterans of El Alamein subsequently spoke of night turning into day, so heavy was the barrage, and said they could feel the whole desert shake under their feet.

The 9th Division covered itself with glory at El Alamein, but suffered heavy casualties. They were subsequently acclaimed for their incredible bravery and initiative. One battalion of the 9th, the 2/48th, had four Victoria Cross winners, but all posthumous awards. I know everybody has to die, and 'age shall not weary them', but it is nonetheless infuriating that humans seem unable

to resolve problems other than through the sacrifice of
their best specimens. Even on a genetic level it's crazy.

Rommel, in Germany at the start of the Battle for El
Alamein, flew back to Africa too late to stop the Allied
onslaught. It was interesting to read in subsequent years
that Rommel was one of the German generals who sought
to overthrow Hitler and seek an honorable peace. It may
be that he was plotting this when El Alamein called him
back. When he ordered the German withdrawal at El
Alamein he directly disobeyed Hitler's order to 'stand fast
until victory'. Despite the withdrawal and his eventual
defeat Rommel was held in high regard as a decent soldier
by the Australian boys. But he was on the run after El
Alamein. I read many years later that the Allies cracked
Rommel's codes and thus were able not only to anticipate
some of his brilliant moves but to feed some false information into his intelligence system.

After their heroic part in the African campaign Churchill finally consented to the return of the 9th Division to
Australia. In February 1943 I think everybody in Melbourne turned out for their march through the city streets.
People seemed to celebrate non-stop for weeks. The pubs
were bursting and the whole city smelt like a brewery.
We sang 'Swinging Along The Road to Victory' as though
we'd beaten Rommel ourselves:

> Swinging along the road to victory
> (*All*: Have a Banana!)
> Never a job too tough for you and me
> Salute to the army, the boys in navy blue,
> Here's to the air force, and the nurses too
> And now for Australia, shout 'Coo-ee'
> Swinging along the road to victory

Not to be outdone the Australians fighting in New
Guinea were the first to establish tactical superiority
over the Japanese at Buna, Gona, the Kokoda trail, later

at Milne Bay and generally throughout the region, not-withstanding the harshness of the country, their relative inexperience, and the ongoing shortages of supplies and air cover. Sir William Slim the great British general, who was fighting in Burma at the time, wrote later in his 1956 book *Defeat into Victory:*

> If the Australians, in conditions very like ours, had done it, so could we. Some of us may forget that of all the Allies it was the Australians who first broke the spell of the invincibility of the Japanese Army.

The jungle fighting in New Guinea continued to be brutal and relentless but our boys there knew that with the 9th in jungle training in Queensland they would soon be reinforced. When the Aussies were victorious at Kokoda we knew we would eventually win the war. With all our experienced soldiers back in the Pacific region and crack airmen like 'Killer' Caldwell coming back from Britain, bringing with them amazing aeroplanes like Spitfires to attack the Japanese rather than merely defend, you could sense an attitude that we didn't see any need for the Americans to be patronising us any more. After all, what had they done so far? Not much, compared to our forces. We conveniently forgot just how much money, equipment, transport and so on the Americans provided.

The problem was not with the American rank and file, who were getting along well with our blokes, and after the Japanese evacuated Guadalcanal the Yanks were hailed as heroes too. MacArthur kept inferring that our forces were ineffective. It seems he never grasped the complexity of the New Guinea campaign, nor realised just how impossible the terrain was for ground troops and the courageous airmen trying to drop supplies and provide air cover. Apparently MacArthur was always looking at small spaces on maps and demanding unachieveable progress from Blamey. The seasoned campaigners from the Australian 6th, 7th and 9th Divisions were not averse to reminding Americans that MacArthur's only claim to fame in the war was that the Japanese had done him like a dinner in The Philippines.

Uncle Martin came out to say goodbye. He had been sent by 'the Manpower' to work with the CCC (Civil Construction Corps) building the all-weather (later bitumen) roads from Alice Springs to Darwin and from Mt Isa to Tennant Creek. I suppose it would have been a reasonably good experience for him, as he was still physically fit, but in general terms his life seemed to be purposeless. He was such a sad figure, and I used to get angry with the way our family, even Grace, laughed at his antics when he was 'off with the fairies'. Can't you see it's not his fault? I used to seethe. I still do, as over the years the various stories are recounted about Martin. I can only see the photograph of the dashing soldier who went off to fight for his country, whose experiences I traced in my 'Song for Grace'. At the start of the song:

> And Martin writes, Mum and Dad life in the army is grand.

but at the end of the war:

> Martin was shell-shocked and he'd have been better off dead.

I joined the Coburg Central Brass Band in 1943 as a drummer. It was a new band, re-formed really, and it was good to be there at the start and to watch the development of some of the lads into fine players. One family of brothers, Robert, Don and 'Lofty' Beeson all finished up crack musicians. 'Lofty' graduated to the Flinders Naval Band when he joined the navy, but would occasionally play the tuba for us whenever he was on leave. The band used to get lots of jobs, and we'd travel in the back of Stan Fennell's furniture van, sitting on benches and generally clowning about. It was a feature of Melbourne life in those days that people went on picnics in large groups, either by train or in the backs of furniture removal vans. You'd hear singing and, sure enough, a picnic van — as they were called — would cruise past, with everybody happily waving. Today's coaches seem stuffy by comparison.

Being in a band you got a great view of all sorts of things. There seemed to be some sort of march in the city every second weekend to honor a branch of the armed forces. Then there were the regular marches like Anzac Day, May Day and St Patrick's Day.

The St Pat's march was one of the biggest features of Melbourne's year and amazingly, in such a sectarian city, most people watched or supported in some way this big Catholic festival. Coburg Central Brass Band had no religious affiliation, but we always participated. Up Bourke Street we would march, to the top of the hill, where Doctor Mannix sat in an open Rolls Royce and gave us an austere wave as we played 'It's a Great Day for the Irish' on the way to St Patrick's Cathedral, a block from the Victorian parliament.

One job the band loved was playing at the Napier Park Greyhound Races. It was an easy night. All we had to do was march up the straight a couple of times during the night, and then play some tunes in the rotunda. In between we watched the races, had some small bets and received a fee of three shillings each. We all got a free hot dog as well, with all the usual jokes: 'you're about to eat the beaten favorite from the first race.' Unfortunately we only got the Napier Park job every six months. All the other bands wanted to work there too.

In the summer months there were Massed Bands days at different sporting ovals. As well as the various competitions for the bands there would be woodchopping, tug-of-war, cycling and running, perhaps competitions between fire brigades, with lots of people using the day as a picnic outing. We were only a D Grade band at first, but advanced quickly to C Grade. We were rank amateurs, though, compared to some of the A Grade bands, including Coburg City, who looked down their noses at poor cousins like us. We were just a bunch of kids, with three or four very good adult players. Our conductor, Mr Selwyn, was a fine trombone player in the Regent Theatre orchestra. Kids nowadays find it hard to believe that once, when you went to the pictures at the toffier theatres like the Regent or the State (on the corner of Flinders and Russell Streets, now the Forum Revival Centre) there would be a 20-piece orchestra. They would play for about 20 minutes and then the films — always two films plus cartoons and shorts — would roll. Even in the suburban theatres like the Padua in Brunswick, there would be someone playing a Wurlitzer organ, which magically rose from a pit.

Band practice was at the McDonald Reserve in Bell Street every Wednesday night from 7.30 to 9 p.m. and then again on Sunday mornings when we'd also practise marching.

After I'd been in the band a few months I noticed a girl always standing at the corner of Sydney Road and Urquhart Street, every Wednesday evening. I tried to ignore her for a few weeks, but one night, as I walked past her, she said,

'Hey, do you know Len Kline?' Len played the euphonium.

'Yes,' I replied, blushing and very unsure of myself.

'So do I,' she responded. There was an embarrassed silence and I stammered out,

'Well, I gotta go to practice,' and scurried off.

It dawned on me that she was waiting for me, and that threw me absolutely. I must admit that if she hadn't been there on future occasions I'd have been disappointed, for she seemed pretty (for a girl) but our exchanges didn't get past the 'Hello' point for a couple of weeks. I used to get hot flushes from the time I turned into Sydney Road near Pentridge.

'What can I say that doesn't sound stupid?' I roared inwardly to myself. I'd practise some smart remark mentally, but then find I couldn't get it out, even to myself. Perhaps she would like me to do a fancy drum roll? I always carried the drum, taking it home to practise. Maybe I could demonstrate how Jack Dyer took a high mark? It was always the same. She'd be there, all expectant, and all I could do was blush, stammer and squeak,

'H'lo'. She must have thought I was the dumbest creature imaginable, so decided to take the initiative.

'My name's Elsie,' she said, about four weeks into our affair. 'Good,' was all I could muster, and even that came out with a quiver to it, I was so nervous. I knew it was coming.

'Well, what's yours?' What could I say? I hated being called Teddy. So I wanted to say, laconically, 'Hi. Ted Egan, nice to meet you,' as the Yanks would have done, but I had as much chance of getting that out as saying 'Clark Gable, how about a fuck?' I opened my mouth, but my voice just wouldn't function. I must have looked a real dag, standing there, swallowing, shaking my head like a scrub turkey, trying to talk, but getting nowhere.

She must have anticipated my impotence. She took a little notebook from a pocket in her dress.

'Here, write it down.' She handed me a stub of pencil. I quickly wrote 'Ted Egan' and passed back the book.

'I already knew,' she roared and we both laughed. The ice was broken.

'Who told you?'

'Len Kline.'

For the next few months Elsie and I chatted each Wednesday and I began to leave home earlier in order to

spend time with her. We talked fairly easily about all sorts
of things, until one day she grabbed me and kissed me
right on the mouth. I nearly died.

'Come on,' she said, 'kissing's easy.' Well, I didn't know
what a fuck was, but I knew from hearing other boys talk
that that was where I was heading and it was a mortal
sin, wasn't it? She must have sensed me getting edgy, or
gave me up as a bad job, or both, for she stopped coming
to meet me soon after. I guess she found someone a bit
more forthcoming.

I tried to put girls out of my mind, and that was fairly
easy, given my great love of sport. I was a bit small yet
to play handball against the big kids on the main court,
but I played on all the side courts which meant any space
of brick wall in the college grounds. Left hand, right hand,
butt, hit out, on the full, come on Ted, one day you'll clean
them all up.

There were about forty boys in Brother Nash's class,
which was called 'First Year'. Nowadays it would be called
'Year Seven'. I was eleven, most boys were thirteen, a few
were fourteen. They were a good bunch of kids, with no
real snags or bullies. That was a feature of the Christian
Brothers Colleges as I experienced them: no bullies, no
gangs, no stupid initiation stunts. We had a few real
characters, but the biggest problem at the Brothers was
the push for high academic achievement. It was easy to
find reasons why less talented boys should be encouraged
to go elsewhere, so we had a fairly high dropout rate.

One boy I was sorry to see go was Neil Somers. He
was a very funny kid, with a gruff voice and tight curly
hair like a Merino ram. He had drilled a tiny hole in the
gap between his front teeth, and he could hold a reason-
able-sized quantity of milk or water in his mouth.

'Watch this,' he'd say as he walked up to some unsus-
pecting mug.

'Excuse me,' Neil would say to the mug, 'I think I've

got something in my eye.' The mug would come up close, peer intently into the proferred eye, and would then cop a great squirt of milk or water down the front of his suit, and we who watched would hoot with laughter. Like all true villains, Neil could handle the aftermath of his daring. Size was no deterrent, and he did it to some of the biggest kids, but if they retaliated by starting to chase him Neil would head for the Brother on playground duty and say:

'Sir, this big bully's going to belt me'.

Kevin Sheedy, the Richmond champion who later became Essendon's coach, used the same tactics to upset players on the opposing team. One day Sheedy ankle-tapped North Melbourne champion Sam Kekovich at the start of a Grand Final when silly Kekovich offered to shake hands. When Kekovich started to chase after him, Sheedy immediately appealed to the umpire: 'Look at this brute.' Kekovich spent the rest of the game chasing Sheedy without laying a finger on him, and Richmond won the premiership. Again.

But poor old Neil Somers was told that a technical education might be the best prospect for him. A pity I felt.

On a regular basis we had visits from old boys recently ordained as priests or professed as Christian Brothers. This was blatant recruiting. We were constantly urged to 'pray for a vocation' and these visitors always started out,

'Yes, ten years ago I was a kid like you, sitting in that very desk, and one day God answered my prayers and called me. Well, here I am, fellers, and look at me. Happy!' I kept a low profile on those occasions, because I knew my own vocation was so strong I didn't need any prompting or urging. To have indicated an interest in the religious life would have set me up as a crawler, for that was how I viewed the kids who were forthcoming and asking all the questions. I must acknowledge it was forceful proselytising, especially when you met men of the

calibre of Father Jim Tough — the very name was straight
out of the *Champion* comics — who was once Captain of
the College, reputed to be good enough at football to play
in the VFL, the great Victorian dream. He had 'given up
the worldly life' to become a Blessed Sacrament priest.
They were a religious order who concentrated their lives
on prayer, contemplation and perpetual adoration of the
Blessed Sacrament. He looked stunning in his white robes,
complete with hood. I must say the 'uniform' impressed,
but the perpetual adoration's not glamorous enough for
me, I thought. I preferred the big audiences, oops, congregations, and the power of people like the
Redemptorists. I could see myself swinging majestically
into the sanctuary in black robes, flamboyantly taking off
the mediaeval cape to show that I was really a nice bloke,
giving the women the benefit of my better profile, pausing
for silence, a couple of amazingly subtle jokes and then
blasting them out of their pews as I roared: 'And what if
you were to die this very night?'

My cousin Frank Brennan from Perth didn't make all
that much impression on me at first, but he did dispel
the myth spread by the army boys that the fellows in the
air force were 'pansies' or 'blue orchids'. Mind you, the air
force boys called the soldiers 'footsloggers', the inference
being that they wouldn't be intelligent enough to get into
the air force. Frank had been in the Middle East in Syria
with the army, but then changed to the air force as an
air gunner. He was a terrific looking bloke and I began
to watch him closely. I realised not only that women of
all ages just flipped over him, but men liked him too.
Today, we'd say he had 'charisma'. Oh yes.

His full name was John Francis, which made him
Mick's Jack in the Brennan list of Jacks, but just as his
brother Len (Leonard Michael) chose to call himself Mick
when he joined the air force, Frank discarded his Jack.
We called him 'Frunner'. I checked out his mannerisms:

the way he pursed his lips before a disarming, flashing smile; how he wrinkled his forehead to frame his strong Brennan nose; how, when concentrating on something he whistled little tunes through his teeth, and the tiny gold filling in one front tooth gave a little flash; the artlessness of presenting his best profile; and the manner in which he was able to show what a great physique he had without having to resort to the Don Athaldo poses. I thought to myself: here's one to follow. It had already been agreed that I looked more like the Brennans than the Egans, particularly around the nose, so I began to practice Frunner's mannerisms in front of the mirror. One day, to my pleasant surprise somebody said, 'Goodness, isn't Teddy like Frunner!' From that day until many years later I concentrated on being just like Frunner: the way I got my hair cut, the pursed lips, the wrinkled brow, the little whistle and — a few years later, when I controlled my own destiny and could afford such luxuries — a gold filling and two small tattoos.

Frank had a small tattoo on his left hand, an aviator's head complete with helmet and goggles, and the inscription RUNT RAAF. He had done it himself to honor Len (nicknamed 'Runt' because he was the smallest of their family) when Len joined the air force. He also had an eagle on his chest, just the outline, which he had done with a needle and ink in front of a mirror. He must have been a charmer, for even Grace doted on him. She used to call him 'Frankie boy'. He was camped at the Melbourne Cricket Ground or based at Sale in Gippsland for a while in 1943-4 so we saw quite a lot of him.

I came home from school one day to discover Grace crying. This was a rarity, although I had probably seen her cry more than anyone else on our visits to the Shrine of Remembrance.

'What's wrong, Ma?' It was our way of being frivolous with Grace, and she looked like she needed cheering up.

'Kathy died this morning'.

My lovely cousin Kathy Brennan died in the Warrnambool Hospital when she was only thirteen and fifty years later as I write I again cry as I did when I first heard the news. I loved her, as did everyone who came in contact with her. She was everybody's favorite, and just like her Mum: kind, considerate and very quiet. She had some bronchial problem which could probably be easily fixed today, and it was tragic that she died so young. She apparently knew she was going to die and wrote a little letter to her father to prepare him. She collected embroidered handkerchiefs, and her Dad had promised to get her some. Realising she was going to die, and knowing he would be mortified at not getting the handkerchiefs for her she wrote him a note saying, among other things, 'Dad, don't worry about the handkerchiefs. I have plenty already.'

Her family was devastated. They took her body back to the farm for an overnight vigil and the family and the neighbours said the Rosary, Irish style. The next day she was buried at Tower Hill cemetery, near Koroit.

Aunty Rita was very depressed and not long after Kathy's death they left the farm at Dennington and came to live in Melbourne. It was a big move, but with Bob again in the army, as were Frank (that's Bob and Rita's Frank, not Frunner) and Artie, and Leo wanting to join up, it was decided to move to the city. They bought a large brick house in Donald Street, Brunswick, not far from us, and it became another centre for friends and relations who were in the services. We used to visit Donald Street often, and loved going there. The Coburg Egans got on well with the Brunswick Brennans, and our parents had been best man and bridesmaid at Bob and Rita's wedding, so they were very close friends as well as relations. Bob and Rita were generosity itself. Bob was on army duty locally, so got home most weekends. They didn't have as many singing-style parties as we did, but there was always lively discussion going on. And cards! There were some monumental card games on their big dining room table: euchre, solo, bridge, forty-fives, poker, crib. We Egans were introduced to lots of new servicemen, from the Western District, and Grace and Pop could always establish some sort of connection having been born in the Western District themselves.

Rita succeeded in having Frank discharged from the army. He was only 14, but already had been promoted to corporal! Frank was furious when Rita went to the authorities and in a year or so he enlisted again. Leo was older than Frank, but smaller, and wanted to join the army but Bob wouldn't sign army papers. I guess his own experiences in France's trenches told him to keep his sons out of the type of hell he had endured. He did finally consent to signing papers for Leo to join the air force.

I loved to sit and listen to Pop and Bob talking politics. Bob was a few years older than Pop, and Bob's early letters from various parts of Australia, and indeed from the front lines in the war, indicate a great feeling for early Labor ideals. He and Pop were both socialists while at the same time staunch Catholics, and in those days the two were not considered incompatible — in fact Doctor Mannix encouraged it. Political power for the common people was the hope of all those who had lived through the Depression and had seen how the working classes were just pawns in the power games of capitalists. These two self-educated men could have been political science lecturers. They knew every member of parliament, state and federal, and they followed parliamentary debates closely. Both were articulate, and it was fascinating to hear them discuss world affairs at such an informed, detailed level. Frank, too, was a politics buff. He used to subscribe to *Hansard*, and often would sit in the gallery at State Parliament House.

Eileen was a very pretty girl, very much like my sister Pat in looks and expressions. She joined the WAAAF and looked very flash in her blue uniform. Margaret, Judy, Betty and Peter all enrolled at St Margaret Mary's School in North Brunswick, and settled into city life well. Betty provided a new connotation to the word 'flash' when Rita bought her a lovely red dress with a Red Riding Hood cape and bonnet. Betty paraded in front of us all and said, 'Ain't I a 'slash' guy?' She certainly was.

Kathy's death demonstrates how serious it could be to have medical problems in those days, before the arrival of wonder drugs like penicillin. Polio, tuberculosis, pneumonia, were all killers, and people spoke in hushed tones if loved ones had to go 'to Fairfield' (infectious diseases hospital) or 'to the sanitorium'.

Our sister Peg developed 'a spot on the lung' at around this time, and was confined to bed for eight months. Pop always insisted that her illness was brought on by Holbrook's sauce: 'It's that bloody black sauce she plasters on everything,' was his considered medical opinion. Grace told him to 'pull his head in' which was the latest rejoinder established in the wonderful Bluey and Curley comic strip. Peg was set up on a bed in the lounge room for most of the time, so she could have company. She had a little folding table-cum-desk which enabled her to eat meals, read a book or write letters, but the main medical advice was that she was to do nothing strenuous. She used to sit by the window and watch us playing on the street, and sometimes we would get her to adjudicate when there were disputes in games.

A good mate of mine, Dixie Anderson, lived in Bell Street and he used to ride over on his bike most nights, for two reasons. He liked chatting to Peg, and he could copy my homework. Dixie was amazingly worldly and, although he was academically dependent on me, he could give me the most profound insights into everyday life. He was hopeless at French at school, but invariably announced his arrival with *'Voici Dixie'*. There was a woman in our street named Dulcie Connors and she was quite good-looking. One night Dulcie walked past and Dixie gave Peg a wink and a knowing look and announced:

'Elle a les belles jambes n'est-ce pas?'

In the next couple of tricky years Dixie was going to be a good friend to help explain the mysteries of life. That's if I could separate fact from fiction. Grace said of Dixie, 'He could kid you up a tree and then chop it down.' He was just so sharp. He could tell you the most blatant piece of rubbish with a deadpan face. He was constantly getting me to look up 'seamy' words in the dictionary, insisting that his dictionary at home had given him definitions that I could never find. He told me to look up 'fart' insisting that his dictionary described a fart as 'a short explosion between the legs'. I could only find some meaningless stuff about *(vulg.)* 'emission of gases from the anus'. Then he insisted that in his dictionary a 'bastard fart' was 'a little stinker without a pop'.

Peg's illness was something of a blessing in disguise for her. The number of blokes coming to 'court' her, as we called it, increased during her illness. One bloke in particular seemed to be in with a real chance. He was Jack Gleeson, in the army, on leave from New Guinea. Peg knew him vaguely from childhood. Jack's skin was as yellow as butter from taking atabrin tablets to prevent malaria. He was a bit of a hero, for he already had two of the little blue 'wound' stripes on the forearm of his tunic. It was interesting to hear Jack talk approvingly of the Americans, particularly the support they provided with their air force and their generosity with things like food and cigarettes. It was obvious that our boys were on subsistence rations compared to the Yanks. Jack didn't seem to mind that Peg wasn't able to go out during his leave. I guess he had had enough action for a time and welcomed the chance to just sit and chat.

Our boys were starting to get the ascendancy in New Guinea. The fighting was still bitter and conditions hideous, but they nonetheless beat the Japanese at Lae, Finschafen and Milne Bay. Indeed, the war was starting to turn around in our favor. A crippling blow to Japan was administered in the Bismarck Sea when the Australian and American air forces sank eight troop ships and four destroyers seeking to transport 10,000 Japanese troops to reinforce Lae. It was an absolute slaughter and regrettably thousands of Japanese survivors of the shipwrecks were strafed and killed in the open sea. What a dreadful thing war is. Such base actions are considered necessary and are rationalised in the history books written thereafter. When the other side does it we call them barbarians.

The Russians had the Germans on the run. Africa was secured by Montgomery. Sicily was invaded, as soon as the Mediterranean was controlled by the Allies. Eisenhower was getting ready for the invasion of France. The Americans were well and truly involved in all theatres of war, and there would be no more complaints about their late arrival. All of Australia's army forces were concentrated in the Japanese war, but thousands of our airmen still served in Europe with great distinction. The Big Three, Stalin, Roosevelt and Churchill, met at Teheran and began to draw up plans for the future of Europe.

As for me, I went to 'the slave gang'. It was common practice for kids to take a holiday job for half of the six-week long Christmas break from school. In that way you were introduced to the principle of paying board. (Hello? Teenagers of today, are you still there?) You paid your board for the entire holiday, and anything left over became your pocket money to be used on trips to the swimming baths, the pictures, Luna Park, skating, and so on, during the remainder of the holidays. Anderson's Hosiery Mills was just near the Batman Railway Station and the word went round that they were taking kids on for the holidays. I was signed up and began work as an 'assistant presser' in the factory. Fifteen bob per week. Sal was luckier. She and Delia French worked in 'Stationery' at Coles and also had some responsibilities in the lolly (sweets) department.

The Andersons (no relation to Dixie) had some members of their family who were 'deaf and dumb', as we in our ignorance called it in those days, and so they employed many people who could only 'talk' with their hands and through facial gestures.

It was eerie working there, for the only sound was the steam engine which powered the various presses. No wireless. No talk. But, boy, did we work. I was assigned to a senior presser who was easily able to demonstrate the routine to me with appropriate actions. Great baskets of socks were tipped into a bin and we had to fit them on flat wooden leg-shaped boards in lots of twenty, feed them into a slot in the press like putting slices of toast in a toaster, clamp down the lever to press the socks, and, while this was happening, get the next batch ready and fold the previous batch, which we then neatly packed into boxes. We stood for the entire day. It was non-stop work from 8 am to 5 pm, except for lunch and two smokos. I used to go home exhausted, and I speculated to Grace that I thought the deaf and dumb people could once talk, but had been taken prisoner and put into 'the slave house'. This jokingly joined the family admonitions as we went anywhere. Grace would say, 'Don't talk to any strangers or next thing, there'll be a needle in your leg and you'll finish up a slave at Anderson's Hosiery Mill.'

Bluey and Curley were created during the war by Alex Gurney

13

Ve Haf Vays of Making you Dance

I don't know who gave him his nickname, but it was perfect. He was straight out of a George Raft movie. I often mentally replaced his Christian Brothers' habit with broad-brimmed black hat, black suit, black shirt, white tie, white spats, and black patent-leather shoes. One day I suggested to John Murray, the class cartoonist, that he should draw such a picture. He did it perfectly, adding a Tommy gun for good measure. It was a great hoot for us Second Year boys.

His name was Brother J A Edwards, but we called him 'Slick'. He was a big fat bloke with impressive jowls and plastered-down, jet-black hair. He had not long come down from Queensland, and we were to be reminded of that for the next two years. He threw up his hands in disgust on the very first day and said, despairingly,

'The boys in Queensland would pick that up in one second flat. What are you, nincompoops or something?' It was a good start to a volatile two-year relationship none of his pupils would ever forget.

Slick was the exact opposite of Brother Nash. Nashy

was always in control, cool, analytical. Slick was likely to
start the day with six 'cuts' each, just to show us there
was no animosity. He would crack heads together and belt
us over the ears. He threw chalk and blackboard dusters
to punctuate a furious outburst. He would go into apo-
plectic rages and scream at us. He would single us out
for vitriolic individual abuse. Here's what he thought of
Vern Wilson:

'I can see you in five years time Wilson. Standing on
the street corner, spitting in the gutter, out of a job,
useless.'

Another of my mates, Geoff (Lou) Lynch had long,
straight hair — not unlike Slick's own hair in fact. Slick
blasted him with:

'Yes, Lynch, you with your rat's tails. You'll be sitting
up in some scungy bar, wondering why you never learnt
anything at school. I'll tell you why, son. It's because
you're basically stupid. Genetically bereft. That's why.'

And all the time we were reminded of those wonderful
boys in Queensland. I met a few of them later!

For a while we were absolutely petrified. One day,
when he 'kept us in' until almost 5 p.m., against a normal
3.30 p.m. release. I was so afraid of him I was not
prepared to ask permission to go to the toilet, and pissed
my pants. What humiliation! Vern Wilson didn't help
when he pointed to the pool under my desk and said:

'Sir! Sir! The roof's leaking!' This on the second floor
of a three-story building. I think at that point Slick
realised he had taken things too far, for he let us go home,
but not before giving Vern a belt over the ear for good
measure. I was mortified by this experience for years.
Vern Wilson used to delight in relating the incident, but
I could only manage the wryest of smiles which sought to
conceal the shame and anger I felt.

I quickly came to Slick's attention. Youngest in the
class again, I was a dreadful show-off, always, as part of

my insecurity, looking for laughs from the bigger boys. I
was into daring practical jokes. One day when Slick was
called to the door to speak to Brother King, I sneaked
from my desk and dipped the blackboard chalk in the
flower vase. Slick returned to the blackboard to resume
the geometry theorem we were doing.

'Where was I?' he asked.

'You were showing us about the square on the hypot-
enuse, Sir,' I volunteered, looking around the class for
approbation from the bigger boys. Slick beamed one of his
rare smiles in my direction, which added to the moment.

'Yes, thank you, Egan,' he said, and grabbed the chalk
to go to work on the right-angled triangle he had already
drawn. The wet chalk skidded down the board. Sitting up
innocently in front of Slick was Puggy Dwan, a beaut kid,
but one who always needed reassurance in everything he
did. After a footy game Pug would come up and say:

'Hey, Ted, do you think I played any good today?'

We all took great pains to look after Pug's ego:

'Sure, mate, you were terrific.'

So here's poor Pug, looking up at Slick with trusting eyes.
Slick undid all of our counselling in one second flat. He
hurled the chalk at Pug's head.

'I suppose you think you're funny, Dwan.' Pug threw
me a look which clearly said 'thanks, shithead,' but the
other kids all had a laugh. Fortunately, Pug forgave me
when I apologised, and we stayed good mates.

I had been caught out at other times, and Slick made
me sit in a dual desk with Dixie Anderson, right at the
front, within head-banging or cuffing range. I was always
late into class, spending vital last seconds of recess time
on the handball court. Slick would say:

'I'm sure your parents are going to be thrilled when
they look at your report, Egan. Then they'll know they
are getting good value for the hard-earned four pounds

ten a term that they're paying to the North Melbourne Handball Club.'

The constant, predictable abuse and hammering eventually backfired on Slick. It must have been physically exhausting for him, dishing out four or six 'cuts' to each of twenty boys, as often happened. A hundred mighty swings must have taken a bit out of him, and we sometimes felt concerned that he might have a heart attack. His face would be almost purple with effort. Although I was only twelve at the start of Second Year most of the boys were fourteen or fifteen, some of them big tough kids. Keith - known, naturally, and appropriately as 'Chesty' - Bond for example would have been six feet tall and thirteen stone. The boys respected the cloth to the point where they knew they weren't allowed to punch out the Brothers, but some of them looked very capable of doing it. Only a few boys showed any sign that Slick hurt them with the strap: most of us developed the tactic of leaving the hand extended at the end of the punishment, more or less implying that we could handle a few more cuts if he liked. It must have been both infuriating and counter-productive, but Slick never let up. He had sufficient control, or cunning, to refrain from hitting the bigger boys around the ears — that would have really been stretching his luck. Boxes on the ears were for little squirts like me, guaranteed not to hit back. All a bit cowardly, I thought. Mind you, he did hurt on some occasions. But I for one never let him know.

I have thought about this a lot over the years, trying to establish reasons for it all, seeking to apportion blame. On the one hand it must have been frustrating for the teachers dealing with immature teenage boys, and there is no more boneheaded species on the planet. Also, we seemed to delight in generally being dumb and obtuse. I also knew that, for my part, Grace was right: 'You can lead Teddy Egan, but you'll never push him.' Mind you,

Grace was into the lash too. But I think of men like Uncle Bob, or my own Dad. They wouldn't have had to resort to the knuckle to get the best out of kids. I think that often some of the very worst people are engaged as school teachers, and that our approach to the education of kids needs a total rethink. But there I go again.

My own son, Greg, put me on the spot recently, when I was talking about the 'physical' side of my schooling. I had asked his boys, Rory and Jack, my grandsons, if they ever 'got the cuts' at school. They didn't know what I was talking about, so I started to discuss Slick.

'So why did you send me to the Brothers?' asked Greg, bemused. I wasn't too sure what the correct answer was, but I guess that, at the time, there seemed to be no alternative to Greg also 'going to the Brothers' and I had been assured by his generation of teachers that the old days of the knucklemen were long since gone. The paradox of it all is that a poll among the hundreds of boys taught by Slick would probably reveal a majority of the opinion that he was 'a good teacher' and that 'the discipline didn't do us any harm'. I can't make up my mind.

Slick did get terrific examination results and that was important to the Catholic cause. To assess their academic attainments Catholic schools had to submit their pupils to the public examination system. They welcomed this challenge because of their ongoing claims to State Aid, and felt that continuing good results must inevitably eventuate in justice being achieved. Slick had an amazing knack of predicting an examination paper, almost to the point where you felt something shonky was afoot. Not only could he forecast the questions, he could tell you with unerring accuracy what approach the examiners would (not 'might') like you to take.

The best example of this follows. The American psychological guff about 'how to bring up children' was just starting to permeate Australian society, and we were supposed to be impressed by books and films which told us that American teenagers were ever-so-cute, articulate, rich, thoroughly spoilt, white, and thus eminent role-models for Australia. The word 'co-ed' had hit the airwaves, screens and pages of the media. Slick said to us one day in about June,

'I'm starting now to prepare you for the final examinations.' (The exams were in November: this was the sort of emphasis placed on passing exams at the Brothers.) He went on. 'In the English Expression paper there will be - you can bet on it - an essay topic 'Do you believe in co-education?' Now boys, we all know that co-education is just American-inspired nonsense, not good for boys or girls or the education system. But the examiners will want you to say it's great, and definitely the way to go in the future. Jot down these points, and forget them the moment the examination is over.' Sure enough, he was right. 'Is co-education a good thing for Australian schools?' just happened to pop up on the exam paper. I came third in Victoria in English in the Second Year final exams, having written this very convincing essay that girls and boys needed one another's company through school life if they were to share their lives on a mature level as adults. Yuk.

It was hard to concentrate on school with so much happening around the world. It was 1944 and the Americans were making up for their late entry into the war with some stunning successes in Sicily, where their 7th Army combined with the British 8th Army to drive the Germans and Italians to the Italian mainland. Mussolini was deposed and Italy surrendered to the Allies only five days after the invasion. But the Germans fought on in Italy. It's not widely known that the new Italian government then declared war on Germany. In Britain, as Eisenhower prepared for the invasion of France, the publicity machine made him one of the most popular figures of the war. Everybody knew him as 'Ike' and his open face beamed at us from all quarters.

When the long-awaited invasion of France took place on what became known, from a codename, as D-Day, 6 June 1944, our joy knew no bounds. Surely this was the start of the downhill run to victory? A million Allied troops were landed in France. Australia's involvement was confined to the RAAF, who played an important role in the air war. The Germans were not giving up yet. They launched savagely erratic flying bomb and rocket attacks on London, not achieving any military success but killing thousands of civilians. The Germans insisted that these attacks were reprisals for the saturation bombing of cities like Hamburg, Dresden and Berlin by the Allies. German troops braced themselves to defend the Fatherland at the Siegfried Line, but we had bad news for them, didn't we?

> We're gonna hang out the washing
> On the Siegfried Line
> Have you any dirty washing, Mother dear?

In the Pacific the Americans overran the Marshall Islands and then relentlessly began to drive the Japanese ahead of them, taking one Pacific island after another, and isolating the Japanese on the islands south or west of their front, in a tactic called 'island-hopping'. MacArthur had one eye on Japan and the other on the Philippines, where he sought to fulfil his promise to 'return'.

The Australians were driving the Japanese from the New Guinea mainland and in April 1944 they captured Madang. Thereafter, it was an arduous grind north-west towards Borneo along the New Guinea coastline by Australian and American ground forces, supported by superior air and sea cover. At the same time guess who was given the dirty work of clearing out the Japanese from the islands of New Britain, New Ireland and Bougainville?

Fierce hand-to-hand campaigns were to go on for the next twelve months. General Blamey was subsequently blamed for committing Australian troops to the inevitable prospect of heavy casualties as they sought to eliminate the isolated and desperate Japanese, who were prepared to die rather than surrender. The American policy in similar situations was to leave them to 'wither on the vine'. Blamey's response was that these were Australian Territories which had to be restored to peacetime activity, and there was no alternative to the tactics he imposed. Nonetheless, the Australians suffered dreadful casualties before they killed or captured the last Japanese.

There was much heated debate by the armchair warlords of Melbourne, but when Jack Gleeson eventually returned after what must have been horrendous experiences in Bougainville he quietly said:

'It's over. It's best forgotten about.'

A huge naval battle waged in the Philippine Sea was to be one of the most decisive of the war. It was certainly the biggest conflict involving aircraft carriers the world had ever seen. The Japanese were comprehensively beaten, losing three aircraft carriers with all their aircraft and pilots. At the same time the Americans invaded the Marianas, capturing Guam and Saipan. The strategic importance of the Marianas was not lost on the Japanese, for with America in control at Guam invasion of Japan was possible. Our advance neared their homeland, as theirs, in 1942, had neared ours. When it was announced that 50,000 Japanese had been killed in the Marianas campaign, General Tojo's Cabinet was forced to resign. (It did not save Tojo's hide, though: he was subsequently executed as a war criminal.)

The Allied pincers were beginning to tighten on the various fronts. In June 1944 the Allies entered Rome. In August deGaulle led the Allied forces into Paris. In Burma Generals Slim and Wingate were poised to drive the

Japanese northward through China, aided by Chiang Kai Shek and the Chinese Nationalist Forces. After heavy naval and air attacks on Japanese strongholds MacArthur finally kept his promise: the Americans, led on the ground by the brilliant General Eichelberger, landed at Leyte in the Philippines and began the bloody preparations for the invasion of Luzon. And I was still in short pants. I knew I might never make that uniform.

Most of the bigger, older boys in Second Year were in long 'uns. Many of them had started to shave, or should have. Some were prevented from shaving by acne and the most obscene pimples, pussy little blobs, often with little whiskers sticking through. I was lucky. I never had one adolescent pimple, and kids who did and do have my sympathy. Adolescence is bad enough without pimples.

One of the great advantages of educating boys and girls separately is that boys don't have to get into the stupid business of trying to impress girls through horseplay and loud guffaws. If only they knew how moronic they look and sound. Growing up is frustrating for both sexes, but boys are a few years behind girls in terms of personal maturity through the teenage period. The Christian Brothers didn't do everything right, but their philosophy seemed correct to me, and still does. Keep the boys on their own, give them lots of sport or other physical activity, provide challenging schoolwork to keep their minds fully occupied, and at the same time seek to instil in them the code of ethics which will prepare them for the time when they are less stupid and ready for the outside world, and female company. At the same time I have to acknowledge that at teachers' colleges and in first-year university courses it is often the boys and girls from Catholic colleges who have the greatest problems handling the new found freedom without going mad or impairing their studies. At last they have thrown off the shackles of Reverend Mother or Brother Superior. I guess the total solution is to have less dominant staff so that students can impose more self discipline. But it won't just happen, you've got to make it happen — said Ted Egan, the bloody old smart-arse.

I approve heartily of the way the Christian Brothers spoke about women. Bachelors, celibates, what would they know about women? Plenty, in terms of basic respect. They imparted the message that the Christian Brothers, as an Order, were very strong on devotion to the Blessed Virgin Mary, the Mother of Christ.

'Boys, if you want to be Christ-like, and surely that's the reason why you're here, you should accord all women the respect you would offer your own mother, in the same way that Christ honored the Blessed Virgin,' said my cousin, Brother Des Kilmartin. I heard other, less eloquent Brothers say similar things so often I am sure they made a profound and beneficial impression on the vast majority of boys they taught.

While the Brothers disapproved of co-education they certainly weren't training us to be homosexuals or celibates. Their basic approach seemed to be that life would sort itself out as long as they provided the necessary framework. Girls could come into our lives if that was what we wanted, but later. That certainly suited me, because at the time I thought girls were very definitely to be avoided. So I wasn't too enthused during Second Year when Slick announced one day:

'Boys, next year, in Proficiency, you will be old enough to attend the joint dance with St Aloysius Girls' College, so we are going to have dancing lessons this year to prepare you.'

'Oh, no, Sir!' roared most of the boys.

Slick tried to sound worldly. 'It'll be good for you. One day some of you will get married, although I must say I would pity any poor girl who finished up with the likes of you, Wilson, or you, Lynch. We have arranged for Mr Price of Price's Dancing Academy to come and teach you.'

'Oh, no, Sir, not dancing sir. That's only for sheilas, Sir.' Slick responded with one of his rare funnies:

'Ve haf vays of making you dance,' he retorted, in the Doctor Goebbels voice we all imitated in those days.

Along came Mr Price, a dapper, smiling man. We had to front up on the handball court, most of us electing to dance with imaginary girls, a few extroverts like Lou Lynch, who was a pretty good dancer and not averse to letting everyone know, grabbing brooms and twirling round ecstatically in quarter turns, natural turns and the cross chassis and lock. I kept it quiet that I could already do all the old-time dances, for I didn't want to be labelled a sissy, but I was not averse to learning a few basic steps for the quickstep and the modern waltz. Mr Price was a skilled dancer and demonstrated 'the girl's part' and it was good harmless fun. Slick leered at us from the side-lines, and Dixie Anderson said as he waltzed past Slick, 'I'll bet the boys in Queensland were good dancers, Sir.'

I guess such things as dancing lessons were an acknowledgement by the Brothers that most of us would finish up 'ordinary people' rather than members of religious orders like they were. It must have been difficult for them to relate to ordinary life. When you talked to them you discovered that most had been educated by the Christian Brothers themselves and whisked straight to the novitiate at age 15 or 16. They were basically as uninformed about life and growing up as we were.

Our sports master was Brother O'Connor, a very popular bloke who was called 'Jerry' by the boys. It was left to poor Jerry to organise the one and only biology lesson I had in my entire schooling! I don't know how typical I was of Catholic boys of those days but I had no knowledge whatsoever of bodily functions other than pissing and shitting. As for girls, I was even more ignorant than the

kid in the song who 'thought a "cunt" was something you
were called at school,' for I did not even know any crudi-
ties. Any boy into crude language at North was very
quickly hauled into line by his peers, I'm happy to say. I
still get angry at people who get into effing and blinding
without consideration of who's listening or who might be
offended, even though I take great delight occasionally in
swearing if I think it will assist in making a point in the
appropriate company.

Jerry mumbled his way into the opening of the lesson,
as he put up one of those charts where all your muscles
and nerves and arteries and capillaries are shown. It was
a man, but there was no genitalia, just the various tubes
that took you there. Boys shifted uneasily in their seats,
especially me in mine. But Dixie Anderson licked his lips:
he was going to enjoy this. It seemed to me that Dixie
might have been better qualified to run the lesson than
poor embarrassed Jerry. I wouldn't have known where to
start.

All I knew was that from the time I could talk my
penis was called my 'jockey' and I was not to play with
it or it might drop off. Later I learned that it was a sin
against the Sixth Commandment to play with yourself. I
had had only a couple of vague experiences in my life
which suggested there might be something about 'jockeys'
I didn't know.

Sal has recently reminded me of a day when a few
kids in Higinbotham Street were playing 'hospitals'. I
seem to remember being with a group of girls and boys
and getting into a bit of you-show-me-yours-and-I'll-show-
you-mine, but as I could only have been about three it's
fairly hazy. I do remember the shocked face of Grace as
part of the experience. It must have been some game,
though, for Sal's recollection is that she had all her hair
cut off! Grace had long hair at the time. She cut off some
of her own hair, plaited it into two pigtails and sewed

them into a bonnet which Sal wore all the time. There was only one problem: one windy day Sal's hat blew off, leaving poor little bald Sal howling her eyes out.

My only other penile experience occurred one day when I was about five and got hooked up on a wire fence. 'What happened?' asked Grace when I ran into the house, crying.

'I've cut my jockey off.' There was blood all over the front of my pants. Grace had the pants off me, and me up on the kitchen table in two seconds flat, and seemed very relieved to see it was only a small cut on the scrotum which was bleeding profusely. Grace's level of concern impressed me. There must be more to this thing than I can appreciate, I remember thinking. But I had no idea what for another nine years.

Although I squirmed a bit when Jerry nervously proceeded with the lesson. I was quite interested. Like the others I gave an insecure guffaw when Jerry came to the 'down here' bits. That did not help poor Jerry. He swallowed and then found the courage to say:

'And down here we have the testes.'

'Is that your knackers, Sir?' piped up the disingenuous Dixie Anderson, and we roared hysterically.

'Shut up, Anderson, this is serious,' Jerry snapped, and mumbled his way through the lesson as quickly as possible. I was still ignorant of how things worked, but at least I knew the words 'scrotum' and 'penis' — and 'knackers', which I think is one of the great words. Knackers — knickers — knockers It's a bit like a Latin declension. Only more fun. *N'est-ce pas, Dixie*?

I was pleased that Slick seemed to work out eventually that I was brighter than I led people to believe. He would sometimes say, with a knowing look:

'How did you manage to get that right, Egan?' I met him a few years later as an adult. I came down to Melbourne from Darwin and went for a game of handball to the Christian Brothers' College in South Melbourne.

Slick was principal there by that time. He was absolutely charming.

'Thought I recognised that three-wall serve,' came this familiar voice from the back of the court.

'Gooday, Brother.'

'How are you, Ted?' We chatted briefly and I wish I had had the courage to ask him why he had been such a bash artist but I didn't. I was certain I would have responded to better treatment at school, but I suppose our behavior at that time didn't help. Yet it must have registered that the more he roared, the denser we became, for it became part of our ritual to give him reason to find cause why we didn't compare with the boys in Queensland. Mind you, he may have been saying at South Melbourne that 'the boys at North would pick that up in a minute flat'.

He certainly seemed to enjoy meeting me as an adult, and if he ever admitted to such things I wouldn't mind betting I finished up one of his favorites at school. I certainly never let him down at exam time. One day we were studying a play for English literature titled *Elegant Edward*. It was about this English toff, who was also a robber. Slick, in a rare moment of levity said to me:

'And why do you think he was called "elegant", Edward?' Little turd that I was, but, as the son of Joe Egan, and not about to be outdone in the play-on-words game, I preened myself, made sure everybody was listening and looked him straight in the eye, but deadpan and said:

'Perhaps it was because he was 'slick' at everything he did, Sir.' The boys chortled. Slick pursed his lips, screwed his eyes ruminatively, and gave me a 1-all look. My dad would have been proud of me.

I passed Second Year with good marks, second in the class behind 'Rock' McLaughlin, and First in Victoria in Latin and commercial principles. During the long holidays

I worked at Jack Squalizza's fruit shop on the corner of Moreland and Sydney Roads, so I was able to have a yarn occasionally with Nigger O'Reilly. I wanted to get to know Nig better, but he was always too busy for young kids like me. His eyes were constantly darting around, looking for a sale, just as his forefathers would have smelled out a kangaroo for dinner. Our conversations didn't get beyond 'Gooday Nig' from me and 'Owyergoinmateorright?' from him. But I remained a devoted admirer of The Master.

For about three months I stopped trying to look like Frunner. Cornel Wilde was a popular filmstar and the Cornel Wilde haircut became a fashion for all boys. Elaborate waves - a bit like Bob Hawke's — were the go, and when my dark hair grew a bit longer it began to curl, so a lot of the customers at Jack Squalizza's shop thought I was Italian. Jack's offsider, Gravio Arena, used to go along with this. He taught me simple little bits of Italian, and when a lady asked for a lettuce I would look imploringly at Gravio, and he'd say:

'Una lettuga, Theodoro.' I'd run and get a lettuce and he would say, 'He'sa from Italia, Missus, he no speaka da Inglese.' As the weeks went by I would occasionally forget, until the women would say, 'Hasn't he picked up English quickly?' I would quickly revert to type, give them a few flamboyant hand gestures to display Latin nonchalance, and say something like, *'Mutatis mutandis'* or *'Quod erat demonstrandum'*. Rhubarb Vaselino wasn't in it. The fruit shop was great fun, much better than Anderson's Slavehouse, and because, as Grace said, 'the Egans are great fruit eaters', I gorged myself between serving customers.

Over the Christmas holidays I shot up as getting taller used to be described in pre-drug days. I grew several inches. My school suit was not going to fit me for Proficiency (third-year high school) so I decided that part of my wages from the fruit shop (15 shillings per week plus a bag of fruit each day) would go towards buying a suit with long trousers, plus two pairs of underpants! And I got them. I thought I looked pretty flash. I must have sensed some imminent changes in my life.

Back to school we went for 1945 expecting an easy year with Jerry as our main teacher, but a roar went up when it was announced that Slick would be teaching us again.

'I guess it's some sort of penance for me,' sighed Slick, and we boys looked at one another. He seemed a little mellower. For a good three minutes. Until he backhanded Vern Wilson. We quickly got back into routine and there was a sense of expectation throughout the land that the war would finish during the year. I had practised handball a lot during the Christmas break, and Lou Lynch and I were now the best two players at North, so we dominated the big court each recess period, 'paying our dues to the North Melbourne Handball Club' as Slick constantly reminded us. We were both picked for the inter-collegiate competitions, and I surprised everybody by winning all but one game in the Under 14 competitions against all other Christian Brothers' Colleges.

I was picked for a few games of footy in the Under 15 representative team, and did reasonably well, although North was not very strong in those days. We had some great individual footballers like Jacky Rogan, who later played VFA for Coburg, Gerry Marchesi and Kevin Smith who played for North Melbourne, and my good mate Vern Wilson. Vern was selected to play for Footscray Firsts while still at school. We were ever so proud of him, for he was only 16 and the press photographers came to North to photograph him working away at his desk.

'I was too compassionate, Wilson. I should have told the journalist what a moron you were and that you couldn't in fact write,' was the Christian Brother's way of keeping Vern's feet on the ground.

I have the strangest bag of memories of the year 1945. President Roosevelt died in April. My cousin Artie Brennan died from rheumatic fever just before VE (Victory in Europe) day in May. Mr Curtin died in July, the atomic bombs were dropped on Hiroshima and Nagasaki in August and the Japanese surrendered. We became aware of the horrors of the German concentration camps and the Japanese prisoner-of-war camps, and the Nuremberg trials were conducted. And Slick read us *Man Shy*.

It was a fascinating turnaround for him. Out of the blue one day he announced:

'I'd like to share with you a book I've recently read. It's about a calf.' Is this some sort of sick joke? I wondered. But I was immediately entranced by Frank Dalby Davidson's wonderful, simple story. Slick used to read us a chapter each day, and that in itself was a delight, school for enjoyment's sake, and no exam question at the end. I decided to seek out other books and stories about Australia, for my reading for pleasure had been restricted to the William and Biggles books and *Champion* comics. Maybe Henry Lawson might not be just an aberration. And maybe Slick would have had an easier time all round if he had occasionally relaxed with us in other ways.

And who knows what would have happened had Roosevelt lived? Would he have ordered the atomic bombing? We were all sad, too, that Mr Curtin died, just before Australia celebrated the end of the war to which he and his country had contributed so much. It was generally felt that our prime minister had hastened his own death by his uncompromising committment to the safety of Australia, and he deserved to be remembered as a great national leader. He was succeeded briefly by Mr Forde, but then the Labor parliamentary party selected Ben

Chifley to be prime minister. Joe Egan and Bob Brennan shook hands.

'At last,' said Bob, 'a working man as PM.' They had a cup of tea and toasted the engine driver from Bathurst.

Artie Brennan is buried alongside Kathy in the Tower Hill cemetery at Koroit. Bob and Rita had some terribly sad moments in their lives, and we shared their family's grief when Artie died, for he was a lovely boy, only twenty-two years of age, when rheumatic fever took him. When I gave Auntie Rita a hug she said to me,

'I want you to have Artie's suits, Teddy. He had two very nice Fletcher Jones suits.' She was trying not to cry. 'Frank's in the army again, and Leo's too small for them, so I want you to have them now that you've grown into such a young man.' In that sad way I came to be the best-dressed boy in the Proficiency class photographs of 1945.

Mussolini was dead: shot and strung-up, upside down to be mocked and vilified, captured by the cameras. Hitler and his mistress, Eva Braun, shot themselves and had ordered their bodies be burnt. Apparently they feared the same fate as Mussolini. We didn't think Hitler was dead at the time, and rumors persisted that he had fled to South America. Germany was divided. Good, I thought: the Russians know how to handle Germany. If it was left to the Poms and the Yanks they'll let Germany re-arm in 25 years time and they would start their nonsense all over again. I no longer minded the thought that I wouldn't get into uniform. Everybody had had enough of the war.

Because I wore long pants I was allowed to go to the VP (Victory in the Pacific) celebrations on the night of 15 August 1945. The Brothers were quick to remind us that the war had finished appropriately, on the feast day of Our Lady's Assumption into heaven. The connection between the horrendous atomic explosions and the fact that the Virgin Mary was always depicted as being assumed into Heaven on a mushroom-shaped cloud seemed to escape them. We had the scheduled Holy Day of Obligation so I went to Mass that morning and that night travelled by tram, on my own, to Brunswick Town Hall, where the big celebrations took place in the streets. They had set up a stage on the roof of the verandah of the Gas Company building, and there was a concert and community singing. Thousands of people were in crazy mood. Girls were wearing soldier, sailor or airman hats and they kept forming into crocodiles — single lines — and they danced through the crowd, kissing everybody they encountered. I gave up trying to dodge being kissed after a while, and had a great time watching all the fun. Nana Sheehan's son Stan was one of the comperes. Stan and his partner were known as Izzie and Ozzie after the well-known song which we sang over and over that memorable night

> Is he an Aussie, is he, Ozzie
> Is he an Aussie, Izzie, eh?
> Is it because he is an Aussie
> That he makes you dizzy, Izzie?
> Has he jazzy ways and does he
> Make you go all fuzzy-wuzzy?
> Make you dizzy, does he Izzie?
> Is he an Aussie, Izzie, eh?

MAN-SHY

A STORY OF MEN AND CATTLE

by
FRANK DALBY DAVISON
Author of Dusty

Br Slick's reading of Frank Dalby Davidson 's tale about a calf, *Man Shy*, captivated me

14

Here comes
Norma Stitz

I thought I'd die of embarrassment.

'Get a load of Egan, would you?' shouted Ronny Matar, and fifty pairs of eyes focussed on me and my deformity. There were whistles, cat-calls and wolf-howls and I wanted to die. Quickly. Decisively. I could see that quite a few of the boys were sympathetic, but that didn't help in the least. I turned my back on them so they wouldn't see the tears in my eyes, and I laboriously folded and refolded my clothes and furiously stowed them in the swimming pool locker.

'You rotten, cruel bastards,' I said, almost audibly.

It wasn't the few little pubic hairs that I now sported, for I knew from my odd, furtive, sin-endangering glances that all of the boys were long-since similarly adorned. No. It wasn't that. But I had grown the most seductive little set of tits a fourteen-year-old boy ever produced, and they were at last common knowledge. It was easy enough to keep them covered at home, but swimming was compulsory at North and we went to the Brunswick Baths every Wednesday. Summer of 1945–46 saw me exposed.

I didn't like swimming much. I had just learned to swim and could only do graceless, belly-flopping dives, whereas kids like Roy Rebesco, Ronny Smith and Peter McLaughlin were like dolphins as they happily frolicked around in the pool, and won races for North at the Combined Colleges Swimming Carnival at Richmond Baths each year. We less amphibious types had to be content with cheering them on to the finish line and going into frenzied deafening war-cries:

> Cadibarra Wirracana Yarrawonga Yah
> Talangatta Wangaratta Oodnadatta Hah
> Nullagulla Wullagulla Whish Bang Wah
> Cynosura Cynosura Yah Yah Yah
> North, North, Yah Yah Yah
> N-O-R-T-H North!

Swimming to me was not enjoyable at all, but rather the means of staying alive when forced to enter the deep end.

After Ron Matar, who was a good mate of mine, had unwittingly humiliated me, I jumped into the shallow end of the pool and studiously began to practice underwater swimming, hoping I could get through the session without attracting any more attention. But each time I surfaced it seemed I was still the day's major attraction.

'Make way for Lana Turner, fellers,' and 'Here comes Norma Stitz,' they called. Boys can be so cruel. The water only made my tits more protuberant and I felt like one of the big Friesian cows at the Show.

My tits were tight and pear-shaped and the nipples were bold red painful knobs. They had been developing for two months. Why didn't somebody tell me that in a few short months they would flatten into better-than-average pectorals? The agony of adolescence. Paradoxically, at the point where my own tits began to protrude I became interested in the same development in girls. I put a photo of June Allyson alongside the revered Jack Dyer (Number 17, 6 feet 1 inch, 15 stone 7 lbs) and the immortal Phar

Lap (Night Raid-Entreaty, ch.g., 16.3 hands) above my bed on the back verandah. Grace didn't mind June Allyson, who was in a lot of films about that time, always with her cute, girl-next-door smile and her gee-shucks, throaty voice. I first put up a picture of Susan Hayward but Grace said:

'She looks like a bit of a hussy to me,' so it was taken down. Grace did not know that I also had a photo of the 'sweater girl' Lana Turner, wearing a tight white sweater, tucked away, under my 'tick', which was what we called mattresses in those days. I used to gaze at Lana, longing to touch her, although only starting to know why.

I idolised Lana Turner but I always felt guilty as I looked into those cheeky, knowing eyes. I'd inevitably salivate as I imagined the ravishing tits under that sweater, longing to cup them in my hands, and look at them, and then slowly suck them, as I did in my dreams about her. I'd never seen real tits or a naked woman and there were no explicit photographs in books, newspapers and magazines, but I was able to imagine Lana in fairly graphic detail.

It was always the same dream. I was walking, searching for Lana, knowing that I would eventually find her. She would invariably emerge from a pool of water, naked, her blonde hair throwing off sprays as she saucily shook her head. I'd go to her and we'd hold both hands and look into one another's eyes. We'd walk away, ever so relaxed, composed, smiling. We'd then kneel, facing one another. I would cup both my hands under her tits and begin to suck them, hungrily, slurpingly. Her hair fell over my face and she then scooped her hands into my loins and pulled me towards her. A heavenly, climbing sensation and then the pumping, driving feeling as she took me from myself. I'd wake up, clogged with semen and guilt, my pyjamas thankfully soaking up most of the semen, my mind racing to atone for the guilt. I'd lie there, trembling in the dark, and eventually I'd make an Act of Contrition:

> Oh, my God, I am truly sorry that I have   sinned against Thee, because Thou art so good, and I firmly resolve never to sin again.

A troubled sleep would follow, but I compounded my sin once, rather badly, by congratulating myself that I had selected such a good sort as Lana Turner to share my erotic adventure. Oops, stop it Ted, impure thoughts as well as deeds. What if you died this very night? You'd go plummeting straight into the fiery depths of the eternal damnation of Hell! Think about handball, or cricket, anything except women.

On the pretext of 'going to Donald Street', which was how a visit to Aunty Rita and Uncle Bob's new residence was described, I would go first to St Margaret Mary's Church on a Saturday afternoon in order to have my Confession heard by a strange priest. I could not bear the thought of any of the priests at St Paul's getting wind of my affair with Lana. Especially Father Norris, who had taken over as parish priest when Father McGee eventually died. There was nothing Jimmy Norris didn't know, or couldn't work out. He would have demanded chapter and verse, depth, speed and position at point of climax.

Fortunately, one day as I broached my sin of 'impure actions, once, alone, Father,' in the gruffest voice I could manage as I buried my head in the darkest corner of the confessional at St Margaret Mary's, I encountered a sympathetic priest.

'Don't be embarrassed, son, tell me what happened.'

'Well, I was asleep and I had this dream about Lan . . . a . . . er, a girl, Father, and this stuff came out of my . . . . um . . . er . . . (thank you, Jerry) my penis.' I'll never forget his words, which brought a cathartic wave of relief.

'Firstly, young man, you haven't committed any sin at all. It's part of growing up for boys, and it's called a 'wet dream'. It's a bit of a worry to you, I know, but it's all very normal. Now, I'm not giving you Absolution, for you haven't committed any sin. So, no Penance. But you might like to say a decade of the Rosary to honor Our Blessed Lady and to atone for any past sins you may have committed. Now go in peace.'

Whew! You little beauty! I skipped, and ran to Donald Street, taking several Jack Dyer high marks along the way. What a clever thing the Catholics invented with Confession. First, it gives the Church the control, and the means whereby the set the rules and create the situations which in turn prompt the guilt. Then it, magnanimously, provides the machinery to remove 'the stain of sin'. But only after the sinner acknowledges and submits to the power of the Church as the priest absolves the guilt, mind. It's all super psychology and it's no wonder the Catholic Church has been able to exert huge influence particularly in peasant societies where power can be wielded supernaturally as well as by natural means. *Ego te absolvo.* Thank you Father. That's real power.

Lana Turner has remained on my list of memorable women, but she was about to be supplanted in my affections by Norma Boderick. To this day I love to meet women who have class, who are aware of that fact, and are very relaxed about it. My dear friend Elizabeth Durack is a good example. Aged over seventy, Elizabeth is still a stunning looker, and walks demurely through life, relaxed, although probably aware that every male turns and thinks wow as she enters a room.

Well, Norma Boderick was like that. She used to get on the tram at The Grove each morning. She went to the Domestic Science School in Brunswick. She had been going there about the same length of time I had gone to North, about four years, and I had only vaguely noticed her on the tram in past years. But now, after my initial experiences with Lana Turner, Norma Boderick turned my world inside out. I suppose I must have had erections as a smaller kid, but nothing had ever come (to coin a phrase) of such experiences. I would never have contemplated masturbation even if I'd heard of the word. It would have been a sin, and that was that. Besides, as a future priest I was going to take a vow of celibacy, although I didn't know what that meant either, apart from never getting married, which seemed eminently sensible.

The year 1946 seems in retrospect to have been The Year of the Erection, constant, raging and embarrassing erections made even worse because I knew that everybody, just everybody must be aware that every time I saw or thought of Norma Boderick my dick went straight into pole-vaulting mode. I'd gasp involuntarily, as the blood drained from my entire body into this surging, throbbing painful appendage, while I crossed my knees and looked frantically around for something to divert attention away from this obscene, tent-like bulge in my trousers.

Norma was totally unaware of me. She'd get onto the tram each morning, where a group of North boys would be jammed into the furthest corner. Most of them were either busy copying my homework or talking footy, but from the time the tram passed the Grand Theatre in Sydney Road, Coburg, three stops to go to The Grove, I would start to quiver, in the sure knowledge that any second I'd 'get a horn' as I now knew having an erection was called. I'd grind my teeth. 'Concentrate, you can prevent this,' I'd be screaming inwardly, but the moment the tram reached The Grove I was gone. She would step quietly, confidently, onto the tram, always on her own, never making any fuss, always serenely gorgeous. I'd start my daily idolatry at her feet, and rove over the plain black lace-up shoes, the white bobby sox, the long tanned legs to the pleated navy-blue skirt, the white open-necked blouse, and then her lovely face framed in the cheekily turned-up school hat. By the time I reached the blouse, which tightly suggested her beautifully-formed breasts I'd be sweating and quivering. I'd cross my legs, and wondered if everybody could see the pulse racing in my neck, throbbing to the same beat I could now feel pounding through my dick. My balls swelled inside a tightly-packed scrotum which would have rung like a Chinese gong if anyone (heaven forbid) was to flick it with a stick.

Because she too was travelling on 'Scholars Cocks' (oh, the very thought of the word) Norma was required to stand, like us, even if there were seats available. The trams were always jammed with workers and students. Norma nearly always stood near us, and I learnt every detail of her through unobtrusive glances whenever I got the chance. She didn't have a perfect face by any means, but a couple of little imperfections seemed to make her even more entrancing. She had a tiny chip on one of an otherwise beaut set of teeth. As I could tell from her very demeanor that she was a good athlete I had visions of her getting the tooth chipped playing hockey. I fantasised her in a short hockey skirt and I kept pace with her as her brown legs flashed towards the goal. I ran to console her when the tooth was chipped by an erratic stick. She had a tiny pockmark on one cheek, so that had me imagining her in a hospital bed. I soothed her fevered forehead. As I had these orgasmic thoughts I'd have to dive my hand into my pocket and try to take my dick from a prodding horizontal to a less obtrusive perpendicular, up against my stomach. Then I'd scratch my knee as I tried to cover the bulge with my arm. But my face was always a dead giveaway, I knew. My cheeks were twitching, my mouth contorted, half from the thrill of being in Norma's presence, half from the physical and mental trauma I was experiencing.

I discovered that her name was Norma Boderick when,

one day, she opened a book briefly to do a bit of study. At first I tried to kid myself that, like Elsie before her, it was a means of making an opening with inept me. There was her name and address. Maybe she wants me to write to her, I thought. No. I quickly dismissed that. She hadn't even noticed me. I knew it. She was just totally unattainable. Infuriating. I was mute, powerless. And my balls hurt.

On a wonderful day I will never forget, a wet wintry Melbourne morning, we came together. The tram was terribly crowded, and the conductor was trying to make more room for passengers waiting to get on at Moreland Road.

'Come on you kids, make some room there,' he kept shouting as he pushed us further and further into the corner. Norma was getting closer, even closer. She was taking all the pushing and shoving very serenely. Eventually she was jammed hard against me. I turned side on as our bodies met, my left hand in my trousers pocket fiercely restraining my raging dick, which otherwise would have speared her in the brisket. She was pressed under my chin, and fitted perfectly into my tormented body. I could feel her warm thigh against mine, and the very definite contour of her delightfully taut right tit cradled in the curve of my forearm. There was no point in apologising, or doing anything other than savor the moment. The tram lurched a few times and this enhanced the encounter — for me at least. Our eyes met. Hers were green, feline, friendly, unafraid. She gave a little shrug which indicated, Not much we can do about this, is there? I returned a stupid grin and nodded at her in agreement, my mouth dry, my eyes glazed with ecstasy.

The bliss lasted until Albert Street, Brunswick, where she had to get off. She gave me the most radiant of smiles and said, 'There'll be a bit more room now,' in the huskiest, most seductive voice I had ever heard. And I'd heard June

Allyson and Lauren Bacall and Lizabeth Scott. None of them would ever hold a candle to Norma Boderick. That night, as I lay in bed, in the dark, I re-lived my morning's delight. I gave Norma the most chaste of mental kisses. 'Goodnight my darling,' I whispered in the darkness and began to drift into deep, untroubled sleep. At last I knew the meaning of true—if somewhat unrequited—love. Not even Lana Turner would have a chance of seducing me that night. Not even Lana Turner.

Sadly that day on the tram was my only close encounter with Norma, bodily or otherwise, and I resumed my impotent non-existence. She caught the tram every day, always seeming to know she looked good and made male eyes turn towards her. She seemed supremely confident about life in general. I saw her a few times at the Brunswick Baths, and the sight of her in her red racing Speedos caused me always to seek a seat at the end of the pool, for my blooming dick would leap to attention each time she came into view. I'd sit there, doubled over, a towel covering my encumbrance, and I'd take in her every movement. She was a strong swimmer, and could do the most supreme racing dives which took her into the water with a resounding whack, caused by her delightfully flat stomach and those memorable tits. Then, like the Lana Turner of my dreams, she stepped from the water, dripping, shaking her body unselfconsciously. Great cascades of water flew from her hair, every muscle gleamed and the tightened nipples tantalisingly highlighted the swell of her breasts. Always alone, she seemed an absolute free spirit, and I hope she still is. Norma Boderick, I thank you for the unbounded pleasure I had as your unknown admirer, your Valentine.

Teenage boys are silly enough without having unpredictable things like dicks grafted onto them. I was average-size and I wonder what some of the hugely-endowed fellows have to endure. All those erections keep draining the blood from your head. Your balls swell and you could scream with the pain of it all. It can't be good for you. In later years it's an absolute bonus and the wherewithal for lots of good, clean fun, but I wouldn't wish adolescence on anybody. I'm certain that life in hormonal terms is tougher on women over a total life span, but I can't imagine adolescence being worse for a girl in physical terms than it is for a boy, even acknowledging the advent of menstrual periods. Girls seem to get into a hormonal frenzy as teenagers and that can be a problem, given their reproductive capacity, for while a sexual encounter might be simple and purely physical for a boy, and he might experience no feeling of guilt or sense of being a manipulator, girls seem to take such relationships much more emotionally and seriously. But at least girls don't have to put up with that sudden, irrepressible, uncontrollable dick surging from their loins each time physical or mental contact is made with the opposite sex.

School dances were just agony itself. Nobody was allowed to leave the dance hall, and if you didn't ask some girl for a dance a bossy lay teacher would pair you off anyway. The brothers and nuns weren't allowed to go to things like dances: I guess they had to be kept apart, too. There was no way of avoiding the bodily contact with girls which inevitably caused the beast to surge into gear, revving away as you tried to concentrate on the slow, slow, quick, quick slow of a quarter turn, or the bobbing, swirling Tangoette, where Xavier Cugat's recorded Latin music made the groin eruptions even more unbearable. Dancing was ever so easy alone, on the handball court, but incredibly difficult with an equally nervous girl forced by convention to try to follow you, and at the same time trying to avoid the prodding missile that ground against her hip as you sought to impress her with waltzing ability, an appalling accumulation of cliches, and absolutely banal banter. 'Have you ever heard of a game called handball?'

quickly proved to be a loser. 'Who do you barrack for in the footy?' didn't fare much better, so I tended after a while to say nothing, concentrating instead on my range of Frunner mannerisms to seek to win the girls over with sheer charisma. No luck there, either. It was infuriating that nothing seemed to work, for the girls looked lovely in their taffeta and lace evening dresses, their gloves, and the sprays of flowers in their hair. They smelt delicious, too. I wouldn't have minded some dialogue, and I knew I could talk a bit of sense on some subjects, but nobody seemed to know where to start. And always the prospect of a sudden, maddening erection. Is co-education a good idea for Australian schools? That might have been a good topic, and I could have argued both sides of the debate.

At the end of each dance it was protocol to walk the girl back to her seat, thank her for the dance, and then return to your own position. There you'd be, trying to look nonchalant, walking slightly knock-kneed as you pretended you didn't have a jackhammer of an erection thumping away, again the focus of every set of eyes in the room.

None of the boys, even outrageous blokes like Peter Pannowitch, seemed to be making any headway with the girls, and I think we all went home from the dances glad the ordeal was over. The girls, too, seemed happier in one another's company.

While those days featured agonising frustration all around I still advocate separate education for girls and boys. I don't see the so-called 'freedom' of today as being more enjoyable for kids than the nervous and agonising times we experienced, no matter how hard today's kids like to pretend otherwise. Puberty is just a tricky time for kids. I don't subscribe either to the belief that teenagers should be 'given their way' and indulged with money or amenities and cars. Let them be reminded at all times that it's an adult world, that adults pay the bills and therefore have the right to make the rules. One fine day teenage kids will grow into adults, at which point life is wonderful again. If they don't like that, parents, beat them over the head with your Doctor Spock book.

The advent of peace didn't make all that much difference in Melbourne. If anything, times were duller. The most obvious single thing was the sallow, yellow complexion of the thousands of atabrin-dosed veterans of the New Guinea campaign. Well into 1946 there were still huge numbers of people still in uniform. The euphoria of war was gone, however, and it seemed difficult for people to settle into the unknown reality of what was termed 'the post-war reconstruction' period. Food, clothing and petrol were still rationed, and, if anything commodities seemed in shorter supply. On the question of things being 'shorter' ,a notable phenomenon of the period was the 'Dedman suit' introduced by the Minister of Post-War Reconstruction, J J Dedman. The aim was to save material by cutting cloth to a minimum, so the trousers were stove pipes, the coats were single-breasted and so short in length my dad referred to his as his 'Dead Man bum freezer' suit. A lot of soldiers were issued with Dedman suits as they were 'demobbed' ('de-mobilised' was the official Army term) but most elected not to wear them.

As if the war hadn't cost enough there was the huge expense of its aftermath, and the gradual assessment of the social and psychological effects. We were appalled at the photographs of the men who had been prisoners-of-war of the Japanese, emaciated skeletons with sunken eyes, who looked even more incongruous when they gave unexpected 'thumbs-up' signs to the camera. They looked like living replicas of the millions of dead Jews sacrificed to Hitler's madness: the horrors of Auschwitz, Belsen and Dachau were being constantly presented on the newsreels, and we applauded the announcement that the Nuremberg Trials would bring the Nazi leaders to justice.

Even some of the physically-fit men who returned from the war were having problems re-adjusting, and there were many reports of blokes finding it easier to get on the grog rather than re-settle, for the glamor and the perks of war which the uniform bestows were gone. A lot of our troops were frustrated by still being posted overseas in New Guinea and Indonesia to help restore control, and repatriate 250,000 Japanese still in those regions at the end of the war. The indigenous people of Indonesia took the declaration of peace as their signal to start to rebel against the Dutch, who had been cruel colonisers, and Australian troops played an important part in calming things down, while acknowledging the inevitability of eventual independence, 'Merdeka', for Indonesia, as the country was already being called.

Bob and Rita's Frank joined thousands of others who volunteered for the BCOF (British Commonwealth Occupationary Force) sent to Japan to administer the terms of the Japanese surrender and disarmament. Thousands of ex-servicemen enrolled for university courses and trade training, and there was a sudden boom in housing as War Service Loans enabled thousands of newly-married returned personnel to take on the serious business of resettling into civilian life. There were many more motor cars than pre-war, and every farm seemed to have a 'lend-lease' truck.

During the 1945–46 Christmas holidays I went to stay with a family named Houlihan at Nar Nar Goon, about 40 miles from Melbourne, on the edge of the rich Gippsland country where my grandfather Peter Brennan settled in the 1880s. The scheme was promoted by the National Catholic Rural Movement, which Bob Santamaria, an old North boy, had started, prompted by Dr Mannix, to demonstrate the value of a society based on sound peasant values, where the people would thrive on hard meaningful work and the Church would remain where it should be, in charge. Grace had answered an advertisement in the *Advocate*, the newspaper of the Melbourne Catholic Archdiocese for 'working holidays for Catholic boys' and away I went. There was no mention of payment. It was generally agreed that boys would have a valuable experience and, in return for board and lodging, do some work on the farm.

The Houlihans had a dairy farm, and there was plenty of solid work to do there at that busy time of the year. It was a small, but very productive farm. They had stud Jersey cattle, as well as some other breeds, and Mr (Tom) Houlihan gave me a few books about cattle to read. I literally devoUred these, to the point where I have a surprisingly good knowledge of cattle to this day. As well as helping to milk the cows, and having my first experience of milking machines, I was able to help with the harvesting, and I learnt to drive four draught horses. It was a thrill when Mr Houlihan said:

'You have exceptionally good hands for driving the team.' I came to love driving the horses more than any other task on the farm. Bess, Baldy, Punch and Blossom. What wonderfully strong, good-tempered animals they were, especially when they strained to give that extra effort after you called, 'Stand up! Up there, Baldy,' to the supreme lead-horse. The hot, sweaty smell of them will live with me forever. It was fascinating to be on the seed-drill, or the haycart driving the horses, watching their responses to the various commands, looking on in awe when they either farted or had one of those rich, steamy oats-enhanced shits that only a healthy draught horse can achieve.

Tom Houlihan was very proud of the fact that he was an old-fashioned farmer. He was much older than Mrs Houlihan, and had been a bachelor for many years before winning the hand of the local publican's daughter. They had three young boys, Michael, Tom and Paul, who were nice kids. Old Tom said to me one day:

'There'll never be a tractor on this farm while I'm alive. They simply pack the earth too much.' I must say I applauded his decision to keep the draught horses, which have been so faithful in the farming life of Australia. They also had a good old riding hack, Peter, and I practised horse-riding whenever I got the chance, although I never acquired the skill I would have liked.

An interesting thing happened one night at the Houlihans. Mrs Houlihan said,

'Ted, I'm taking you to visit some friends tonight,' and she took me to a neighbour's farm for a few hours. On the way back to their own farm she said 'I don't want to be too mysterious, but there's a new Catholic secret society being formed to fight the Communists, and they had a meeting at our place tonight.' Their own three little boys had been put to bed, and apparently about forty Catholic men met there that night. I learned later that it was the Knights of the Southern Cross, which came to be regarded as the Catholic Masonic Lodge, replete with all sorts of secret signs and passwords, and the mumbo-jumbo which goes with such cloak-and-dagger operations.

It was the start of the formation of The Groups, who sought to control the trade unions, and it led to the foundation of the Democratic Labour Party, the split with the Australian Labor Party in 1954, and the domination of Australian politics by Bob Menzies and the conservatives for over twenty years. While the ALP reeled in disarray the DLP, particularly in Victoria, wielded considerable political clout, and Dr Mannix and Bob Santamaria had immense influence over the political thinking of people like my Dad, who became a convinced DLP voter. State Aid for Catholic schools was all of a sudden easily achieved as one of the trade-offs for the preference votes of the DLP.

Pat and Terry Toone were married in January 1945 and Pat went to live in Brisbane, for Terry was up north with the army. Then in January 1946 she returned to show off her new baby, Michael, the first of many grandchildren for Grace and Joe. We were all thrilled with the fact that, when Paddy returned to Brisbane, she was the first of our family to fly, on an Australian National Airlines (ANA) DC3 aeroplane. I was jealous.

I passed my Proficiency exams easily enough in 1945 and was promoted in 1946 to Intermediate, where I would be taught by my cousin, Brother Des Kilmartin. We shared the same great-grandfather on the Brennan side. Des was a quiet ascetic chap, who seemed unsuited to teaching unco-operative teenage boys. I am sure he would have been more at home on some immense research project which would have challenged his obvious intellect. I am certainly sorry that I gave him such a hard time, and I guess the turbulence of puberty must have had something to do with my behavior. I became sullen and obtuse, as well as youngest in the class, again, and less mature than the others. In a moment of exasperation one day Des said, almost imploringly, to the rest of the class,

'I'm sorry, boys, but this chap thinks that because he's related to me he can get away with murder.' It was quite humiliating for me, for my antics backfired when the scorn of my classmates was directed at me following his remarks. I remember 1946 as a dismal, frustrating year. Puberty was frustrating. Peace was boring.

I joined the Cadets, but the uniform didn't have the same allure any more. It was interesting, however, to see the transformation that occurred in a few of the senior boys when promoted within the cadet corps, and it provided me with an insight into how the power game affects various people. Pimply-faced monsters suddenly had three stripes on their arm or a 'pip' on their shoulder to cover up their inferiority and convince them they had class. One of the brothers, Brother Rapp, was made an honorary Lieutenant, and didn't he think he looked good in his officer's uniform!

The army drill and marching came easily enough, for I was still in the Coburg Central Band. I didn't mind the trips to the rifle range, and proved to be a fairly good shot with a .303 Lee Enfield.

But my main area of fascination was that our platoon leader, a very intelligent, quiet bloke named Ron Crane, who was one class ahead of me in Leaving, was the only person in my entire time at the Brothers to get the very best out of me. He did it by appealing to our better nature: it was as simple as that. He said to us one day,

'OK fellers, give me the best you've got, and I'll stick by you at all times. We'll show them who's the best platoon in the whole school.' As I marched proudly behind Sergeant Crane on parade I felt like shouting,

'Hey, Nashy, Slick, Jerry, Cousin Des, here's a bloke who knows how to handle me. We could all have had it easier, couldn't we?' I wonder what happened to Ron Crane? I'll bet he was successful in life.

Perhaps the highlight of 1946 was seeing the greatest bowler the game of cricket has ever known. The Sheffield Shield competition resumed, and the Victorian team used Princes Park, Carlton, as its headquarters. (The MCG was being restored after occupancy by the services.) When Victoria played New South Wales I was there at opening time on the first day. I had seen the great Bill (Tiger) O'Reilly in 1937 as a five-year-old, so did not recall much detail. I simply remembered my father's opinion, which I later incorporated into my song 'The Tiger and The Don'

My Dad said, 'Feast your eyes upon
The Tiger and The Don,
For you'll never see a pair like them again,
Don's the greatest bat of all
And when The Tiger's got the ball,

He puts the fear of God in all those Englishmen.'

Aged fourteen and passionately hungry for cricket, I sat
enthralled, right behind O'Reilly's arm. He thundered
in, bowling spinners at a cracking medium pace, but
these were missiles so unpredictable I marvelled that
he didn't get a wicket with every ball. He seemed
unplayable.

> They told me of the Tiger's skill
> And why there was no doubt,
> Batsmen from around the world
> Could never work him out,
> Arms like pistons, charges in, murder in his eye,
> I watched The Tiger's fearsome style,
> And I understood just why.
>
> He was a giant of a man
> Who bowled at medium pace
> But spinners, mate, that went all ways
> Or fizzed up at your face.
> A wrong'un that you'd never pick
> And, if that's not enough
> The type of killer instinct
> That would call the devil's bluff.

The Victorian team had some good players of spin bowling in Percy Beames, Ron Todd, Ken (father of Keith)
Stackpole and Des Fothergill, and they did better than
most would against The Tiger, but he took six wickets
in each innings nonetheless. Incidentally, in those days,
when such things were a regular occurrence, the four
Victorians mentioned also played League (VFL) football
with great distinction. Nowadays it's unthinkable to
have two sporting careers. It was a great match, memorable for one other thing, the debut of a young yellow-
skinned fast bowler, not long back from New Guinea,
and still taking atabrin to prevent malaria attacks. His

name was Ray Lindwall, and even then I knew he was
going to be a champion.

I had pinched a handful of my dad's Havelock Ready
Rubbed tobacco, and bought a packet of cigarette papers.
As I sat on the outer fence, behind the bowler, I felt myself
ever so sophisticated as I expertly rolled a few cigarettes
and then coughed, spluttered and felt squeamish as I
convinced myself this was the 'manly' thing to be doing.
My taste in cigarettes was about to be enhanced (or so I
thought). Jack Gleeson was back from the war, and he
had brought home from New Guinea a suitcase full of
American cigarettes. Jack's courting of my sister Peg was
now fairly serious, and he used to slip me a shilling as
an incentive to go out, and leave the two young lovers to
do a bit of 'canoodling', as kissing and cuddling was called
then. Jack's step-brother George Coyne was in the same
class as me at 'North' and George and I used to go to the
cricket or footy at weekends, but not before helping ourselves to a packet of Chesterfield's or Camels or Lucky
Strikes from Jack's case. Weren't we flash, sitting up in
the grandstand, doing the drawback, blowing smoke
rings? Slick's predictions were being fulfilled.

I blundered through the Intermediate school year,
concentrating more on being unco-operative for Cousin
Des than on school work, and bothered all the time by
the constant agitation of my turbulent dick. I passed all
the exams in unspectacular fashion. At age fourteen I had
had enough of school, and I put it to my parents that I
should leave, and go to work. To my surprise they did not
demur.

'It's your life, Teddy' said Grace.

I think my parents could realise I might be better off
working for a living, instead of getting more and more
bored by school, for I was now a big strong bloke, and
they saw some sense in not 'wasting' more of their money
on unproductive schooling. I went to Houlihan's farm over

the Christmas holidays and again enjoyed working on the harvest and milking the cows. Tom Houlihan was a good teacher, and I began to think that the best life for me might be somewhere in the outdoors. The country? The bush? Go to sea?

It would be all short term, of course, because one day I was going to surprise them all and become a priest. Perhaps in about four years.

15
Itchy Feet

I had heard a great deal about my cousin Bill Brennan, from Western Australia, and he made a colossal impression on me when I met him in 1946. Bill left home at age fifteen. During the war, in the Merchant Navy, he travelled all over the world, and came under heavier fire than the vast majority of people in the three armed services. Among other things he participated in the Allied landing at Anzio, in Italy, as a crew member of the British merchant ship *Fort Meductic*. A few weeks later, still on the *Fort Meductic*, they were bombed and strafed by enemy fighters near Augusta in Sicily. Their ship caught fire when petrol exploded and Bill was badly burnt on the legs. He spent several months in hospital, but came out pretty fit. He served right through the war and then returned home to Western Australia. He was only twenty when the war finished.

Bill and his brother Frank (the much emulated Frunner) brought their father, Grace's brother Michael Brennan, for a visit to their relations in the 'eastern states' as they put it. Bill and Frank had both put in a stint at Yampi Sound, on an iron-ore mine in the far north-west of Western Australia, and came to Melbourne

223

loaded with money. Bill had nicely augmented his considerable earnings at Yampi by winning a huge treble on the
racehorses, including the 1946 Melbourne Cup winner,
Russia. He won several thousand pounds. The two brothers were very generous with their money, and both wore
clothes conservative in taste, but of the very best quality.
Bill was into suits, and obviously had quite a few of these
which he had acquired in various parts of the world.
Frank was a more casual dresser, but I particularly liked
what I subsequently called 'WA trousers'. They were
tailor-made, navy blue serge, no side pockets, so they
fitted snugly round the hips.The legs flared gently into
bell-bottoms, about a 22 inch circumference. There was a
half-belt made from the same material, with a plain silver
buckle. I would be into these as soon as I could afford
tailor-made trousers, I promised myself.

Bill and Frank were totally self-assured and meticulously groomed, and this made a huge impression on me.
I continued to study and copy Frunner's mannerisms,
even more now that I was older and able to observe better
that he was an absolute charmer, without ever seeming
to try. Bill and Frank were good role-models for a teenage
boy who had just left school. I was no longer the youngest
in the class, a show-off kid. I was a young man, bigger
and stronger than average. In those days having an
Intermediate Certificate at age fourteen was also better-
than-average academic qualification. I was able to pick
and choose from many different jobs available to such a
young man.

Having spent all those years at sea during the war,
Bill Brennan was very mature. I listened avidly to him
and Frunner as they discussed life in general with my
parents and their dad and Uncle Bob. I have never met
anybody better organised than Bill Brennan, and if life
seems to happen easily for him it's only because he has

thought things through. I'll never forget that he said, in 1946:

'I'm going to work hard until I'm about 40. Then I'll take things easy, travel around Australia a bit, until I'm about 60. I don't need to travel overseas, I've done that. But at 60 I reckon I'll be ready to settle down, perhaps even take a steady quiet job somewhere.' I've always felt that this was good sense, especially the post-sixty idea of taking up a new career, for that is often when people, having sown their wild oats and raised their families, are best suited for productive work. The sooner they open careers like teaching to older, experienced people the better. Have retirement between forty and sixty, when people are physically fit enough to travel and do enjoyable things. Let them take their families with them. Bill's philosophy seemed very sound to me and still does. He basically followed his planned course and today, with his wife Liz, he leads a very relaxed life playing lots of golf, lowering the odd frosty schooner of beer, and retaining the physical fitness necessary to enjoy life to the full. Fortunately he worked sufficiently hard pre-fourty not to have to worry about the post-sixty job, but he did take the odd stint on a ship to keep his hand in and keep his union membership current.

Frunner was well-organised too, in some respects, but had nothing like the long-term perspective of Bill. Frunner was generous to the point of embarrassment. If you said 'That's a flash shirt,' he'd have it off and give it to you. He lived absolutely from day to day, but like Bill, was extremely fit and insisted that health was the only thing that mattered. Money was just something you could always obtain by a sufficient amount of work, but you did not get too carried away about it.

Having been discharged from the air force Frunner had to find a job. In his brief working career before the war he had been a very good modeller of things like the 'three plaster ducks' everybody subsequently had on the wall and Bullamakanka immortalised in song. But the war had given him itchy feet and he wanted a bit more excitement from life. He decided to follow his younger brother Bill, and go to sea. Bill planned to work on ships plying the Australian coast. He'd had enough of international travel for a while. As an experienced seaman Bill simply joined the Seamen's Union and a job was secure. But the only way anybody else could get into the Seamen's Union was to have experience at sea. It was what we would call a Catch 22 situation today. So Bill and Frank got some of Bill's international discharge papers, changed the name from William Joseph Brennan to John Francis Brennan, poured oil on the papers, jumped on them to make them look warworn, and thus Frunner joined the union and the two of them began to work on the coastal ships.

Like Frunner, Bill Brennan had two tattoos. Their visit to Melbourne was sufficient incentive for me to have my own two tattoos, a small sailing ship on my left arm, and a Popeye-style anchor on my right arm. I felt that if I had them done then I would look like an old hand when I was ready to take up my maritime career. I had made that latter decision when Frunner said to me, as casually as he did all things:

'Sing out when you're ready, Ted.' (You beauty! He called me Ted!) 'I'll take you round the world.' Why not? It seemed like a great idea to me and Frunner made life look so simple.

'If you want to do something, just do it,' he said. It was agreed. In a couple of years he'd take me under his wing. In the meantime I could do anything at all really. It didn't matter what. Dozens of choices were available.

But hang on, Ted, you're going to be a priest. It was decision time. I was a totally convinced Catholic, nicely enmeshed in a net woven from the variegated strands of

security and guilt. I knew that if you obey the rules and
don't ask too many questions the Church will sort out
your life for you and you'll finish up with the only reward
that really matters, eternal life in the sight of God, in
Heaven. The alternative involved eternity also, the never-
ending physical pain of Hell. The worst feature of Hell
was not going to be the pain, but the loss of the sight of
God. Remember the simple old man sitting in the church,
Ted.

'I look at Him and He looks at me.'

Ted, if you're going to get to Heaven you must take
the course God wants you to follow. If you have a vocation
to be a priest and don't accept that calling it won't be the
stony-broke motherless end of things, but, by jingo, you
might forgo the first-class, one-way ticket in the lounge
seats and the dining car of the train to Heaven. What are
you going to do? Fritter your life away shovelling coal on
some ship (Frunner was a very menial stoker) or put on
the creams and play tennis like Justin McCarthy? Risk
being just another face in the crowd or deliver those fiery
Redemptorist sermons? Can't you hear yourself? 'What if
a truck knocked you over as you walked from this Church
this very day? Would you be at peace with your God?'
Can't you see yourself administering the Last Sacraments
to grateful old ladies on their deathbeds, smoothing their
troubled brows as you lever them straight into the arms
of Jesus? And how about that Yankee bloke, Father Fulton
Sheen. What a charmer! He's packing them in in thousands as he gives his eloquent sermons about the
Communist threat. There's no choice. Really.

When in doubt cats wash and Catholics pray. A novena
Ted, that's what St Aloysius Gonzaga would recommend.
As its name implies a novena involves nine consecutive
days of prayer and concentration.

I wasn't just a Sundays-only Catholic. Since altar boy
days I had regularly attended Mass on weekdays and

popped in 'for a visit' when passing any Catholic Church, for they were always open to the faithful. I always felt that a necessary part of going to Mass was to fast and abstain from food and drink, as required, and then receive Holy Communion, the Body of Christ, Corpus Christi. I had never voiced my private concern that the priest celebrating Mass not only consumed the Body of Christ in the form of the Host (the wafer), but also drank the Blood of Christ in the form of the consecrated wine, as happened at The Last Supper. Was the priest more privileged, I wondered? The general public, the 'faithful' as they were called, were simply given the Host — and a smaller one than the priest had! I tried to reassure myself with the knowledge, no, the belief, that the entire Body of Christ was incorporated in the tiniest crumb of the ciborium full of consecrated Hosts distributed by the priest at the Communion rails. That was why, if the priest dropped a Host he, and only he, with his consecrated hands, was allowed to touch the Mystical Body, pick it up from the floor and consume it himself. It seemed a bit unhygienic to me, but then consuming the Body of Christ could hardly be unhygienic, could it? After all, God created the germs so He can also dispel them, can't He? Something of an answer to my questions about privileged priests and the Blood of Christ were the unhygienic practices of Anglicans and others for whom (we smug Catholics thought) Communion merely incorporated a piece of yesterday's Tip Top loaf and a swig of wine with everybody sharing the germs as they drank from the one chalice. And *their* clergy didn't even have the Apostolic power of Transubstantiation! Come on, Ted, that's a bit uncharitable. Come on! Faith, Hope and Charity, and the greatest of these is Charity. Well, OK. Leave it that that's all right for the Protestants, they only have small congregations. You'd need a mighty big chalice and a lot of wine to cater for all those thirsty Micks.

And how about Joey Walker, the Downs Syndrome boy, self-appointed dog evictor of St Paul's, who used to send us into paroxysms of mirth as he dived among the kneeling congregation to capture a stray dog? Joe used to front up for Communion several times, because everybody smiled at him. He impressed all and sundry by pulling on his white gloves as he walked to the Communion rails. How would Joe fare if we had Anglican-style Communion? Come to think of it, how would God judge Joe on the Last Day? Very kindly, we felt, but we weren't sure.

All of these unanswered questions were just part of being a convinced Catholic. There are many things you can't, couldn't, and need not understand, we were told. Don't worry about these things. Just have Faith. It was a bit like an encounter I had with Slick during a Maths lesson one day. He said, pounding away at the blackboard as he wrote the figures, 'The Queensland boys would see this in a flash. If you want (thump, thump) to divide one fraction by another (thump, thump) you simply invert one fraction and multiply. There you are, (thump, thump) three-quarters divided by one-sixteenth. Turn the one sixteenth over, to become sixteen over one. Cancel out (thump, thump). Four into sixteen equals four. Three times four equals twelve. Three-quarters divided by one-sixteenth equals twelve. *Quod erat demonstrandum*. Got that, have you Wilson? I thought not!'

I put my hand up.

'What do you want, Egan?'

'I want to know why, Sir.'

I thought he'd explode. His face went even 'more purple.

'What do you mean, son, why? You don't ask why! You do what I tell you and you'll get 100 per cent in your exams. That's why, son!' Being a Catholic was a bit like that. Pass the exams. You don't need to know why. Only that it's good for you.

For nine days I went to Mass and received Holy Communion at St Paul's. I also attended St Francis' Church in Lonsdale Street, Melbourne, regularly, where they had Perpetual Adoration of the Blessed Sacrament, and I prayed for guidance on the question of whether I had a vocation or not. At the end of the novena I decided I did not have a true vocation, but that I had simply been impressed by the power and glamor bestowed by the uniform, 'the cloth' which I had been taught to respect so much. Well, I thought, that's that. What else does life have planned for me? In a couple of years I'll be going to sea. By that time Frunner will have discharge papers of his own to forge from John Francis Brennan to Edward Joseph Egan. Shouldn't be too difficult. Just drift for a bit, Ted. You've had a fairly strenuous school life. Relax.

I took a job at the Moreland Timber Company, in Moreland Road, Brunswick. I was the junior clerk, paid two guineas a week, a fairly good wage. It gave me enough to buy some clothes and start smoking in earnest, as well as paying my board. I put my name down for a tobacco ration from a shop in Moreland Road and considered myself quite an adult, as I smoked openly, an expert roller of cigarettes and just about the best blower of smoke rings. The senior clerk, a bloke named Graham Aplin, was quite miffed because I could work out 'super feet' in my head and tot up columns of figures quicker in my head than he could achieve on his adding machine. So he found lots of shitty jobs for me to do, didn't he? Didn't worry me much because I had my dreams to dream. London. New York. Bill Brennan always said Rio de Janiero was the finest harbor in the world. Why not Rio? I remembered one of the Bel Canto choir's songs:

Go rolling down to Rio
Roll down, roll down to Rio

I'd like to roll to Rio
One day before I die

Look out Carmen Miranda. *Ole!* What's that Graham?
Sixteen twelve-foot lengths of four by two? That's 128
super feet. Of course I'm sure.

I had my tattoos done at Dick Reynolds (no connection
with the famous footballer of the same name) Tattoo shop
in Flinders Street, Melbourne. They cost seven shillings
and sixpence each, total fifteen shillings. It hurt a bit
getting them done, but I was fascinated to watch as he
shaved my arms and then went to work with the needle,
freehand, to create the tattoos. It was like watching a
thread of cotton being placed under your skin. Dick said
to me, 'How old are you, Snow?'

'Eighteen,' I replied, not very convincingly.

'Your old lady will have something to say about this,'
he ventured. I remembered Frank Brennan's tactic.

'She's dead,' I told him. It was only a little lie, I felt.

'That's sad,' said Dick, as he drew in the last seagull
at the side of the sailing ship and then added his trade-
mark (as I discovered in subsequent years as I met dozens
of blokes with the same tattoo) which was a dot under
the seagull.

'It's about to shit on Lord Nelson's head,' he explained.
He then stuck two brown paper patches over the tattoos
to soak up the droplets of blood mingled with the blue
veins of ink on my shaven arms.

'There y'are, mate. Best fifteen bob you'll ever spend.
The coppers will have you spotted for ever.'

He was right. Not so much about the value. Or the
cops. About Grace. And not that she was dead, either. She
was very much alive, and swinging. It was the last time
she ordered me into the washhouse.

'You're not too big for me yet, Teddy,' she thundered
as she held me with one hand and whacked me around

the legs with a strap. It was all a bit demeaning for a young man with two tattoos, but as she only seemed half-serious about it we both went through the motions of the punishment to fit the crime. Thereafter she was as fascinated as I at the way the tattoos healed. The scab fell away and I was left 'marked for life, no better than an earmarked bullock', as Grace put it. They'll look great in a couple of years time, I thought to myself. The other young blokes will have new tattoos. I'll look like an old hand.

Then Grace and Pop took a big and strange decision. Peg and Jack had recently married and Grace and Pop decided to sell them Number 4 Higinbotham Street. Grace and Pop would move to work for the Christian Brothers at Victoria Parade College, East Melbourne, Grace to work as cook for the Brothers and Pop to act as caretaker and cleaner. Sal took a job there there also, as Grace's offsider. Tim enrolled at 'Parade', as the college was called. That left me to establish a niche somewhere. I stayed with Peg and Jack until Pat and Terry moved in with them when they returned to Melbourne. Then I moved to Donald Street and stayed with Aunty Rita. My workplace at Moreland Timber Company was within walking distance.

In April 1947, as I visited Grace and Pop at the little cottage they had at Parade, I was fronted by Brother Crennan, the principal of the college.

'Your parents have been telling me about your schooling at North Melbourne. You seemed to do fairly well. I've seen your school reports. A bit lazy, but nothing that couldn't be sorted out. Why don't you come back to Parade and get your Leaving Certificate? Intermediate's not a good enough qualification for jobs like the public service, you know.' I suspect that Grace and Pop had put him up to it, concerned that I might be feeling abandoned, which I wasn't.

'But the first term's over. I'd be too far behind the

others,' I replied, hedging a bit, but suitably overawed by his daunting presence.

'You have to pass five subjects to get your Leaving Certificate,' said 'Snoz' Crennan, nicknamed thus on account of a huge nose, which was much more aquiline and formidable than that of his namesake Jimmy 'Snozzle' Durante. And Snoz was certainly no comedian. He was very used to being obeyed, explicitly, implicitly, any way you like it. 'I'll enrol you just for five subjects instead of the normal seven. It will mean you have no room for failure. A smart boy like you could get through the course in two terms, and the Leaving Certificate will be a handy piece of paper in later life.'

Although I didn't like Snoz then, or now, he was right on all counts. I was subsequently very glad I had that extra two terms at school and got the piece of paper. The job at the timber yard was fairly boring, so I gave notice and left.

Graham Aplin graciously said 'A bit more schooling won't hurt you.'

I restrained myself. 'Thanks Graham. Good luck with your calculations.' He was too dumb to realise that I was having a shot at him.

It meant that I moved into the little cottage at Parade with Grace and Pop, Sal and Tim. It was a bit crowded, but that didn't matter much. I didn't like too many of the Brothers, but I was on the spot and thus able to concentrate once more on my great love, handball, for Parade had a good court. I quickly established myself as one of the better handball players at Parade. I also played in the Parade Under 15 football team, as well as getting a few games with the First 18. Tony Ongarello, who later played for Fitzroy, was our full forward. I played fairly well, but took a savage whack in the mouth in one match as I tried to smother a kick for goal. I got a broken jaw and lost a front tooth, and endured a couple of weeks of inconvenience and pain. I was given a little denture to wear, but as soon as I could afford the dental treatment I had a bridge inserted. It didn't diminish the great love I had for Aussie Rules football, which was going to take me into exciting new experiences in the next few years, although I had no inkling of that in 1947.

They were a good mob of boys at Parade, and I fitted in well, with no 'prior convictions' to tell against me. I was bigger and better-adjusted so I didn't have to play the role of youngest and most mischievous. I managed the school work well enough to get through the exams, but I was not one of the great achievers, academically, for there were quite a few really smart kids in my class. And I was a term behind them, playing catch-up through the year.

Kurt Schuster, one of the Vienna Boys' Choir, was a classmate, and he was a champion fellow. I was impressed that Kurt was such a well-trained musician, even though he was only about eight when the war began and the choir members were interned in the form of becoming St Patrick's Cathedral choir. Kurt had not specifically studied music since that time, and his boy soprano voice had long since broken, but he was a good pianist and seemed to know just everything about music in general. Kurt was a good Aussie Rules footballer and played for Parade's First 18. One day he took a heavy knock on the field and was quite concussed. He ran to me. 'Ted, who's vinning?'

'We are mate, but only just,' I replied.

'Are ve all out on the field?' he queried, his eyes looking north and south at the one time as they rolled in their sockets.

'Yes Kurt, ve are all on the field, including you,' I told him.

'*Vielen dank*,' was his response as he shook his head and played himself back into gear. I wonder if he recalls being best-on-ground that day.

Sal started to learn Irish dancing, and quickly became

very good at it. She also began to go out with a bloke
named Dick McKenna, who was a member of the Irish
Pipe Band. Sal and I used to go to the Irish Club dances
at Roma House, an upstairs function room in Elizabeth
Street, Melbourne, owned by the Catholic Church. I
enjoyed those nights which were a combination of traditional Irish dancing, all the established old-time dances
and the occasional quickstep and modern waltz. There
were some fiery old Irishmen there every week, and
definitely no 'God Save The King' at the end of the
evening, which was the practice at other dances. At the
Irish Club everybody stood to attention and sang:

> God save Ireland, sang the heroes
> God save Ireland say we all
> Whether on the scaffold high
> Or the battlefield we die
> Oh, what matter if for Erin dear we fall?

Eamon de Valera, the Irish President, visited Melbourne
in 1947, and some of the old Irish patriots met him. The
next Sunday night one of them appeared at Roma
House.

'Shake the hand that shook the hand of Eamon de
Valera,' he roared, and everybody had a good laugh.

De Valera visited Melbourne as part of a big Catholic
Congress, presided over by Archbishop Mannix, who was
still going strong. I used to see him regularly, as he walked
from St Patrick's Cathedral, East Melbourne, where he
had his office, to Raheen, his mansion in Kew. What a
figure he cut! Long black coat, black trousers, purple shirt
front and white clerical collar, he looked to be seven feet
tall. Just as the London bobbies wear their high helmets
to turn a 'Collingwood six-footer' into a real six-footer,
Doctor Mannix wore a silk top hat and just dominated
the scene as he strode fearlessly home, deferentially
waving to those who greeted him, and showing absolute

disdain to the odd drunk who sought to ridicule him. They don't make them like Dinky Dan any more.

At the same Congress Pop and I went to hear the American, Bishop Fulton Sheen. He was scheduled to preach at the Exhibition Building in Melbourne, and the place was jammed full on Catholic Men's Night. On to the stage he swept, and it almost made me wish I did have a vocation. He paused for dramatic effect, and then said:

'Gentlemen, I wish to speak to you about Communism.' For about an hour and a half he took us through the Communist dogma and aims, the domino theory, the threat to the Church and to civilisation itself. At the end of his eloquent sermon he said, as an organ swelled into an introductory chord right on cue:

'And now, I understand you all know a hymn called "Faith of Our Fathers".' Did we ever! Catholics are not good singers as a rule, but it seemed the dome of the Exhibition Building was pushed upward as about twenty thousand men and boys joined him as he led the singing and conducted us into deafening coherence:

Faith of our fathers, holy Faith
We will be true to Thee till death
We will be true to Thee till death.

We welcomed the resumption of Test cricket, first with a visit from Lala Armanath's Indian team, and then the Poms. Just before this the Services team, made up of our boys who had been overseas during the war, toured the major states. They were led by that delightful character of cricket, Lindsay Hassett, and we saw for the first time the player whose name was on everybody's lips, Keith Miller. When the Services team played a match at St Kilda Oval Miller hit one immense six right over the main grandstand

We were thrilled that our family friend, Bill Johnston, was selected to play for Australia, and we smacked our lips in anticipation as we heard the results of the Tests in Brisbane and Sydney, for we knew that Pop, Tim and I would be at the Melbourne Test. The mighty Bradman was back in full array, and Australia was about to develop into the greatest team that has ever played Test Cricket. We beat the Poms easily, but one had to feel sorry for them, for their ranks of cricketers must have been savagely depleted by the war. But what a thrill to be old enough to appreciate players of the talent of Bradman, Morris, Barnes, Brown, Lindwall, Loxton, Miller, Tallon, McCool, Toshack and Johnston on our side, and Hammond, Washbrook, Hutton, Edrich, Bedser, Voce and Wright for the Poms. In the Melbourne Test Lindwall and Tallon, a bowler and a wicketkeeper, smashed the Poms all over the field in a mighty batting partnership with Lindwall hitting 100 and Tallon 92. In his short career Don Tallon definitely, in my opinion, established himself as the greatest-ever wicketkeeper. But what bowlers he kept to!

We saw a bit of Bill and Frunner through 1947, as they were working on the coastal ships. Frunner got me all excited when he said one day, 'There's an old English coal-burner, the *Mahia*, being refitted for return to England in about six months. I'll get on the crew and take you with me.'

To my surprise Grace did not object. She liked Frunner and felt it would be a good adventure for me. It was hard to concentrate on school work, and each weekend I would go to Victoria Dock to see the old *Mahia*, a derelict ship if ever there was one. But what the hell, it was going to start my life of adventure.

To my dismay I switched on the wireless one morning in August 1947 and heard the announcement:

'The British freighter *Mahia* was destroyed in a huge

fire this morning at Victoria Dock. Ten workmen have
been killed in the explosion which started the fire.

I went to the dock and saw the ruined hulk, and that
put paid to my first big prospect of world travel. Never
mind, I thought. Something else will turn up.

What had pleased me was Grace's encouragement. Pop
didn't mind, for he was definitely a peace-at-all-costs man,
and deferred to Grace in most things. I think they both
envied me my youth and the prospect of doing things not
achievable for them when young. So I bided my time: 'I'll
knock this school business over and away I'll go. Somewhere.'

So I concentrated on handball, winning the Victorian
Under 16 Championship. To a much lesser extent I
slogged away at the school work and eventually passed
the Leaving Certificate exam. It was a valuable qualification, giving automatic access to the Commonwealth and
State Public Services. Typically the Christian Brothers
encouraged us to sit for entrance exams for numerous
other areas of employment. I passed all of these, so at the
end of the year began to contemplate a bewildering array
of opportunities for employment. Kids who have just
passed their HSC exams today will probably be interested
to know that at the end of 1947 with an equivalent
qualification I had the choice of working for any branch
of the Commonwealth or State Public Service, the Commonwealth Bank, the ES&A (later ANZ) Bank and the
State Savings Bank of Victoria (later called the State
Bank of Victoria and destined for a sticky end). I merely
had to indicate a preference and I could start work
anywhere.

Because I had no immediate prospect in the adventure
stakes I took a job as a junior clerk with the State Savings
Bank. Theirs was the highest pay rate. It was easy enough
work. I was posted to the Western Branch, on the corner

of Spencer and Collins Streets, working in the School Bank section. In those days most State schools had bank agencies and kids would put sixpence or a shilling a week into their accounts. It probably involved more clerical work than it was worth in banking terms, but the bank felt it would ensure kids stayed with the bank as adults.

At lunch time each day I walked to the wharves at Station Pier and Victoria Dock and looked longingly at the ships. I had no great interest in the ships themselves, in the way that some people just love ships and trains, but they represented adventure and travel, getting off on my own to lead my own life. I didn't like living at the college at all, particularly once I left school, for I was by this time fairly disenchanted with the Christian Brothers as an organisation. I felt that a few of them were absolute charlatans. No names, no packdrill.

The elocution teacher at Parade was Miss Kitty O'Shea. As her name suggests she was Irish, a very cultured lady, with that delightful lilt to her voice all educated Celts achieve when they show how English should be spoken. One day I returned to Parade after work at the bank. There was Grace, all beaming and bright-eyed.

'If you want to travel, Miss O'Shea says she can get you a job working in Queensland. She has some friends who have a racehorse stud. Are you interested?' Was I ever!

With the greatest of ease it was arranged that I would leave the bank and go to Queensland. Miss O'Shea gave it to me with absolute Irish simplicity.

'Go to Queensland by train. Just send a telegram to Andy Maguire, Kialla Stud, Greenmount, when you're ready. Greenmount is between Warwick and Toowoomba. Andy will be there to meet you.'

16

It's Mighty up in Queensland, eh?

'But who in the hell are you? What's it all about?'

Not a very good start. Dithery old Kitty O'Shea had forgotten to let her dear friend Andy Maguire know about me, even of my existence. I had, as advised by her, booked my train fare, one way to Queensland. I had sent a wire to Mr Maguire telling him my date of arrival.

Here he was, meeting me at Greenmount Railway Station as Kitty promised, but looking ominously likely to send me packing. In fact, if the train had not steamed out of the station to continue its tedious journey to Toowoomba before he had accosted me, I feel certain he would have insisted I stay on board.

I drew in a deep breath.

'Well, my name's Ted Egan, and Miss Kitty O'Shea . . . ' I looked for some flicker of recognition, but he did not even nod at mention of her name. He pursed his lips even tighter. 'Miss Kitty O'Shea said I could get a job with you. All I had to do was come up here, and you'd meet me.'

'And I have met you,' he responded, 'but what can you do? Why would I want to give you a job?'

'I don't know,' was my brilliant reply. Slick would have laughed his head off. The rules of dialogue, Egan. Always be clear, concise and courteous. I was feeling pretty miserable, and it must have shown, although he remained ungracious.

'Well, it looks as though I'm stuck with you, so I'll have to sort something out. Hop in the car.' He had a very flash Chevrolet sedan, number plate Q 444268, (although why the number stuck in my memory forever I'll never understand), certainly the best motor car I'd ever been in. I sat in the front seat alongside him and we drove the miles from the little railway town on the Darling Downs to his thoroughbred horse stud, Kialla.

Despite my forlorn feelings I could not help but admire the lovely, rolling downs country, sparkling green after the early winter rains. There were some rocky timbered hills which framed the lush blacksoil plains, and all the stock were rolling fat. Not a word passed between us. First one to talk loses, I guess we were both thinking. I sneaked a couple of curious glances at the forbidding Mr Maguire, whose battered profile suggested he might have stuck his head into a chaff cutter at some stage. His thick glasses kept sliding down the ridges of the most misshapen nose I had ever seen. His impaired vision probably contributed to his totally inept car driving. I was relieved when he zig-zagged to a halt inches from the front gate. I sprang from the car to open the gate, anxious to do anything which might impress my new master.

Mr Maguire took me to the men's quarters, and handed me over with a resigned sigh to an elderly man with the most cherubic Dickensian face. I was instantly relieved, for I could see kindness written all over him. After Mr Maguire had mumbled something about me which obviously conveyed the message that I was yet another burden in a troubled life, he drove off to his own house, a palatial sprawling white mansion, perched above manicured lawns, facing south to a beautiful panorama of some of the best grazing and farming country in Australia.

'I'm a Ted, too,' said the kind man. 'Ted van Dreick, and believe it or not, I'm the cowboy. Not the American style, but the Queensland style of cowboy. I milk the cows and do the gardening.' He showed me into a frugally furnished little room, one of five which shared a common verandah. The men's quarters was a neat little galvanised-iron building, consisting of the five bedrooms plus a laundry. In my room there was a single army bed, a chair, and a kerosene lamp.

'Take no notice of the boss,' advised Ted. 'As long as the stud runs smoothly he doesn't bother us too much. You'll be well-advised to keep right out of his way until he gets used to you. We'll sort out a place for you. I'll talk to Bert. He's the farmer, and a jolly good one too. He'll find plenty for you to do. And it won't be long and all the new foals will come along. They're all supposed to be born on the second of August, you see.' I didn't see. He began to explain. I was starting to relax, and Ted was an easy talker.

'All horses have their birthday on the first of August each year, so if a foal is born on the thirty-first of July it turns one the next day, and that's no good in the racing game, is it?'

I nodded. I unpacked my suitcase, which he told me was called a 'port'. 'It's short for portmanteau. You'll find a lot of things different in Queensland.'

I told him briefly of Slick, and watched his reaction when I asked, tongue-in-cheek, whether people, but especially boys, were in fact smarter in Queensland, as Slick had suggested.

'You'll have to wait and find out, won't you?' said crafty old Ted to disingenuous young Ted.

He filled me in on Andy Maguire, and the Kialla stud. Andy had been featherweight boxing champion of Australia. He must have been a better pug than his battered face suggested. He had saved most of his pugilistic earnings and used the money to finance a brief but spectacular career as a bookmaker. Marrying into a family with a good social profile in Brisbane, he then advanced his own status by purchasing Kialla.

Although he had no prior knowledge of the racing game other than through bookmaking, he began to read and learn a lot about bloodlines. Whether by good luck or acquired expertise he bought a Gainsborough stallion from England, lightly-raced, but a good prospect at stud. Its name was Emborough. Ted said that Emborough was definitely a one-man horse, and Andy Maguire was the man. He'd owned the big chestnut stallion for ten years, and came to love him more and more, particularly after Emborough sired one of the greatest-ever Australian racehorses, Bernborough, from the unknown mare Bern Maid. Being very well-informed about the racing game I knew the detail of the career of the mighty 'Bernie', whose last-to-first wins had electrified Australia for the two years he raced in the capital cities before being snapped up by the Americans for stud duties in the United States. I thought Kialla was going to be an interesting place. And it was.

Ted van Dreick and I had our meals with the farmer, Bert Tavender, his wife, and their twelve-year-old daughter, June. The Tavenders were from Somerset, England, originally, and were lovely people. Ted was right. Bert was an excellent farmer, and I was assigned to him until the foals were born. Bert and Ted negotiated with Mr Maguire a wage of two pounds a week plus keep for me . Bert taught me more in a short period than anyone else in my life, before or since. He was methodical and painstaking without ever being boring. I helped him with yardbuilding, and ever since I have looked askance at other stockyards. Bert's yards were built to absolute precision,

and to last a hundred years. For the first time in my life
I was learning to use tools. He showed me how to use an
axe and an adze and how to mortice posts, snugly fit the
adzed rails, and then secure the join with a neat Cobb &
Co twitched wire.

'A good Cobb & Co twitch is stronger than nails or
bolts, especially when you use bush timber' he reckoned.

We had two International tractors, which started on
petrol, and then you switched over to power kerosene.
Bert taught me to plough and to harrow, and to work the
seed drill. I was an enthusiastic learner. We had to
prepare and sow all the available paddocks on the 1500-
acre stud, for Kialla grew all its own grain — wheat, oats,
barley and maize, as well as quick winter crops like millet
for green feed, and lucerne which was constantly cut and
stacked in the hay shed.

In addition to all the thoroughbred horses there were
a few cattle and sheep. The sheep were all used as 'killers'.
I used to ride out and muster these, and then help Bert
as he slaughtered them. Kialla was totally self-sufficient
in meat and most other things. There was something to
learn every day, and at night Ted and the Tavenders were
full of information about all sorts of things.

The new foals began to arrive in August, and I got an
idea of the complexity of stud life. While their foals were
still quite small it was desirable to 'bring the mares on'
again, to prepare them for the next foal which, ideally,
would be born on the second of August next year. To
stimulate the mares we had a beautiful little 'teaser' pony
named Jerry, a dapply-chestnut 'galloway', as I now discovered a pony of 14.2 hands was called. To remind me
of my own teenage agonies — which had not been 'put on
hold' nor 'held in abeyance' but rather, in true Christian
Brothers style, sublimated by lots of interesting hard work
— it was fascinating to watch Jerry. He would prance
around his yard, all erect, looking like a pre-incarnation

of David Boon. He'd sniff and snort and rear and fart. One day, as Ted van Dreick and I watched him from our front verandah I found myself smiling wryly as I wondered how a Jerry-style approach might have impressed Norma Boderick or the St Aloysius' girls. Not too well, I was thinking. Like a pork chop in a synagogue. Ted must have read my thoughts.

'Subtlety is what you need in this courting business, young feller. Take my advice. When you meet a nice girl stick your dick in her hand and then cry. It works every time.' And the wily old bachelor gave me an enigmatic wink.

The brood mares certainly found Jerry exciting, for they kept backing up to him and pissing everywhere. Jerry would smell their piss. He'd curl back his top lip in delight, and then nuzzle their ears and gently bite the mares along the neck and around the back legs. The mares squealed with frenzy. After a few days of this Mr Maguire would pronounce them ready for service, but not by poor Jerry. He was a bit like me, consigned to celibacy for the moment. But the stud did have a few mares which Jerry served each season to keep him in form.

Emborough or the other stallion, a beautiful black horse named Roadhouse, would do the deed with the thoroughbred mares. Roadhouse was also imported from England, retired to stud after winning the Ascot Gold Cup, one of the most famous races on the British racing calendar. He, too, was lightly raced but was as yet unproven as a sire.

While a mare was being served my thankless job was to try to hold her foal in check. The presence of the foal helped keep the mother placid, less likely to kick out and damage the stallion's valuable equipment. As an extra precaution against kicking we'd put trotting harness on the mare when we took her to the stallion, and the combination of the harness, the presence of her foal, and

Jerry's stimulus usually caused the mares to be reasonably amenable, even if squealing and prancing about. But try holding a foal while the stallion is brought out, rampantly prancing the last twenty yards on his back legs, snorting and rearing onto the mare's back. You'll never get more action in your life. The foals would shit and piss all over me, and jump and kick at the same time. I'd be fox-trotting around the yard with one arm under the foal's chest, the other under its tail, with Andy Maguire helping immensely by roaring:

'Can't you hold it steady, son?'

Old Andy loved it when the mares were being served. I guess he was totting up the money (for Emborough's stud fee quadrupled after Bernborough began to win his races) but he also obviously loved to watch 'Gene' (after Gene Tunney) as he called Emborough, do his stuff. Because he was the only one who could handle Emborough at any time, and especially when he was about to serve a mare, Andy would lead the big stallion out of his stall, and somehow control him until the big chestnut mounted the mare, his great rigid dick prodding hopelessly off-target as he bit into the mare's mane. Andy's moment was at hand. With great ceremony he would sweep away the mare's tail, grab Emborough's dick with both hands, and ram it into the mare like a German artilleryman feeding a huge shell into Big Bertha. Andy would watch the mating with great satisfaction, then he'd return the stallion to its stall and a good feed. I'd re-unite the foal and its mother, and then head for the shower.

We were getting stalls ready for the previous year's foals, about to be prepared for the yearling sales, when an ex-jockey named Joe Jennings joined us at Kialla as stud groom. Joe was a funny little bloke, with a disconcerting blue spot in otherwise brown eyes, and the tiniest pimple on the end of his tongue. Joe constantly reminded us of the day when 'I won me six grand'. Apparently he was working for a stable which had a monumental win with one of their horses. Joe had spent his £6000 in three months of nightclubs and gambling in Sydney. He talked constantly of the 'rorts' of the racing game, and each tale was spiked with 'scores' (£20), 'ponies' (£25), 'monkeys' (£50) and 'spots' (£100). I was assigned as Joe's offsider, and it was fascinating to watch him handling the yearlings, and quietly and efficiently breaking them in. I was mainly consigned to the onerous jobs like 'doing out' stalls, which meant raking out the soiled straw, cleaning the stall and putting in new straw, and preparing feeds, but I didn't mind, for I liked the smells of hay and chaff and healthy horses, and it was a great satisfaction to see the results of our grooming and the way in which the yearlings' coats were enhanced when we added things like raw eggs and linseed oil to their feed.

Out of the blue one day Andy Maguire said to me:

'It's a quiet time for the next couple of months. You can finish up next Friday.' I was dumbfounded, certain he had used me up and then decided to pay me back for arriving unannounced. You bastard, I thought. I wondered how I might predict future bosses if they were going to be as volatile as he was. I think he may have been a bit drunk on the day, although I was not very good at spotting the effects of alcohol. Bert had told me Andy gave the Scotch whisky a big nudge occasionally. When I told Bert and Ted of the sacking they were furious.

'Unfortunately, it's typical,' they said. Bert went on: 'You watch. He'll realise in a couple of days we have to start harvesting in a couple of months. He'll offer you your job back'.

Sure enough, about three days later, up fronts Andy.

'I've decided to give you another chance.' I looked right into his myopic eyes and gave him the icy, eyes-tightened, I-think-you'd-better-back-off stare that has only 'Graced' my countenance about five times in my entire life.

'I've already lined up another job in Toowoomba,' I lied, and felt really good as I haughtily turned my back on him and resumed cleaning out the stall.

Ted and the Tavenders were consoling, and I left Kialla with mixed feelings, but certainly grateful for their company and my learning experiences with them. A subdued Mr Maguire at least had the grace to drive me to the Greenmount Station. He mumbled 'Good luck' as he left me to catch the rail motor to Toowoomba. I suppose he wasn't a real bad sort of a bastard, but he was a bastard nonetheless. There are grades of bastardry, as I was beginning to learn.

In Toowoomba I felt like a real adult as I strolled into the foyer of the Federal Hotel in Ruthven Street, my port in my fist and a few quid in my kick, and booked a single room. I had saved about twenty pounds, so I was able to spend a few idyllic days, ordering steak, two eggs and onions for every evening meal at a nice cafe, reading the newspapers, having a haircut, going to the pictures twice and taking some photographs with a Box Brownie camera I bought. Toowoomba was then one of the loveliest cities in Australia. Still is.

At the Federal I enjoyed for the first time a good hotel breakfast. Ever since, wherever possible, I avoid meals in motel or hotel rooms, preferring to shower, dress, and go to the dining room to soak up the luxury of reading the morning paper while getting stuck into a solid breakfast of 'chaff' (which Ted van Dreick taught me to call cereal), bacon and eggs, a pot of weak black tea, toast and marmalade. Your day can't fail after such indulgence.

I thought it was time to go home. Not that I was homesick. On the contrary I was loving the new-found freedom, and particularly enjoyed anonymity and the fact that nobody knew my childhood foibles. People treated me on my merits. But I wanted to start to get organised for some real travel, where I could learn languages, and soak up the detail of other countries, for I felt that 'the real thing' could only be found overseas. Apart from a few words like 'port' equalling suitcase and 'duchess' equalling sideboard, added to the local propensities for pie-eating and Rugby, I found nothing incomprehensible, or mysterious about Queensland. No intrinsic genius to them either, Slick. So what was the point of staying? Get back to Melbourne, and contact Frunner, Ted. He seems to have the clues about world travel, and the jobs that get you there. South America, Ted, that seems to be the go. And now that you can ride a bit better, maybe a cowboy's life is what you need. A *gaucho*. A real cowboy. *Hasta la vista*.

Not just yet, I thought. I had noticed that all Queenslanders loved to say 'out west' with a glazing of their eyes. They reckoned it was 'mighty' out west.

'The real Queenslanders are out west, Ted. It's just mighty around Quilpie and Thargomindah,' Ted van Dreick had mused, his coastal-fringe eyes lighting up with nostalgia. Everybody else was the same. Say 'out west' and they'd go into orgasm.

So I strolled into Gower's Employment Agency in Toowoomba, and met a friendly lady behind the desk.

'Looking for work, son?'

'Got any jobs out west?'

'What are you, a ringer?'

'No, I've never done any shearing.' I was thinking of the song 'Click Go The Shears':

> The ringer looks around
> And is beaten by a blow

'Oh yes, "ringer". No, I didn't mean a shearer,' she laughed. Up here in Queensland we call stockmen "ringers" — they "ring" the cattle when they're on watch at night. I thought with your laughing-side boots you must be a ringer.'

I was flattered, and pleased she had noticed my new

elastic-sided riding boots, Cuban heels and all, made by R M Williams, 5 Percy Street, Prospect SA, where I now knew all bushmen bought their clothes, ordering from the extensive mail-order catalog. The boots added two inches to my height and heaps to my morale.

'So you're obviously not a ringer. Where have you worked?'

'Kialla Stud, Greenmount,' I replied, a bit cagey. I didn't want it known that I had been sacked, however unfairly. She was quick to reassure me.

'What, did old Andy tramp you when things got quiet?' I nodded. She nodded. We smiled.

'He's an old bastard,' she said nodded agreement. I was feeling good. The lady ruffled through her cards.

'He does it all the time, old Andy. Here's one for you.' She pulled out a card. 'Good employers. Cowboy-butcher at Myall Park, Glenmorgan. Can you milk cows? Probably only a few house cows.' She looked at me speculatively, reassuringly.

'Yeah, I can milk cows,' I half-lied, but I was confident I could become proficient quickly.

'What about sheep? Can you kill sheep?'

I'd never killed one, actually cut its throat, but I had watched and helped Bert, and felt I would be all right after a few tries on my own. I didn't want to be telling too many lies, though, so I used the royal plural.

'Yeah, we used to kill our own sheep at Maguire's.' 'Job's yours if you want it,' she said.

'Is Glenmorgan out west?'

Her eyes rolled with ecstasy when I said 'out west'.

'Well,' she said slowly, 'Glenmorgan's certainly west of Toowoomba. Depends on how far west you want to go doesn't it? Do you like it out west?'

'Never been there,' said the townie from Melbourne, feeling inadequate, like a Muslim who'd never been to Mecca.

'Oh, it's mighty out west. Me dad was a drover round Boulia. Crows fly backwards to keep the dust outa their eyes out west, mate,' she laughed. 'Back to business. No, Glenmorgan's not really out west, but it's on the way. You'd have a mighty time. Now, do you want this job or not? Two quid a week and your tucker, and I can give you a railway pass to get you there.'

Why not? Just for a few months. It was the end of September. Give it a go, Ted. I signed up, and the next day I caught the little old steam train, heading west.

Everybody on the train seemed to be drunk, or on the way. Several offered me a bottle of rum. 'Have a pull, china'. No thanks. I'd never heard of anybody drinking rum before, apart from Long John Silver and his cronies. There were no women in the second-class sit-ups. Most of the men were hard, tough-looking ringers, and I watched them with interest. They had the biggest hats I have ever seen, and I particularly liked the way they walked, jamming the cheeks of their arses together and taking mincing little steps in their RMs. Some of these mannerisms might be worth a run back in Melbourne, I thought. Where've you been Ted? Out west. What, Footscray? Naah, bit further. Had a mighty time.

There were a few of life's losers, gaunt young-old men in their forties, whose eyes told of busted marriages, too much booze and gambling, a hundred jobs, and thereby a bit of acquired talent in a hundred different areas of work experience. Droving, fencing, tank-sinking, yard-building, snake charming (I quickly learnt that railway fettlers were called 'snake charmers'), you name it, these blokes would have assured you they were experts in all or any of these fields.

I listened to a few of them, but avoided eye contact.

'Yeah, I had five years boundary ridin' out round Toompine'.

'Oh, I must have been what, four years on Margaret Downs. Runnin' the camp I was.'

'Fencin'. Don't talk to me about fencin', mate. Never want to see a roll o'wire again. Put up the entire section of the rabbit-proof fence from Nutwood to Wandilla.'

The rum bottles went around. Two things were noticeable.

Blokes would always establish their own bona-fides around the various exploits. So when one said: 'I was horse-breakin' on Beaton Downs in '43' another would say 'Who was runnin' the camp then?' When told it was Les Watson, he'd then say, 'Bloody old Les. He was a hard man. Good man, mind. But by the Jesus, they don't come harder.' There'd be a murmur of agreement, and the rum bottle would do the rounds.

The second thing I discovered was that nobody ever lost a fight.

'By Christ, did I hammer 'im? Well, what's a man to do? I come home and here he is, chockablock up me missus, so I beat the livin' shit out of him.' The others murmured approval.

'Three o' the bastards there were, but I head butted one, kicked the next joker in the nuts, and then finished off the third prick with the old one-two.' On they went, each one propping up his own ego around the exploits of the talker.

'Here, son. Have a charge'.

I suddenly realised I was being offered a rum bottle. I didn't want to be singled out for undue attention. Didn't want to tell them about my confirmation pledge.

'No, thanks.' I feigned a cough. 'Got a cold. Might give you germs.'

He seemed satisfied with that as an excuse for refusing his hospitality. He had a swig on my behalf:

'Where ya headin', young feller?'

'Glenmorgan. Near Surat.' I had studied the map, and wanted to sound like an old hand.

'Ringin' out there?'

'Yeah,' I lied, well aware that the cowboy in Australia was not the romantic figure the American movies portrayed, but the yokel who milked the cows, not yet smart enough to be a ringer.

'Sheep or cattle?'

'Sheep.'

He spat contemptuously.

'Have nothin' to do with sheep, mate. Cattle. That's where the real ringers work.'

He was prepared to be aggressive about it.

'Yeah,' I agreed.

I didn't want to be the first bloke on that train ever to lose a fight, so I opened my book, but he had decided I was dead-boring anyway, and moved on. I pretended to read, but I was in fact watching them all, fascinated. Most got progressively drunker. Some were funny, some moronic, all boisterous. Card games started, and at Dalby they all raced across the railway lines to a pub to get some more rum.

'Rum's a Queensland drink, mate,' said a friendly old bloke when he discovered I was a Victorian. 'It's a mighty drink. You see, you can drink it hot or cold, neat or mixed with anything at all, water, milk, coffee, Bonox, raspberry, cloves. Lemonade if you're a poofter. Goes with anything, rum does. Best drink of all is rum with a beer chaser.'

His name was Alma Ashton, and he was a train drover. He was heading 'out west' - where else? - to pick up a mob of cattle. He would be in charge of them as they were taken back east by train. He had to water the cattle, feed them, and check their safety on the train.

'Alma Ashton. Funny name for a bloke, eh?'

I noticed that everybody tended to put 'eh?' on the end

of sentences, to turn a statement into a question which demanded your agreement.

'Don't know why my parents give me such a moniker. But by the Jesus, mate, it teaches you to fight real good, bein' called Alma.'

I really enjoyed Alma's company. As the train was incredibly slow, and kept stopping, sometimes for an unscheduled hour, we had plenty of time to talk. Or rather, Alma talked. I listened. Avidly. And asked lots of questions, which he was very happy to answer, about cattle, droving, life out west.

Around us the card game continued. Into the serious bit now. The mugs had been eliminated, and the stakes got higher. There were lots of ribald comments about the Queensland Railways.

'What's the bloody hold-up?'

'Oh, the driver's gone off to do a bit o' roo-shootin'. Won't be too long.'

'What would you do if you're on a Queensland train, and the engine driver dropped dead?'

'Fuck him while he's hot,' the others roared in unison.

I said, but not very loudly, I'll admit, 'I reckon I know who taught all you blokes at school.'

The weaker ones had dropped off to sleep in various poses, open-mouths and snoring being common to all. They were everywhere, up in luggage racks, under seats, on the floor, everywhere. Alma and I shared a couple of sandwiches I had bought at the railway refreshment rooms at Dalby. He opened the sandwich, and sniffed suspiciously.

'Not mutton is it? Nah, beef, that's good. Can't touch mutton. Or rabbit. That's underground mutton anyway. Or chook. I'm a beef man. Beef and bread and rum. That's what Queenslanders go for. It's mighty.' I saw my opportunity to join the club.

'Yeah, it's good, eh?' I responded, and almost suc-

cumbed to the temptation to have a swig of rum. It
certainly seemed a powerful drop. Mighty in fact.

We both dozed off eventually, and as the sun rose the
blokes started to groan and fart and stir into action.

'Jesus, who shit in me mouth last night?' asked one
seedy-looking character as he scratched his nuts reflectively.

'Anyone got a heart-starter?' shouted another, and
somebody unscabbed a rum bottle and passed it to him.

'Most of these jokers are OK really,' said Alma. 'They
play up on a trip like this, but some of them are going to
jobs where they won't get another drink for six months.'

I wasn't too sure. I felt a few of them would get a
drink wherever they were, but I was happy enough to
shrug my agreement. They hadn't done me any harm.

I farewelled Alma at Surat, where I was met by Ted
Rooney, the overseer at Myall Park. He seemed a friendly
enough bloke, and we drove to the railway station in an
old square-nosed wartime truck, which was called a 'Blitz'.
There we loaded the truck with supplies, drums of petrol
and diesel, and rolls of fencing wire.

'We're flat out at the station. Got the shearers coming
in a couple of weeks. Hope you're a good killer?'

He looked hard at me. I was nonplussed.

'Butcher. You have done some butchering, haven't you?'

'Yeah, a bit,' I replied, none too convincingly.

'Never mind. You'll soon be good,' he went on reassuringly. 'You'll be killing about twenty sheep a week for the
next six weeks. You'll be a bloody champion by then.'

He did not sound too hard a taskmaster, and he wasn't.
He came with me to do my first slaughtering job. I
confided — I had no alternative — that I hadn't done it
on my own before, but was a good learner. He supervised
as I cut the sheep's throat, and then showed me how to
bleed it properly. I eventually became quite good at it. I
only had to kill the sheep and hang the whole carcass in

the meathouse. The cooks — the homestead cook and the shearers' cook — liked to do most of their own butchering, and they, too, taught me a few tricks.

Myall Park was a fairly typical sheep station, I was told. Forty thousand acres. The class structure was prescribed by the accommodation layout. The Gordon brothers, two bachelors who owned the station, lived in the big old homestead with a lovely rose garden. I was told that Dave Gordon was one of Australia's top authorities on roses, one of the many examples I was to discover of diversely talented people in the bush. I have met some wonderfully knowledgeable people on stations over the years, people who might seem rough and ready when you meet them in town, but who are absolute experts in all areas of what city snobs would call 'the arts'. Most of the toffs think 'the arts' are only practised in the trendier suburbs of the big cities. They might be surprised at how many good painters, photographers, potters, weavers, jewellery makers and writers there are in the bush, quietly following their interests for recreation.

Ted Rooney and his wife lived in a modest but well-appointed house in the middle of the station complex. As overseer Ted was at everybody's beck and call. The ringers and the cowboy normally lived in the men's quarters, but as there were some building contractors on the station we station employees had been put into tents for a while. There were three ringers, plus me, and we had a tent each which was all right. The ringers were Dick Chappelow, Ray Berg and Bede Campbell. Bede seemed to be the butt of all the jokes, but he took it pretty well.

I settled in easily with the three ringers. Fortunately they did not pull rank on me, and I learned a lot from them. They were all country-bred boys, and good horsemen. They were currently mustering horses, and helping a bloke named Lindsay Cant, who was on contract to the station as horsebreaker. The boys loved to ride the buckjumpers, and I had a couple of rides, with the predictable busters.

My routine job of milking the cows, cutting the firewood and doing the slaughtering did not take too much time, so I got a lot of opportunities to help anybody who could use me in any capacity. Ted Rooney liked the fact that I was a self-starter, and he got me to help him moving sheep, getting ready for the shearers, 'the coming of the plague' as he jokingly remarked.

'If you think those blokes on the train were wild, wait until the shearers get here,' he warned.

Ted and I would ride out early in the morning. He had given me a couple of quiet horses to use, and I tried hard to be a polished horseman like he was, but I think you have to be on a horse from childhood, riding bareback, to get that harmony with a horse that seems telepathic, the knees as well as the hands letting the horse know what is expected. I could get by, but I largely felt sorry for the horse, having to carry such an unco-ordinated bulky object on its back.

We had our quartpots strapped to our saddles, and in our saddle bags we had tea and sugar in a little muslin bag, and bread and mutton in another. We'd go first to a watering spot, a dam or a bore, find the freshest tracks, and then (hopefully) follow the tracks out from the water to locate the sheep. It was thick, scrubby country and I must admit I got lost a few times. I realised it was better to let the horse work things out if I couldn't, and I always got back to base all right. At the end of the day we'd take the sheep to some big holding paddocks close to the shearing sheds, where they could easily be mustered again for the shearers.

They arrived, about thirty of them, in all sorts of battered cars and trucks. It was a big shed, with twelve shearers to shear about 80,000 sheep. As well as the shearers there were rouseabouts, a classer, a presser, the cook, the contractor (known as 'The Sweat Extractor') and a few general hands. They settled into the quarters, and again I could witness the class structure as it applied to this amazing base for Australian folklore, the shearing shed. The shearers were on the top rung of the ladder, the rousies on the bottom, generally referred to as 'shearers' punching bags'.

They were all very militant unionists, with rigid rules which they insisted were enforced to the letter. I could see why the pastoralists didn't like them too much. The shearers were the spokesmen for the entire group, and they very definitely didn't tug their forelocks to the squatters. Dave Gordon was a nice bloke, probably more easy-going than most pastoralists, and it was a lesson in diplomacy as Dave and the union rep sorted out the terms under which the Myall Park shed would be shorn.

Everything about the shearing shed happens at the double. I am sure shearing is the hardest physical job in the world, and I think shearers deserve every penny they get. So it's understandable that men who work so hard also play hard, and are absolutely uncompromising that union conditions, won over a hundred years of tough negotiation, are implemented to the letter.

I watched, fascinated. When I got the chance, that is. We, too, were on the run, keeping the sheep up to them, and they were shearing around 2000 per day. But occasionally, when the holding paddocks and the pens were all full I got the chance to see the breakneck pace at which the operation inside the shed took place. Rousies running, fleeces flying, the contractor standing off, aloof and missing nothing. Everything revolved around keeping sheep up to the shearers, and getting each fleece out of the way and the board swept as he dived into the pen for his next customer. Years later I wrote a song about them:

We're Australia's shearers, shearers of the golden fleece,

No-one can come near us, shearers of the golden fleece
We do all the flamin' work
We're up to every lurk and perk,
From anywhere to Back o' Bourke
Shearers of the golden fleece.

It seemed to be non-competitive, a case of each man for himself as they grimly, relentlessly, silently amassed their tallies. But I noticed them stealing furtive, knowing glances along the board as they got onto the easier stages, the 'long blow' or the 'whipping side', where the action for them was a series of long, routine sweeps along the sheep's back and sides. The race to be the 'gun' or the 'ringer' in their sense of the term was uppermost in the minds of the better shearers, for the folklore was perpetuated each night around the quarters as this particular shed and its sheep were compared to others they had known or heard about. The names and the feats of the great shearers of past years were constantly dragged out and the comparisons brought on fierce debates.

And did they play up on Saturday nights and Sundays . . . We all went to town with them on Saturday afternoons, taking our swags and sleeping out on the flat around the Glenmorgan pub. I was surprised there was no music or singing, for I had imagined shearers standing around, drinking 'rum and raspberry' smoking 'shillin' each cigars' and bellowing out songs like 'Lachlan Tigers', but they preferred to leave that sort of nonsense to the bearded folk singers who could share the atmosphere of the shed through the songs. The shearers did not need songs about themselves. They had a bloody hard week behind them, a good advance on their cheques, and they wanted some serious drinking.

Even in the pub the shearers ruled the roost. They sorted out the fights and arguments, that's if they weren't starting them themselves. I used to have a couple of lemonades and watch them, and I learned quickly to camp well away from the pub, where I wouldn't have drunks falling all over my swag through the night.

On the Sundays we'd sit around the grounds of the pub, spilling onto the dusty roads. The shearers got straight into the grog at daybreak. They'd play cards and darts, and if there were no coppers around they'd start a game of two-up. Everything had a betting aspect to it. There'd be feats of strength, like scratch-pulling, where you sat on the ground facing your opponent, both grasping a broom at your feet. Feet locked against your opponent's. Place your bets, gentlemen. At the command 'Pull' the aim was to pull your adversary to a standing position. There'd be high jumps and footraces, and money changed hands freely. If any two blokes got into fighting mode they were told to hold it until bets could be laid, and then the shearers would referee the stoush. It was good, generous, democratic fun.

I stayed at Myall Park until the end of the shearing. It was late December. I booked myself back to Melbourne on the train, breaking the trip at Sydney to spend a couple of days with the much-loved Aunty Mary, Grace's elder sister. I was thrilled to meet again, but this time as a young adult with a bit of travel behind me, the woman who was the hub the entire Brennan side of our family revolved around. Mary was a prolific letter writer, and kept in touch with all branches of the family. In her letters to Grace she always signed herself 'Your aff. (affectionate) sister Mary'. Her nieces and nephews, particularly, liked to sit at Mary's feet to take in her wisdom and the tales of her travels as an adventurous young woman. My own niece, Elaine McKenna, Sal's daughter, carried on the tradition later and eventually wrote, with Mary, a delightful book, *Better Than Dancing*, about Mary's exploits when young. Elaine based the title on Mary's observation that she, as an individualist, enjoyed a girlish fling at roller skating. She felt skating on your own, free, uninhibited, was much 'better than dancing' where, in those days, it was prescribed that women had to follow the lead, however inept, of the male partner. Mary lived to be 101, a wonderful woman.

After Christmas, which I spent with the family, I went to visit the Houlihans at Nar Nar Goon. They asked me to come and stay with them, and suggested I might get into the highly lucrative business of spud-digging, as there was a record crop in Gippsland and prices were high as well, a rare double. Farmers had grown some new varieties like Carmen, Catardin and Sequoia with amazing results. I boarded with the Houlihans, and they loaned me old Peter to ride to the different farms each day where the diggers assembled to dig, bag and load the spuds.

Potato-digging machines had just been invented, and sometimes we'd follow the machines, picking up the spuds, bagging them, sewing the bags and then loading. Following the machines we were paid three shillings a bag. But a lot of farmers were resistant to the idea of machines, and wanted their spuds dug with the fork, as they and their ancestors (many of them were Irish) had always done. I was fairly good at fork-digging, having been taught by my cousin Leo, and I used to get more money digging with the fork than I could following the machines. That was good. It meant more work for me because most wanted to pick up rather than dig the spuds. Digging our own spuds brought four shillings a bag. The crop that year was stupendous, most farms averaging twenty tons of spuds to the acre, and I earned amazing money for the six weeks' season. I could always do over twenty bags a day, sometimes thirty, so I was getting between four and six pounds a day. Thirty pounds a week, when the basic wage was about six pounds. I came back to Melbourne with a cheque for £150, gave half to Grace, and then began to ponder my future.

I met up with a few old North school mates, principally Vern Wilson and Ron Smith. We went to a few things around Melbourne together, and Ron was constantly extolling the virtues of Darwin. Not that he'd been there, but he had heard there was big money to be earned 'up north' as distinct from 'out west'. So he and I decided to go picking grapes at Mildura in northern Victoria, save a few quid there, and go on to Darwin. Ron agreed with me that South America might be a good destination after Darwin. All we needed was the fare. Life was fairly straightforward in those days.

Casually, I mentioned to Pop and Grace that Ron and I had these international plans. They just took it in their stride again, I think pleased for us that we had opportunities denied them. They liked Ron as he had been with me right through my schooling at North, and had kept in touch with them while I was in Queensland.

I was young, fit, reasonably well-educated and I had a hundred quid in the bank. What more could a young bloke ask for? Some sound parental advice, perhaps? Grace took me aside on the day Ron and I were leaving. We were catching the 'grape-pickers' special' train from Spencer Street that night. Grace wasn't coming to the station, so she made her farewells beforehand.

'Now, Teddy,' she said, 'I'm going to give you two good pieces of advice.' Hello, I speculated, what'll it be Grace? Let me have a guess. Don't forget to go to Mass every Sunday? Always say your prayers? Make sure you write home every week? No. None of these, although I guess they were understood as being an integral part of my life. She sat me down and looked hard at me.

'Wherever you go in life, keep sweet with the cook. And always be a good listener'.

Over many years I have pondered and valued more

and more the soundness of that maternal advice, but on that particular day I treated it a bit flippantly. I was anxious to get away and not be bothered with the hugs and kisses, the family farewells. The world was waiting for me. I was off. Up north.

You little beauty.

Index

Acknowledgements

The author wishes to thank the relations and friends who shared the times and the incidents covered by this book, and those who supplied family photographs: Eileen (Brennan) McQueen, Leo Brennan, Bill Brennan, Jim Brennan, Pat Toone, Mick Toone, Peg Gleeson, Shirley Egan, Tim Egan, Gus and Pat Egan; and to my sisters, brother and cousins who put up with my numerous and usually ill-timed phonecalls to seek their wisdom and insight, and refresh my memory.

Thanks to the holders of copyright for permission to reproduce photographs and illustrations from: The Herald and Weekly Times Pty Ltd, Telegraph Mirror Ltd, Harper Collins/A&R Pty Ltd and EMI Music Publishing Pty Ltd; Mike Gillam for both the cover photo and the portrait on page one of the plate section. And also to John Kerr and Annette Hughes, of Kerr Publishing, who guided me in this project, and then provided wonderful support in its execution (to coin a phrase).

In particular, my sister Sal (Shirley), 'pal of my childhood days' is thanked for her incisive memory, proof reading and general scrutiny, and my beloved Nerys Evans, for her computor wizardry, spelling ability, good manners, general encouragement and unstinting love at all times.